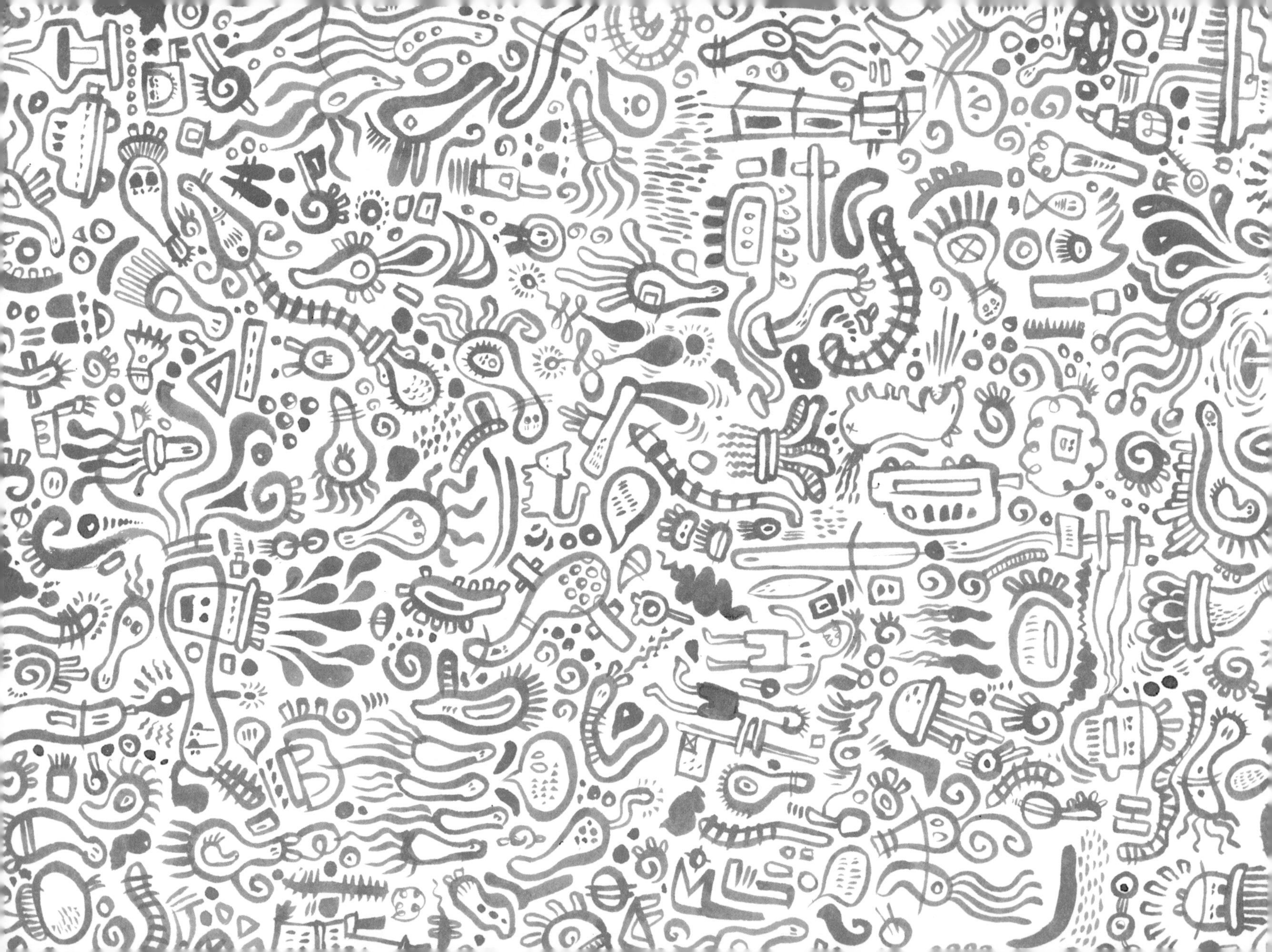

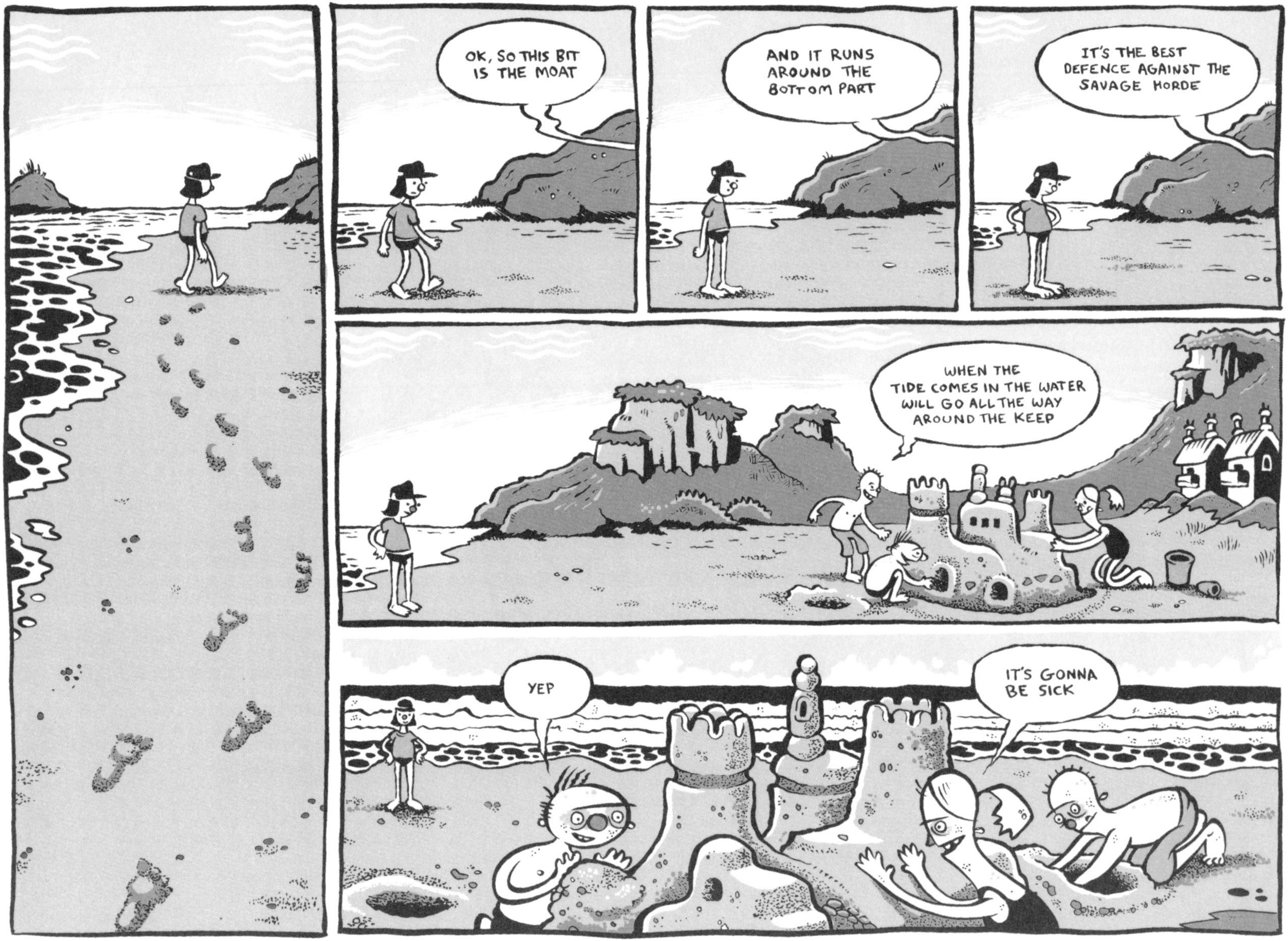
OK, SO THIS BIT IS THE MOAT
AND IT RUNS AROUND THE BOTTOM PART
IT'S THE BEST DEFENCE AGAINST THE SAVAGE HORDE
WHEN THE TIDE COMES IN THE WATER WILL GO ALL THE WAY AROUND THE KEEP
YEP
IT'S GONNA BE SICK

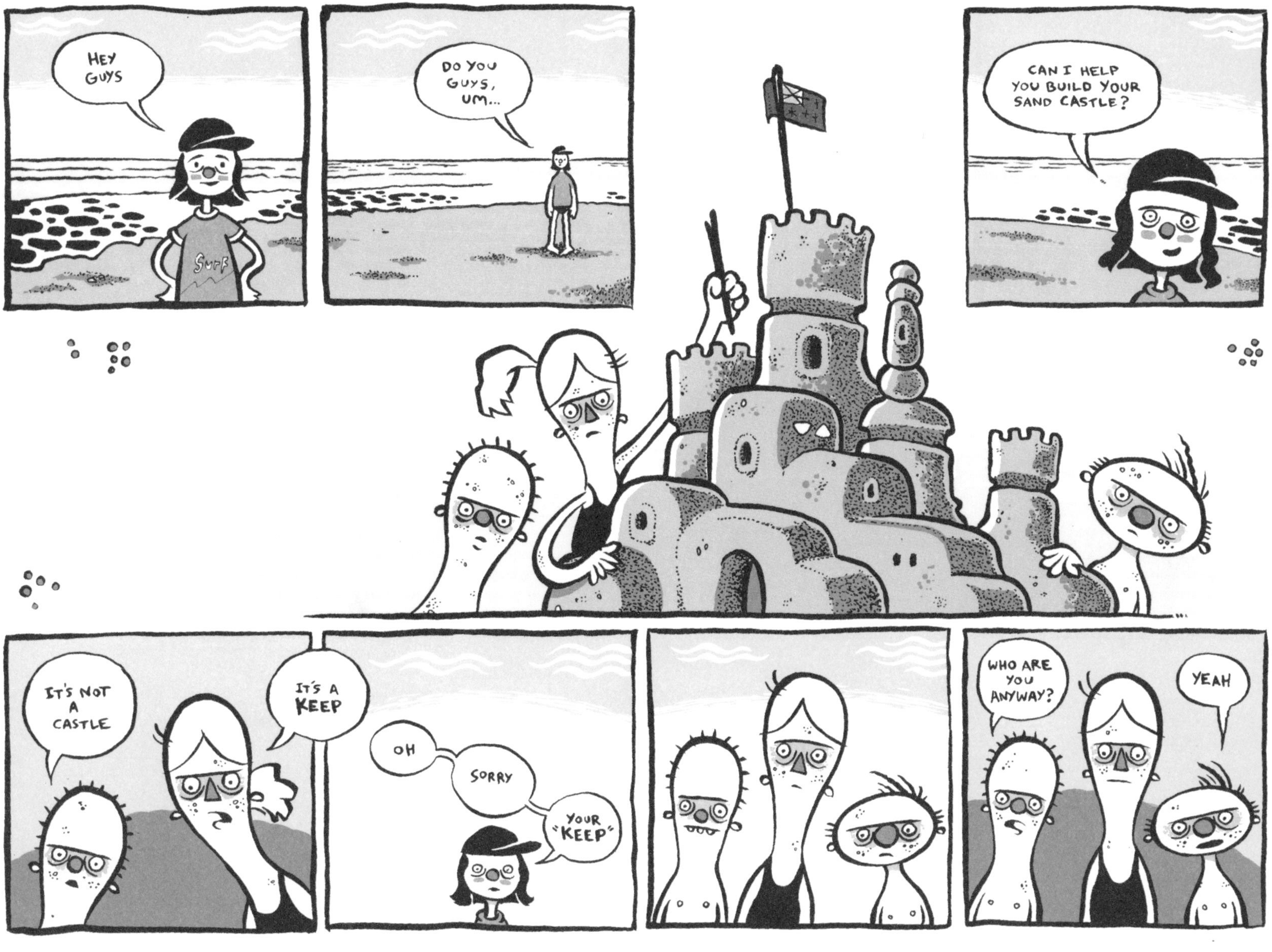
HEY GUYS
DO YOU GUYS, UM...
CAN I HELP YOU BUILD YOUR SAND CASTLE?
IT'S NOT A CASTLE
IT'S A KEEP
OH
SORRY
YOUR "KEEP"
WHO ARE YOU ANYWAY?
YEAH

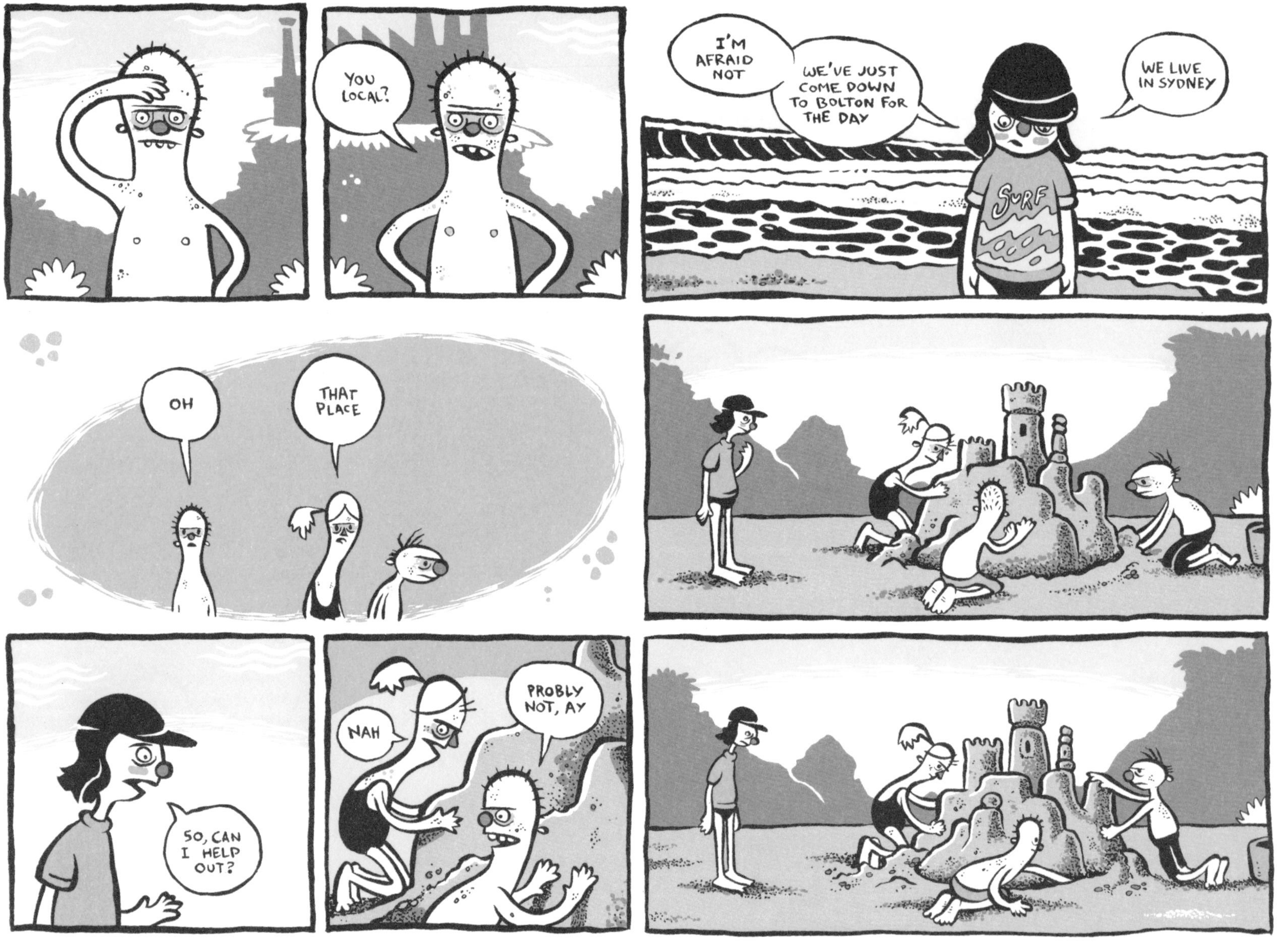
YOU LOCAL?
I'M AFRAID NOT
WE'VE JUST COME DOWN TO BOLTON FOR THE DAY
WE LIVE IN SYDNEY
OH
THAT PLACE
SO, CAN I HELP OUT?
NAH
PROBLY NOT, AY

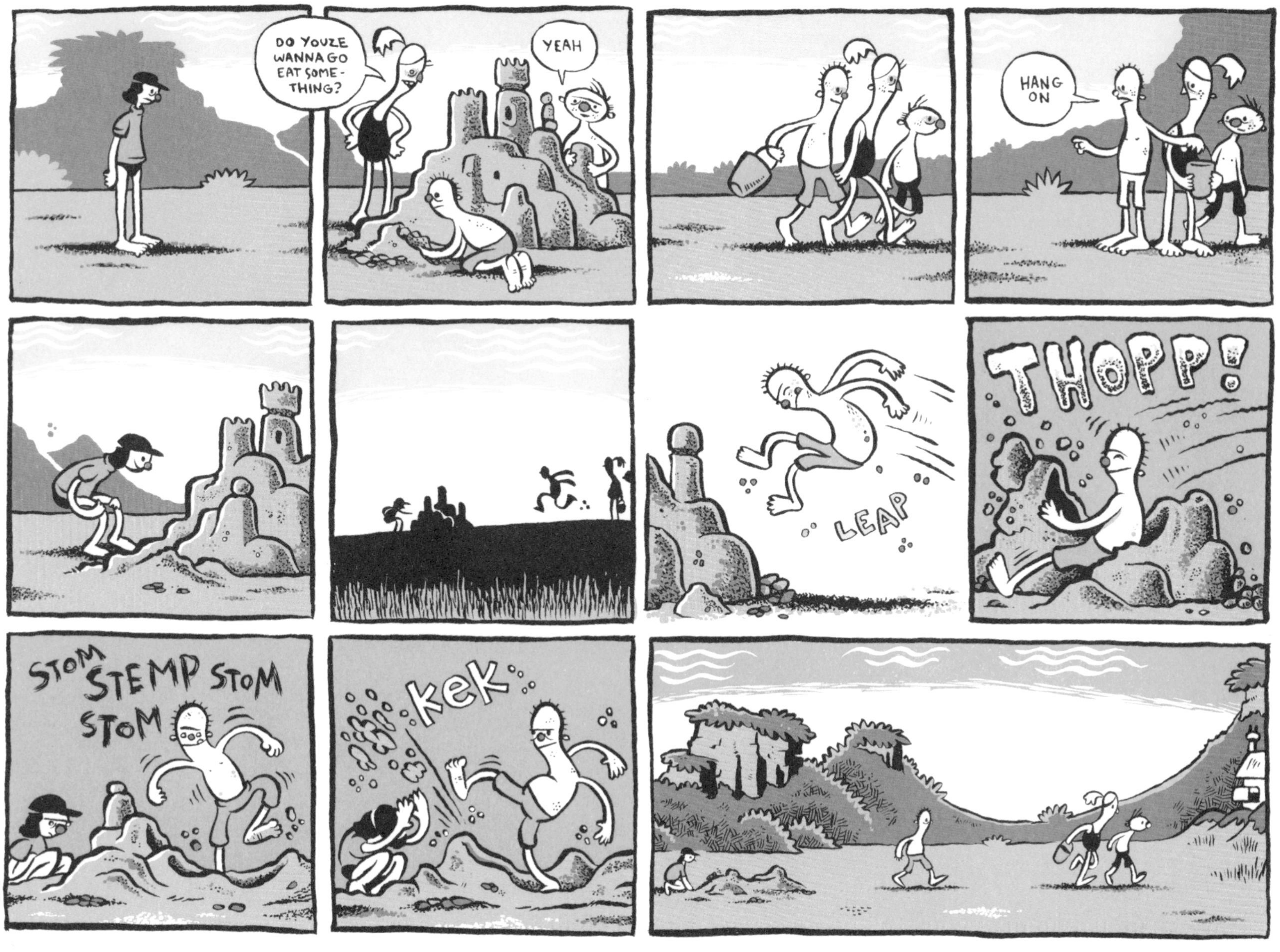
DO YOUZE WANNA GO EAT SOME-THING?
YEAH
HANG ON
LEAP
THOPP!
STOM STEMP STOM
STOM
KEK

 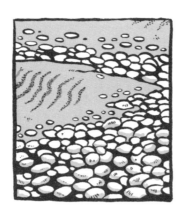 

  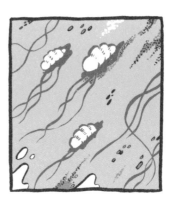

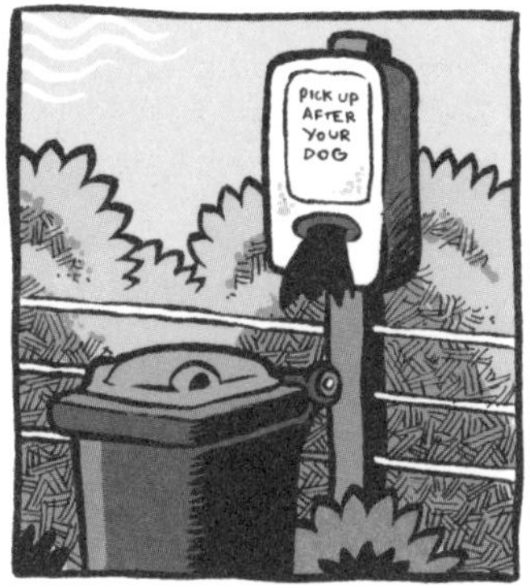
PICK UP AFTER YOUR DOG

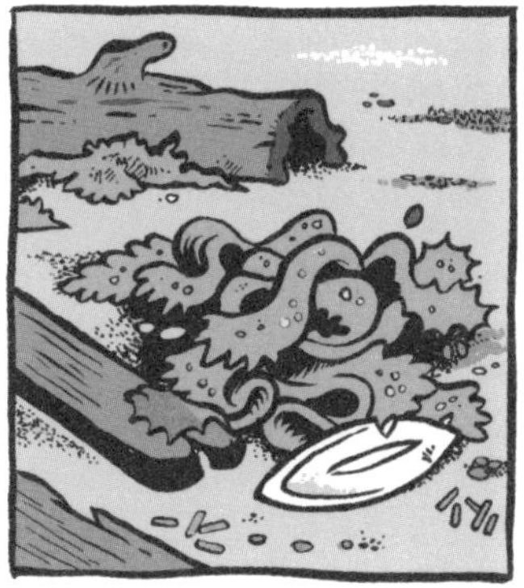

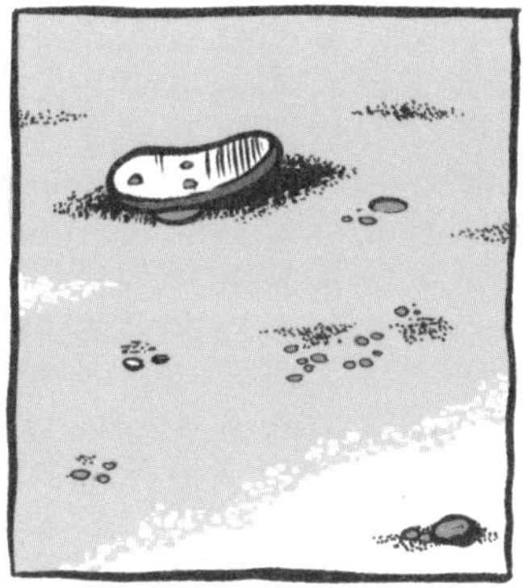

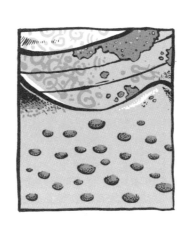

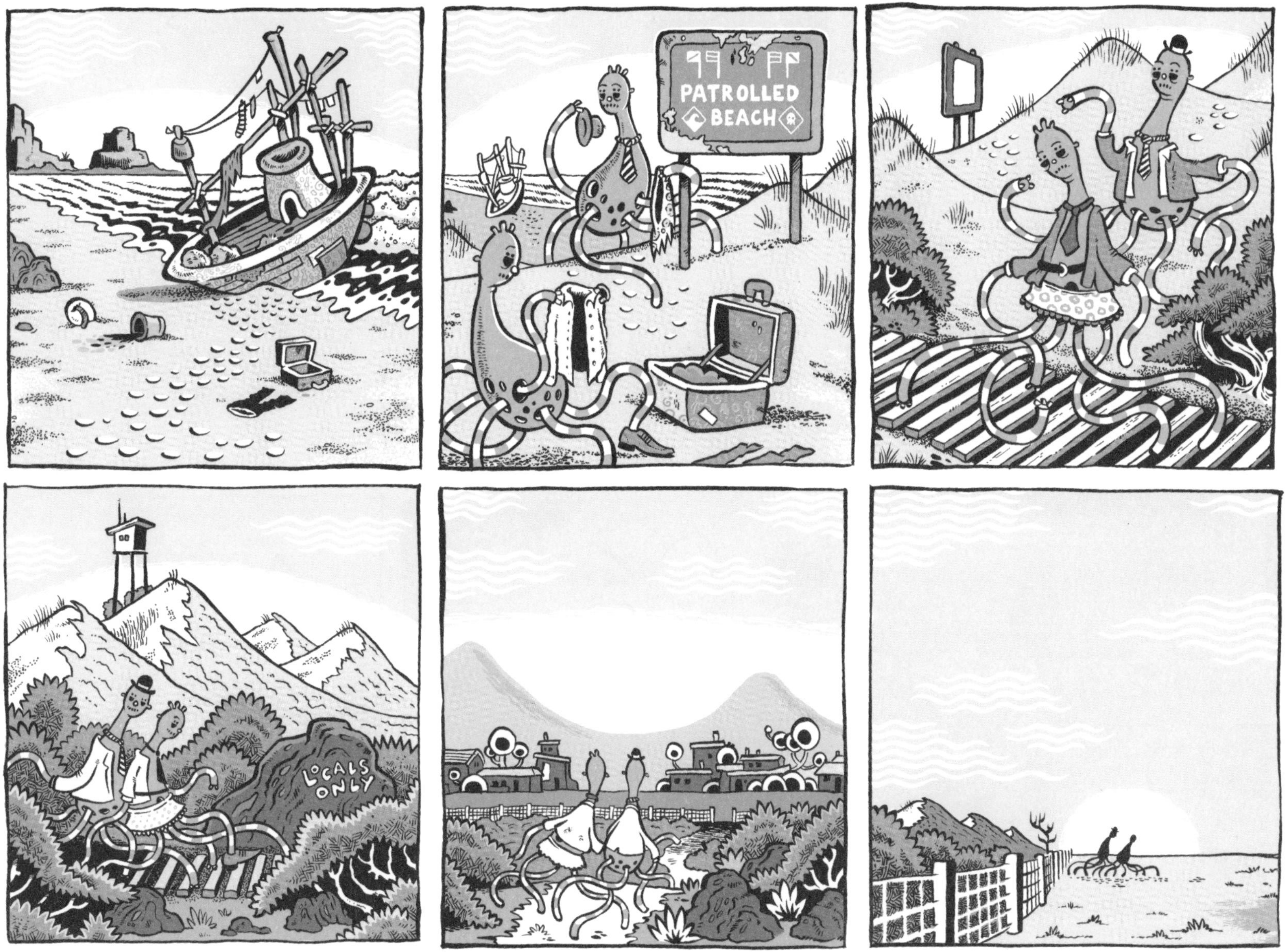
PATROLLED BEACH
LOCALS ONLY

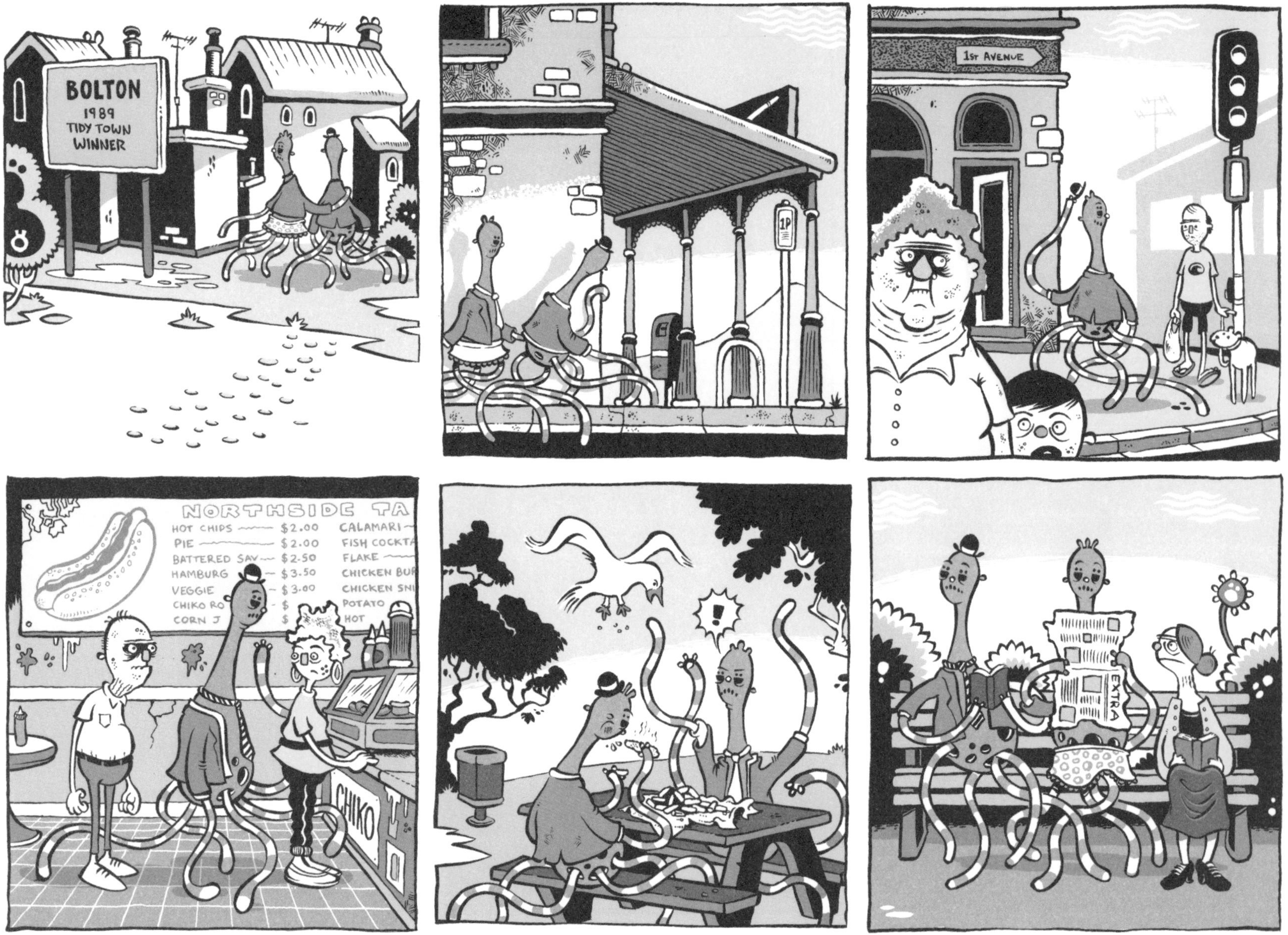
BOLTON
1989
TIDY TOWN
WINNER
1P
1ST AVENUE
NORTHSIDE TA
HOT CHIPS $2.00
PIE $2.00
BATTERED SAV $2.50
HAMBURG $3.50
VEGGIE $3.00
CHIKO RO $
CORN J $
CALAMARI
FISH COCKTA
FLAKE
CHICKEN BU
CHICKEN SN
POTATO
HOT
CHIKO
!
EXTRA

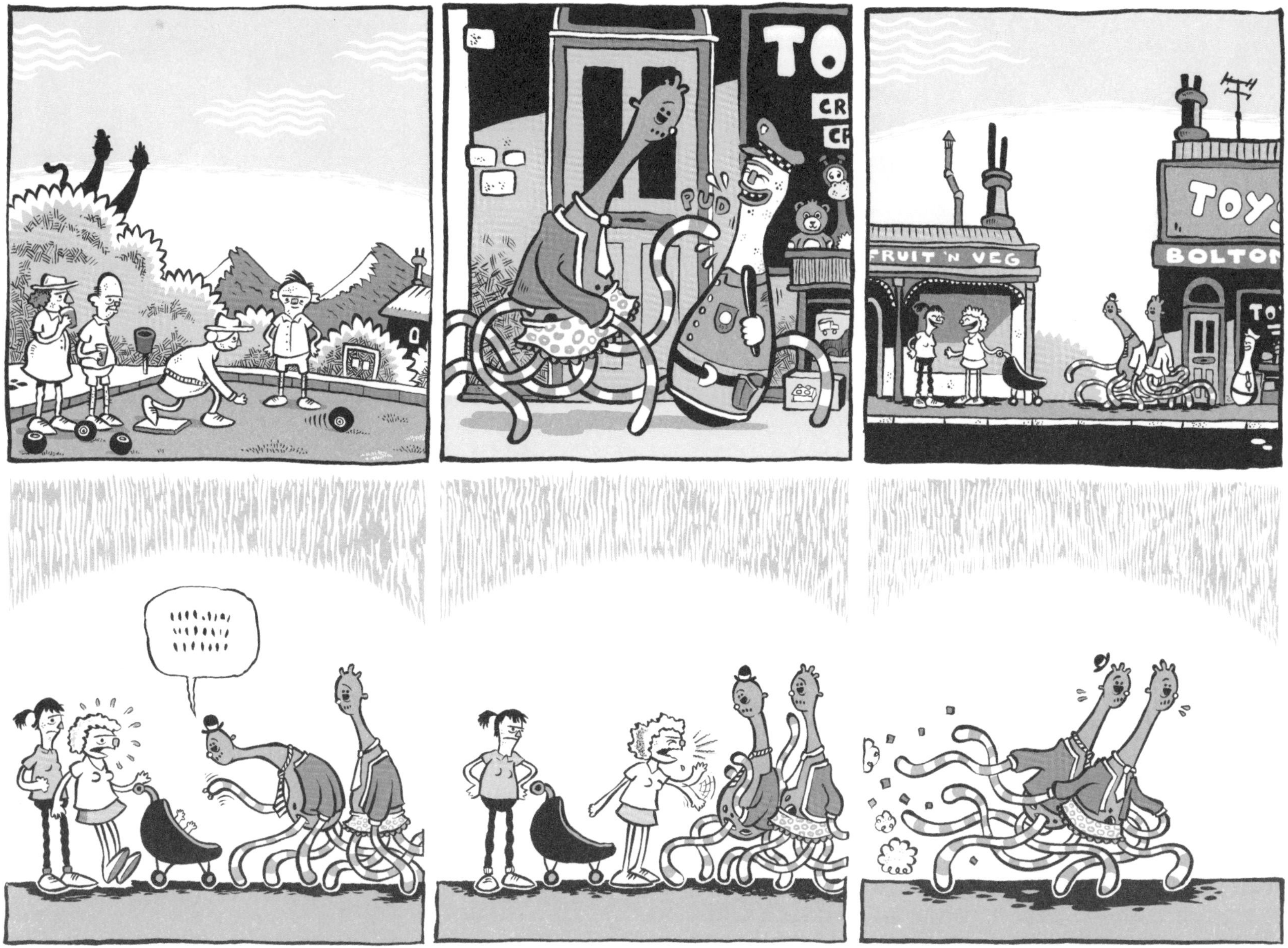
TO
CR
CR
PUD
TOYS
FRUIT 'N VEG
BOLTON
TO

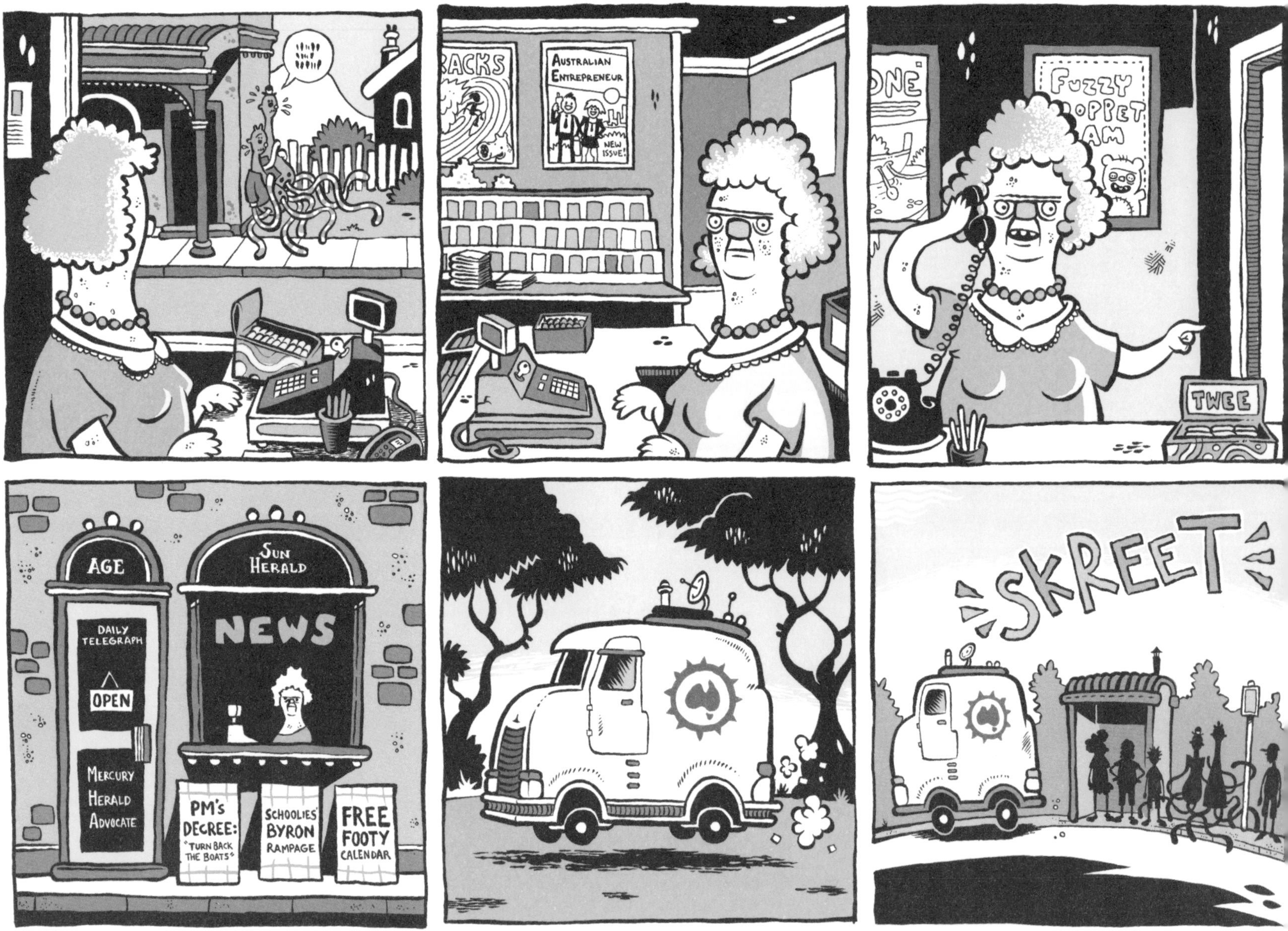
AUSTRALIAN ENTREPRENEUR
NEW ISSUE!
Fuzzy
TWEE
AGE
SUN HERALD
NEWS
DAILY TELEGRAPH
OPEN
MERCURY
HERALD
ADVOCATE
PM's DECREE: "TURN BACK THE BOATS"
SCHOOLIES' BYRON RAMPAGE
FREE FOOTY CALENDAR
SKREET

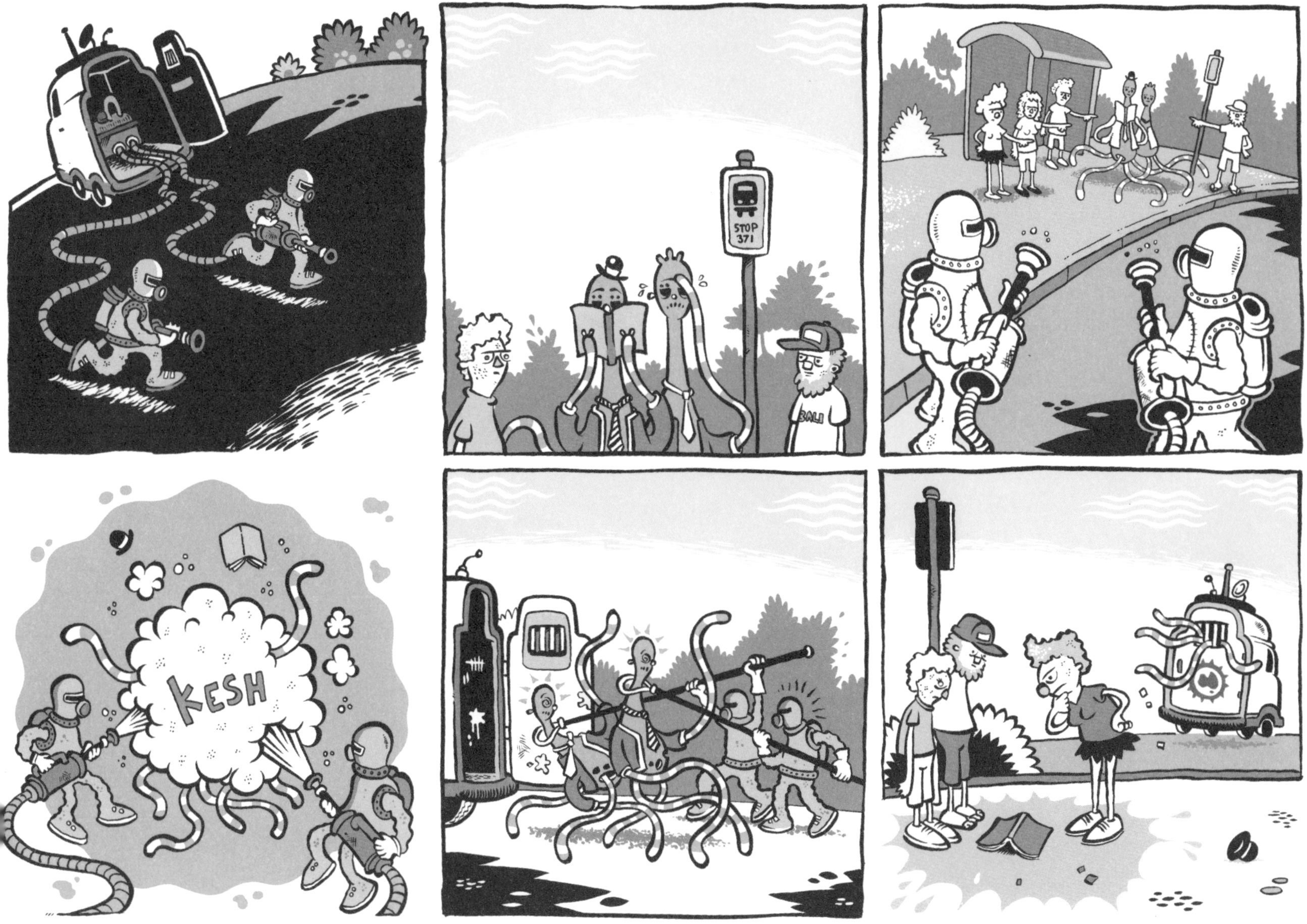
STOP
371
BALI
KESH

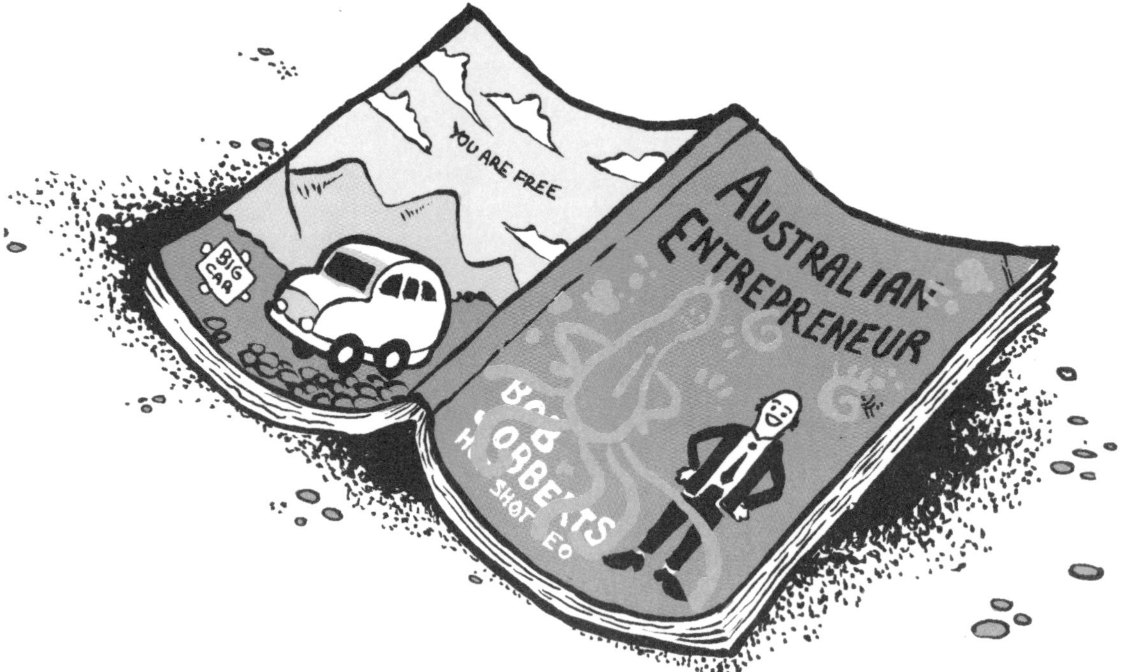
YOU ARE FREE
BIG CAR
AUSTRALIAN ENTREPRENEUR

EVERYONE WAS ARRIVING WITH A SENSE OF FORWARD
MOMENTUM JOINED. EVERYONE WAS TAKING COURAGE
FROM THE SIGHT OF ANOTHER ORANGE MOVING VAN
PULLING IN NEXT DOOR. A FAMILY JUST LIKE US
UNLOADING POLE-LAMPS AND CRIBS AND FORMICA
DINING TABLES LIKE OUR OWN.
    HAVING BEEN GIVEN THE EMPTINESS WE LONGED
FOR, THERE LAY AHEAD THE TASK OF POURING
MEANING INTO THE VACUUM.

        — DAVID BEERS, BLUE SKY DREAM

BLUE 2012 PAT GRANT. PUBLISHED BY THE AUTHOR IN CONJUNCTION WITH TOP SHELF PRODUCTIONS, BRETT
WARNOCK AND CHRIS STAROS, P.O. BOX 1282, MARIETTA, GA 30061-1282, USA. NONE OF THE CONTENTS OF
THIS BOOK ARE COPYRIGHT SAVE FOR THE IMAGES IN THE ESSAY AT THE BACK OF THE BOOK. THOSE BELONG TO THEIR RESPECTIVE
AUTHORS. THE AUTHOR HAS LONG BELIEVED THAT COPYRIGHT IS FOR COMPLETE DAGS AND PREFERS TO LICENSE ALL OF HIS WORK
UNDER A WEIRD CREATIVE COMMONS LICENCE. THE DETAILS OF WHICH CAN BE FOUND AT THE FOLLOWING URL ~~~~
→ www.creativecommons.org/licenses/by-sa/3.0/ ... WHAT DOES THIS MEAN? WELL, YOU'RE FREE TO COPY, DISTRIB-
UTE AND TRANSMIT THE WORK AS LONG AS YOU'RE NOT MAKING ANY MONEY OUT OF IT. BUT REALLY? WHO DOES THE AUTHOR TH-
INK HE IS KIDDING? IF YOU RECKON YOU KNOW HOW TO MAKE A QUICK BUCK PRINTING A BOOK LIKE THIS ONE THEN YOU
AND THE AUTHOR REALLY OUGHT TO HAVE A SIT DOWN BECAUSE YOU CLEARLY KNOW SOMETHING HE DOESN'T. ALL PAGES WERE
DRAWN AND LETTERED BY HAND ON SMOOTH IVORY BOARD AND INKED WITH A W&N SERIES SEVEN SABLE BRUSH, A CROW QU-
ILL NIB AND INDIA INK. SCANNING WAS DONE ON A SCABBY $100 SCANNER THAT THE AUTHOR BOUGHT FROM THE OFFICEWO-
RKS IN COBURG AND ALL OF THE PANTONE COLOURING WAS DONE IN PHOTOSHOP ON AN OLD IMAC THAT ALSO HAP-
PENS TO BE THE DISPLAY CASE FOR THE AUTHOR'S APPLE STICKER COLLECTION. BOOK DESIGN AND PRE-PRESS BY THE AUTHOR
WITH HELP FROM PAT ARMSTRONG AND LEIGH MILWARD, WHO ARE BOTH SILLY ENOUGH TO ANSWER PHONE CALLS FROM
TERRIFIED CARTOONISTS LOOKING FOR DESIGN WISDOM AND SOOTHING WORDS. THIS BOOK WAS EDITED BY NO-ONE, REALLY.
BUT THE STORY WAS WORKSHOPPED BY AN ASSORTMENT OF CARTOONISTS AT THE ATLANTIC CENTER FOR THE ARTS IN FLORIDA
AND THE WHEELER CENTRE FOR BOOKS, WRITING AND IDEAS IN MELBOURNE. EDITING AND PROOFREADING OF MY UNRULY
SENTENCES AND WONKY PROSE WAS BY WORD NINJA ADEN ROLFE WHO THE AUTHOR SOMETIMES MEETS IN THE HALLWAY IN
THE EARLY MORNING WHEN THE AUTHOR IS WEARING NOTHING BUT A YELLOW TOWEL. ADEN ROLFE ALWAYS BEATS
THE AUTHOR TO THE LOO. ADDITIONAL PROOFREADING BY TIM FISHER, BERNARD CALEO AND THE AUTHOR'S AUNTIE SUE,
WHO IS AN ENGLISH TEACHER AND CAN SPELL BETTER THAN YOU CAN. PRINTED IN SINGAPORE BY TIEN WAH PRESS. IF YOU
ARE A LIBRARIAN AND ARE LOOKING FOR KEYWORDS WITH WHICH TO CATALOGUE THIS BOOK WHY NOT TRY SOME OF THE
FOLLOWING: GRAPHIC NOVELS, COMICS, AUSTRALIA, SURFING, RACISM, IMMIGRATION, LOCALISM. IF YOU'RE NOT A
LIBRARIAN BUT SOMEONE WITH A LOT OF TIME AND A WELL ORGANISED COMICS COLLECTION WHY NOT TRY SOME M-
ORE ENTERTAINING KEYWORDS LIKE: SICKEST BLOKE EVER, BORRIE, WOSKIT, SHACKED LIKE A BASTARD, FULLY AY.
THE ENTIRE CONTENTS OF THIS BOOK ARE AVAILABLE ONLINE FOR ANYONE TO READ, AT ANY TIME, FOR FREE, AND THE AU
THOR INTENDS TO KEEP IT THAT WAY. IF YOU LIKE THIS BOOK PLEASE POINT YOUR FRIENDS IN THE DIRECTION OF THE
AUTHOR'S WEBPAGE www.patgrantart.com ~~BUT BE W~~ NEXT TIME YOU ARE BROWSING (NOT SURFING) THE WORLD
WIDE WEB. FEEL FREE TO CONTACT THE AUTHOR AT patgrantart@gmail.com BUT BE WARNED, THE AUTHOR HAS NOT
RESPONDED TO CORRESPONDENCE IN A TIMELY FASHION SINCE 1943. ALL CORRESPONDENCE IN THE FORM OF MINI-COM
ICS WILL BE WARMLY ~~RECIEVED~~ RECEIVED AND DONATED TO THE MICHAEL JACKSON MEMORIAL ZINE LIBRARY, WHICH IS
SITUATED ~~IN THE AUTHOR'S~~ BEHIND THE DOOR IN THE AUTHOR'S BACK DUNNY. LARGE SUMS OF MONEY WERE GRACIOUSLY DEP
OSITED INTO THE AUTHOR'S BANK ACCOUNT BY THE GOVERNMENT AS PART OF THE AUSTRALIA COUNCIL'S EMERGING WRITERS'/
ILLUSTRATORS' INITIATIVE AS MANAGED BY THE AUSTRALIAN SOCIETY OF AUTHORS. FURTHER SUPPORT WAS PROVIDED BY
EXPRESS MEDIA AS PART OF THE 'WRITE IN YOUR FACE' INITIATIVE. THE AUTHOR WOULD LIKE TO THANK THE AFOREMENT-
IONED ORGANISATIONS AND THE BENEVOLENT COMMONWEALTH FOR THE OPPORTUNITY TO WORK FULL-TIME ON A COMICS
PROJECT AND FOR HAVING THE FAITH THAT HE WOULD GET THE LOUSY THING FINISHED. LORD KNOWS, THE AUTHOR
HAD HIS DOUBTS. LASTLY, THE AUTHOR WOULD LIKE TO THANK YOU FOR READING THE FINE PRINT....X

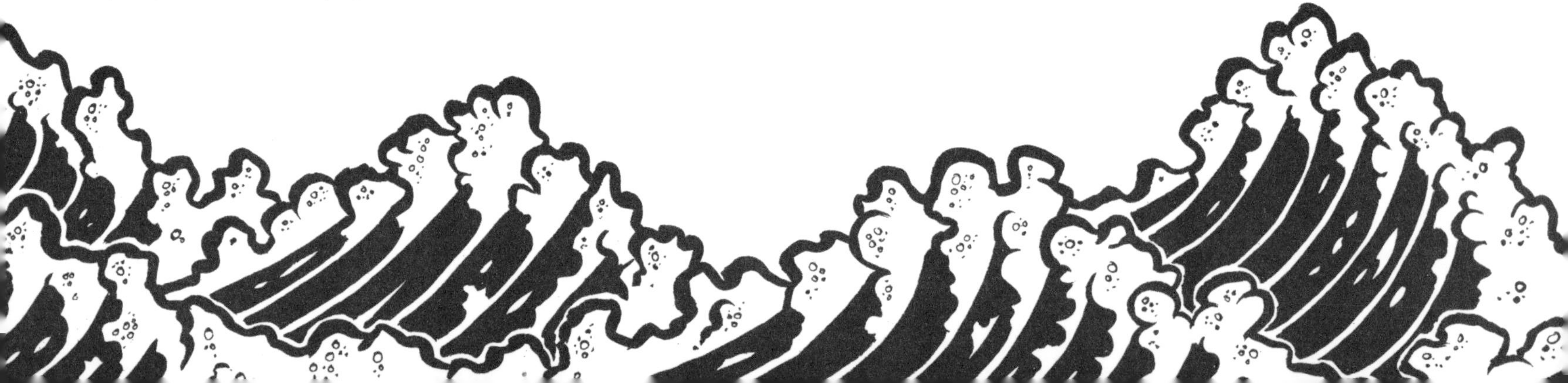

BLUE

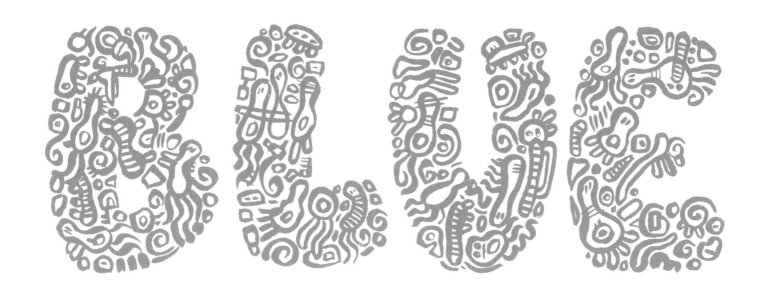

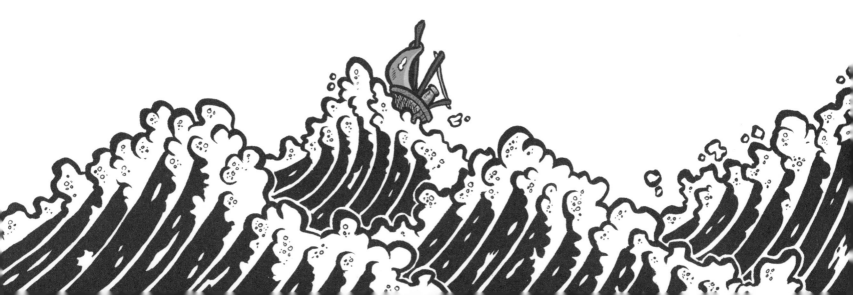

CHANGE AIN'T LOOKING FOR FRIENDS...
CHANGE CALLS THE TUNE WE DANCE TO.
— SWEARENGEN

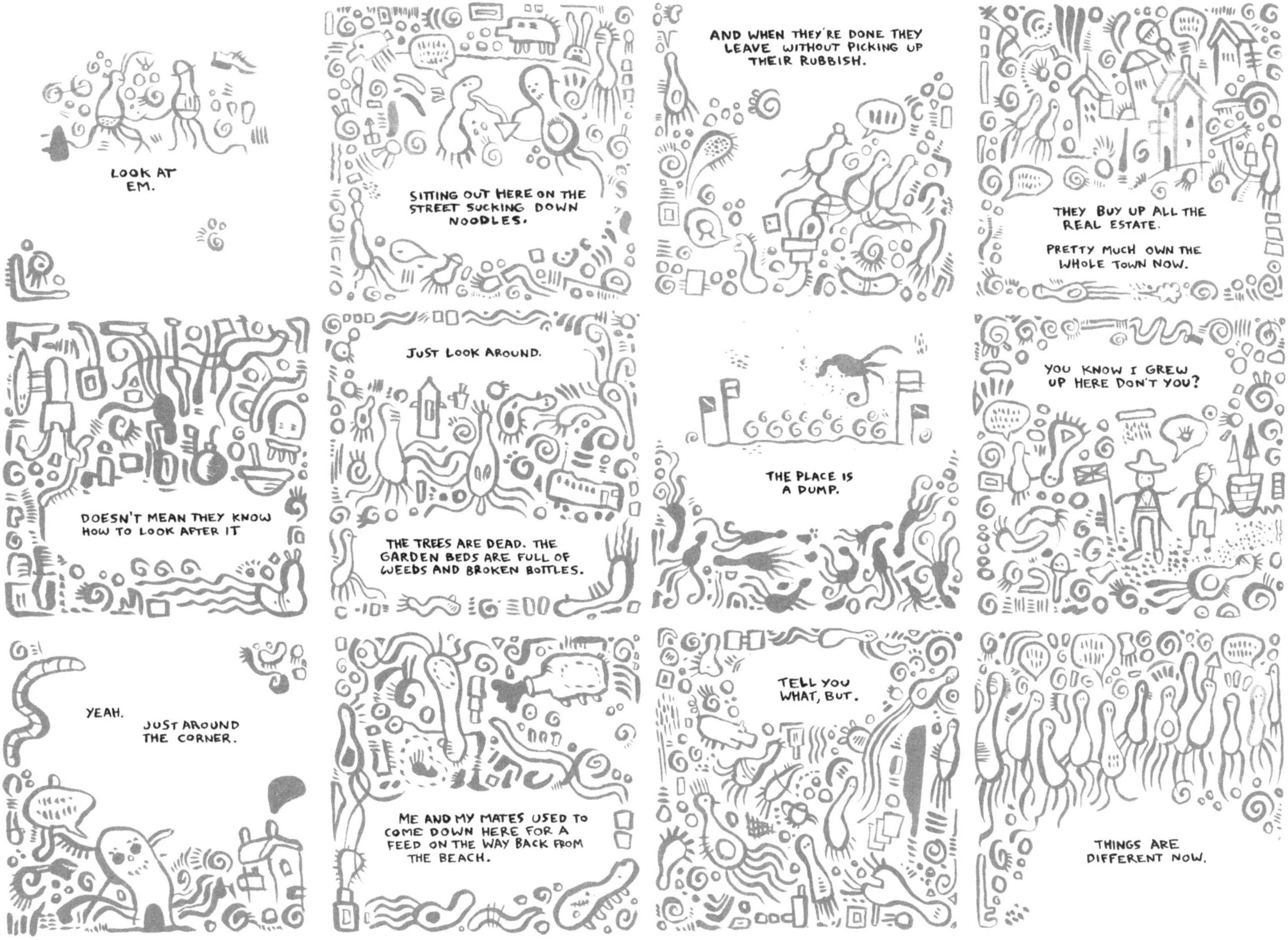

LOOK AT EM.
SITTING OUT HERE ON THE STREET SUCKING DOWN NOODLES.
AND WHEN THEY'RE DONE THEY LEAVE WITHOUT PICKING UP THEIR RUBBISH.
THEY BUY UP ALL THE REAL ESTATE.
PRETTY MUCH OWN THE WHOLE TOWN NOW.
DOESN'T MEAN THEY KNOW HOW TO LOOK AFTER IT
JUST LOOK AROUND.
THE TREES ARE DEAD. THE GARDEN BEDS ARE FULL OF WEEDS AND BROKEN BOTTLES.
THE PLACE IS A DUMP.
YOU KNOW I GREW UP HERE DON'T YOU?
YEAH.
JUST AROUND THE CORNER.
ME AND MY MATES USED TO COME DOWN HERE FOR A FEED ON THE WAY BACK FROM THE BEACH.
TELL YOU WHAT, BUT.
THINGS ARE DIFFERENT NOW.

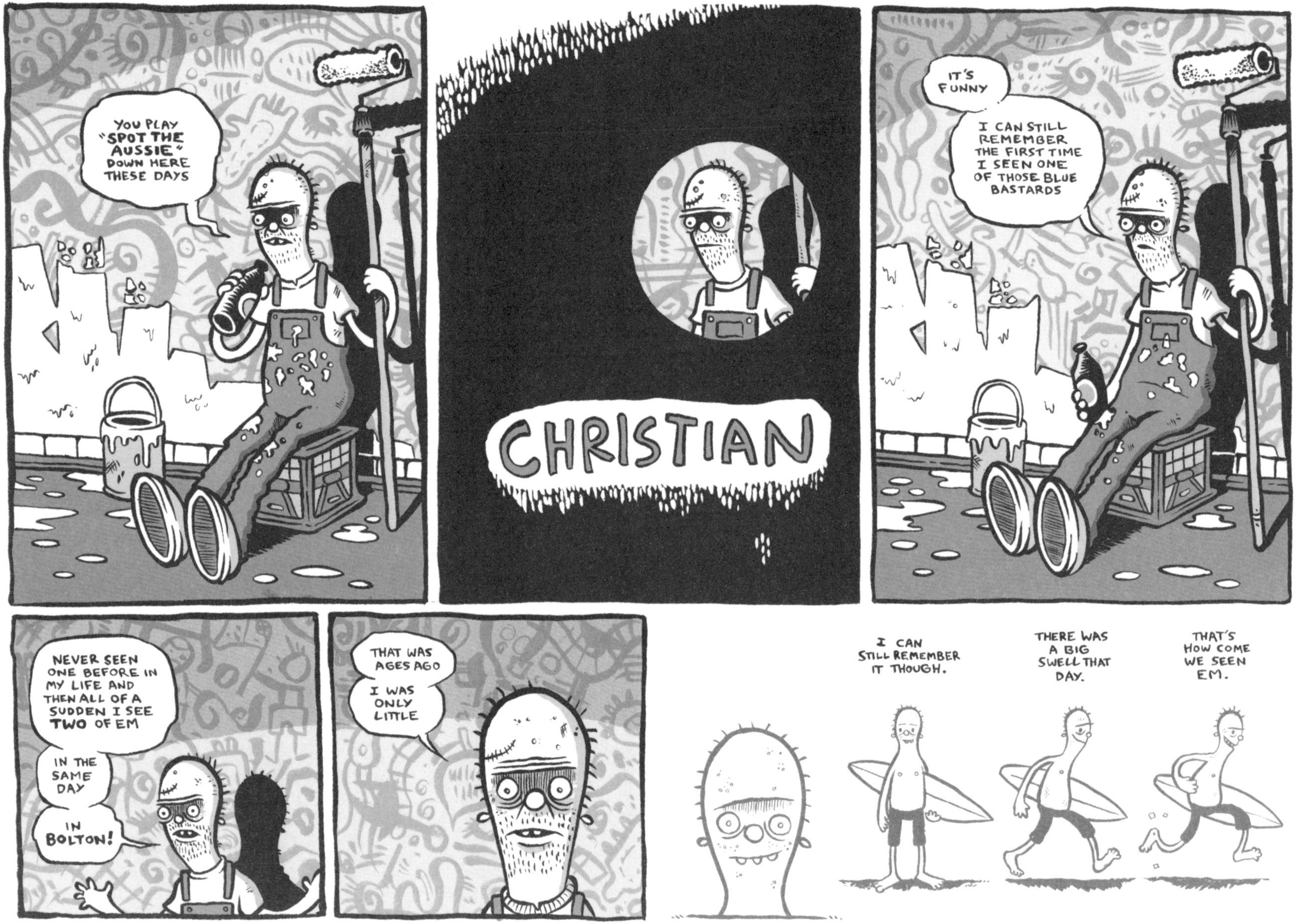
YOU PLAY "SPOT THE AUSSIE" DOWN HERE THESE DAYS
CHRISTIAN
IT'S FUNNY
I CAN STILL REMEMBER THE FIRST TIME I SEEN ONE OF THOSE BLUE BASTARDS
NEVER SEEN ONE BEFORE IN MY LIFE AND THEN ALL OF A SUDDEN I SEE TWO OF EM
IN THE SAME DAY
IN BOLTON!
THAT WAS AGES AGO
I WAS ONLY LITTLE
I CAN STILL REMEMBER IT THOUGH.
THERE WAS A BIG SWELL THAT DAY.
THAT'S HOW COME WE SEEN EM.

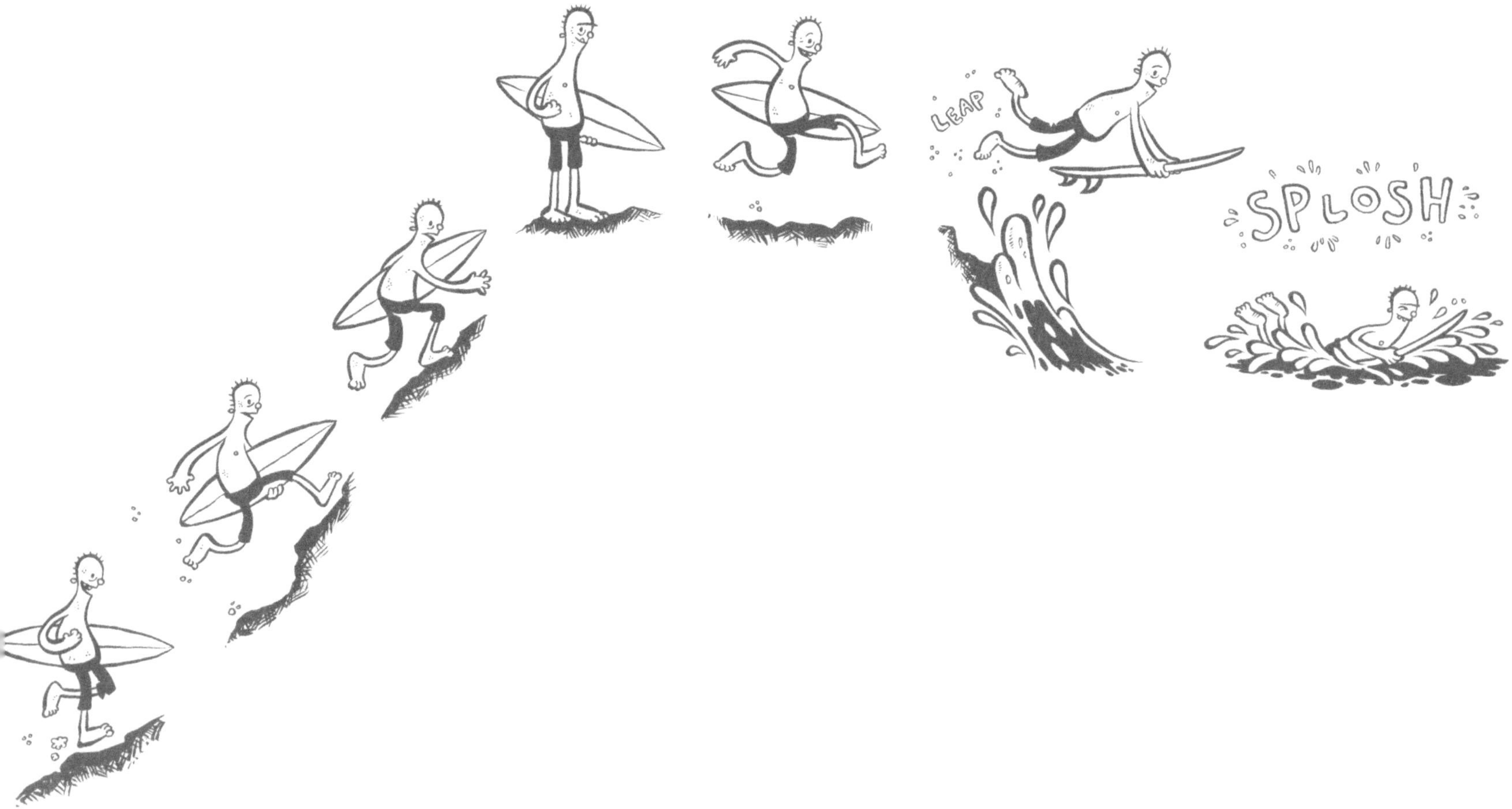
LEAP
SPLOSH

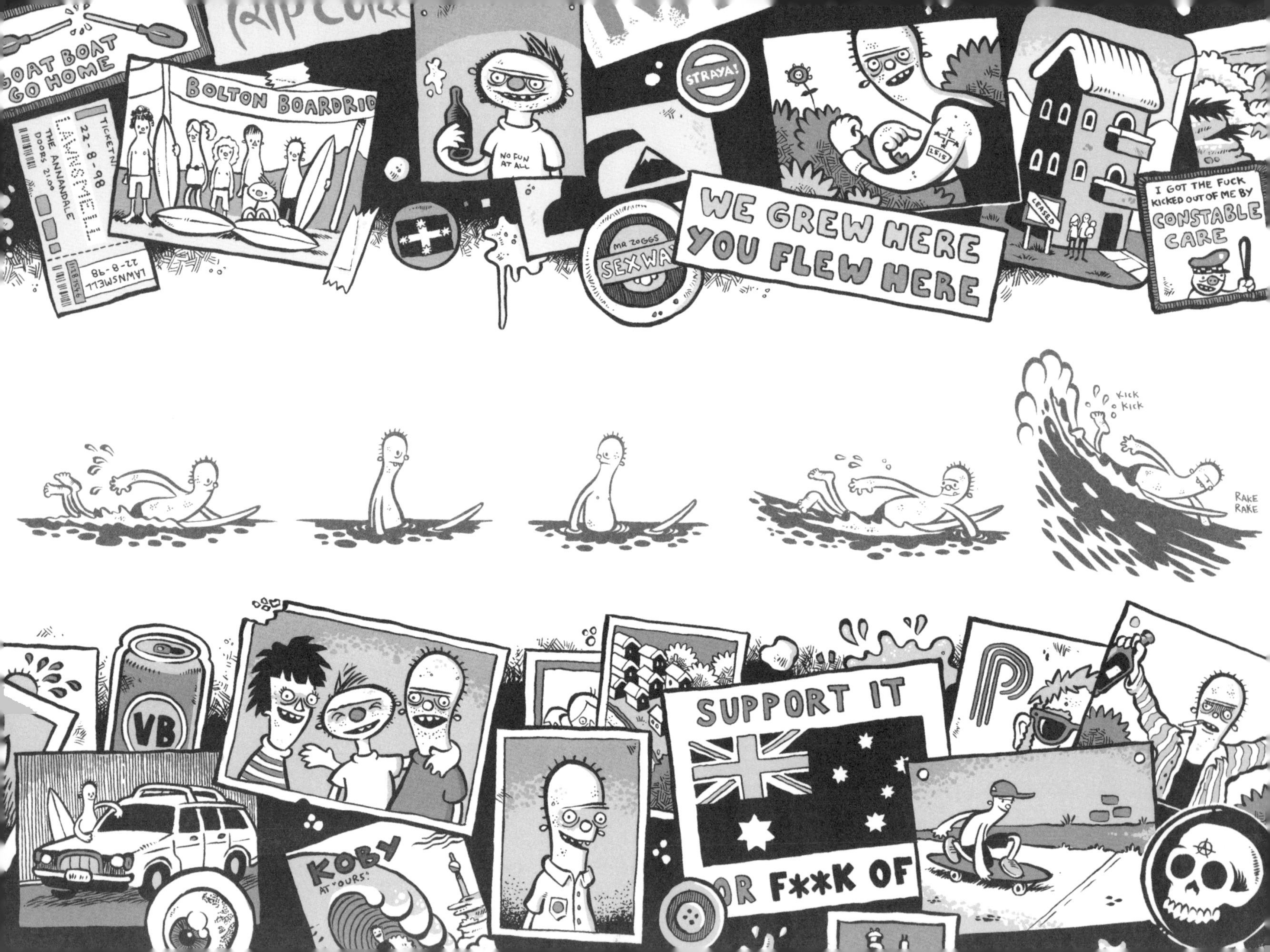
GOAT BOAT GO HOME
TICKET N
22-8-98
LAWNSMELL
THE ANNANDALE
DOORS 21.00
BOLTON BOARDRID
NO FUN AT ALL
STRAYA!
MR ZOGGS
SEXWA
WE GREW HERE YOU FLEW HERE
LEASED
I GOT THE FUCK KICKED OUT OF ME BY CONSTABLE CARE
KICK KICK
RAKE RAKE
VB
KOBY
AT "OURS"
SUPPORT IT
OR F**K OF

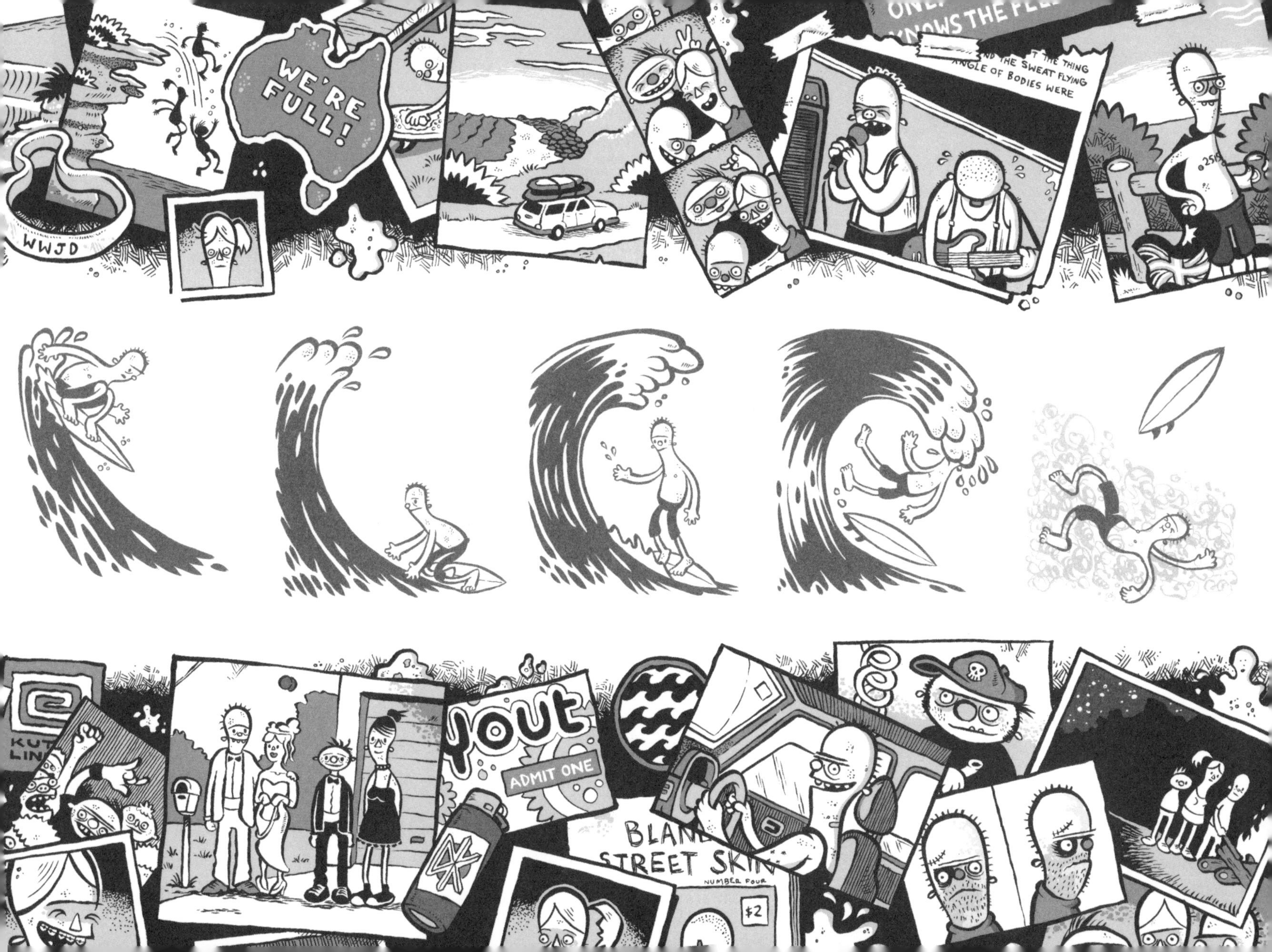

KNOWS THE FE
THE SWEAT FLYING
ANGLE OF BODIES WERE
WE'RE FULL!
WWJD
yout
ADMIT ONE
STREET SKIN
NUMBER FOUR
$2

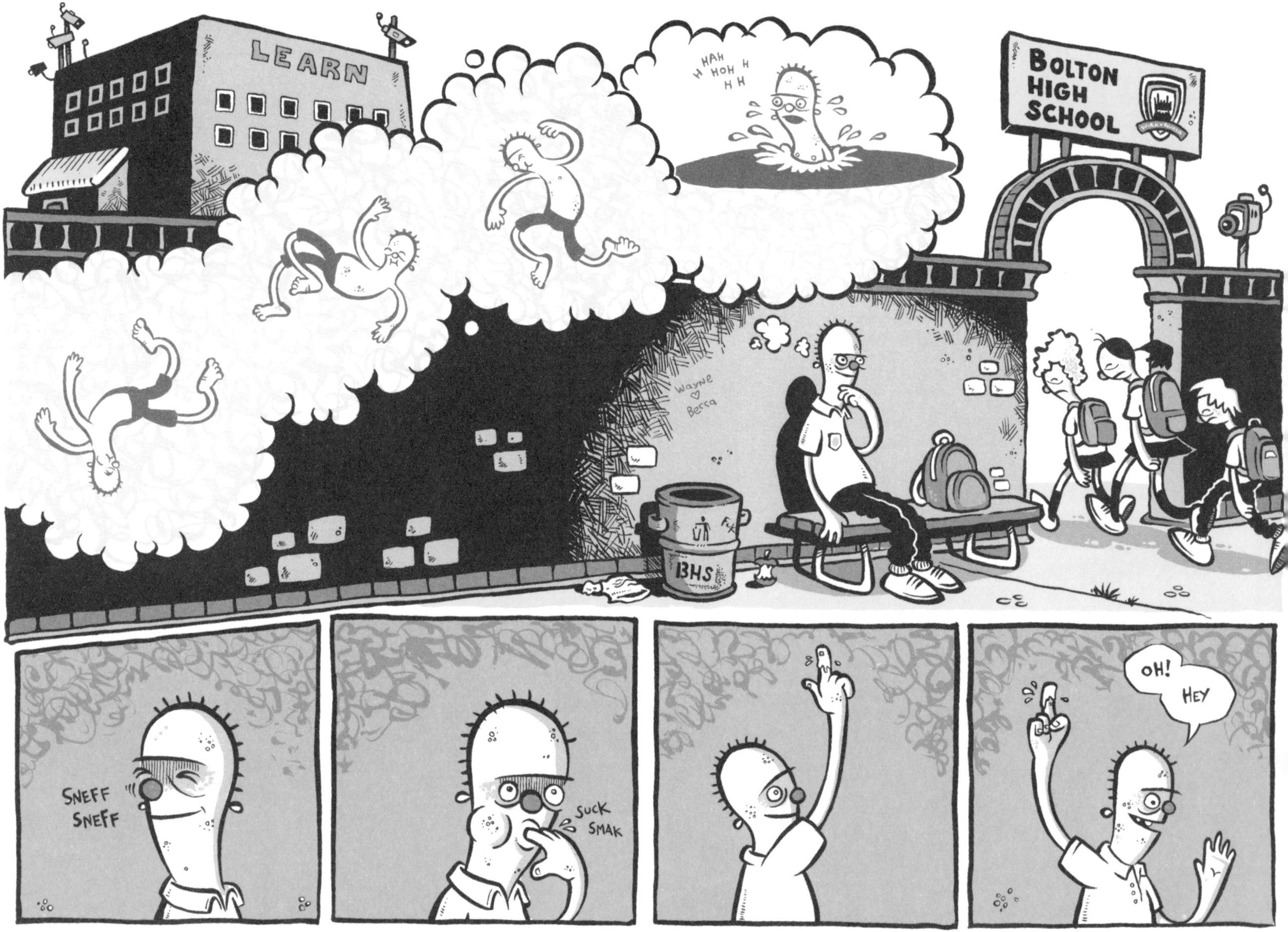
LEARN
H HAH HOH H H H
BOLTON HIGH SCHOOL
Wayne ♡ Becca
BHS
SNEFF SNEFF
SUCK SMAK
OH!
HEY

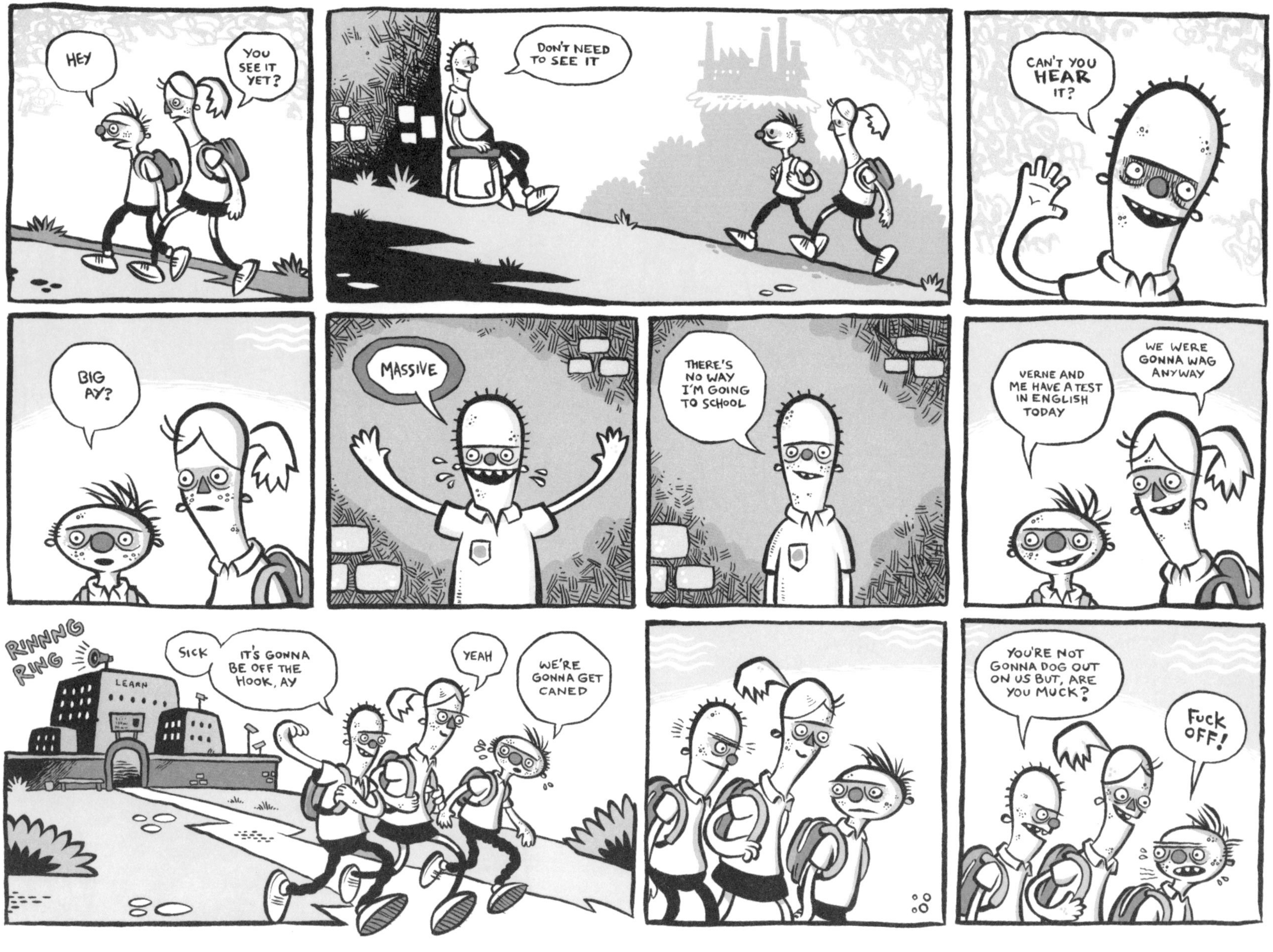
HEY
YOU SEE IT YET?
DON'T NEED TO SEE IT
CAN'T YOU HEAR IT?
BIG AY?
MASSIVE
THERE'S NO WAY I'M GOING TO SCHOOL
VERNE AND ME HAVE A TEST IN ENGLISH TODAY
WE WERE GONNA WAG ANYWAY
RINNNG RING
LEARN
SICK
IT'S GONNA BE OFF THE HOOK, AY
YEAH
WE'RE GONNA GET CANED
YOU'RE NOT GONNA DOG OUT ON US BUT, ARE YOU MUCK?
FUCK OFF!

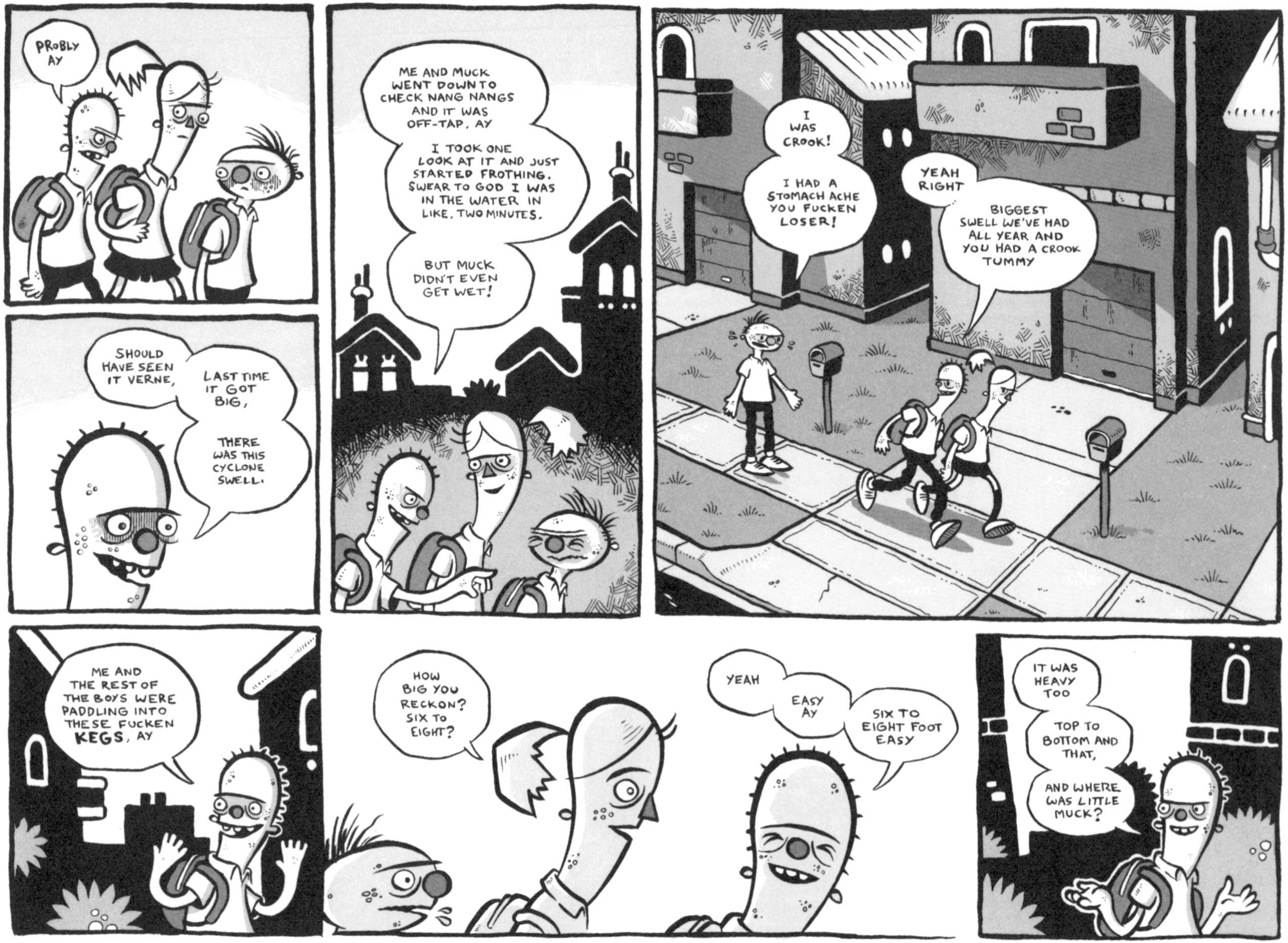
PROBLY AY
SHOULD HAVE SEEN IT VERNE,
LAST TIME IT GOT BIG,
THERE WAS THIS CYCLONE SWELL.
ME AND MUCK WENT DOWN TO CHECK NANG NANGS AND IT WAS OFF-TAP, AY
I TOOK ONE LOOK AT IT AND JUST STARTED FROTHING. SWEAR TO GOD I WAS IN THE WATER IN LIKE, TWO MINUTES.
BUT MUCK DIDN'T EVEN GET WET!
I WAS CROOK!
I HAD A STOMACH ACHE YOU FUCKEN LOSER!
YEAH RIGHT
BIGGEST SWELL WE'VE HAD ALL YEAR AND YOU HAD A CROOK TUMMY
ME AND THE REST OF THE BOYS WERE PADDLING INTO THESE FUCKEN KEGS, AY
HOW BIG YOU RECKON? SIX TO EIGHT?
YEAH
EASY AY
SIX TO EIGHT FOOT EASY
IT WAS HEAVY TOO
TOP TO BOTTOM AND THAT,
AND WHERE WAS LITTLE MUCK?

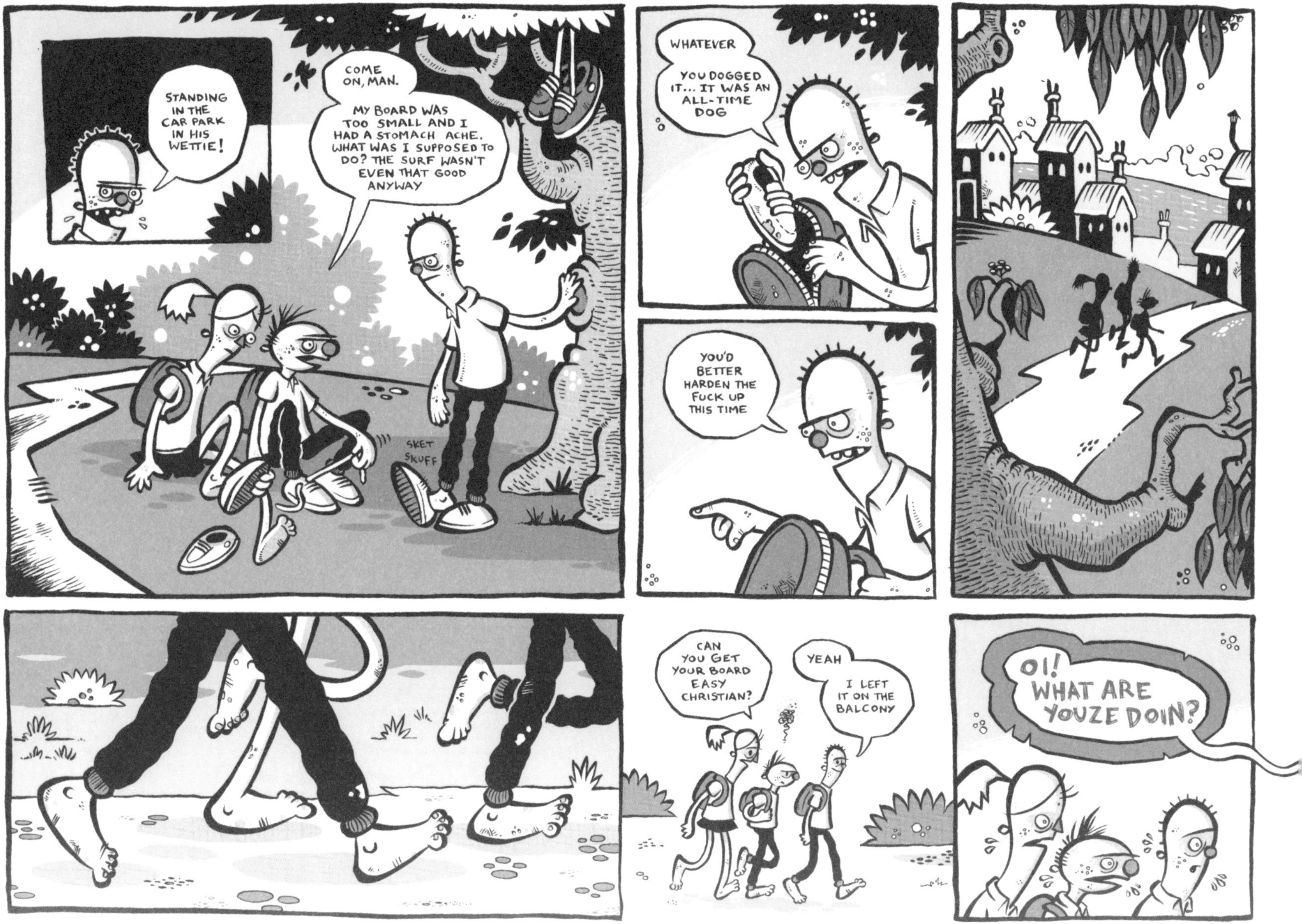
STANDING IN THE CAR PARK IN HIS WETTIE!
COME ON, MAN.
MY BOARD WAS TOO SMALL AND I HAD A STOMACH ACHE. WHAT WAS I SUPPOSED TO DO? THE SURF WASN'T EVEN THAT GOOD ANYWAY
SKET
SKUFF
WHATEVER
YOU DOGGED IT... IT WAS AN ALL-TIME DOG
YOU'D BETTER HARDEN THE FUCK UP THIS TIME
CAN YOU GET YOUR BOARD EASY CHRISTIAN?
YEAH
I LEFT IT ON THE BALCONY
OI! WHAT ARE YOUZE DOIN?

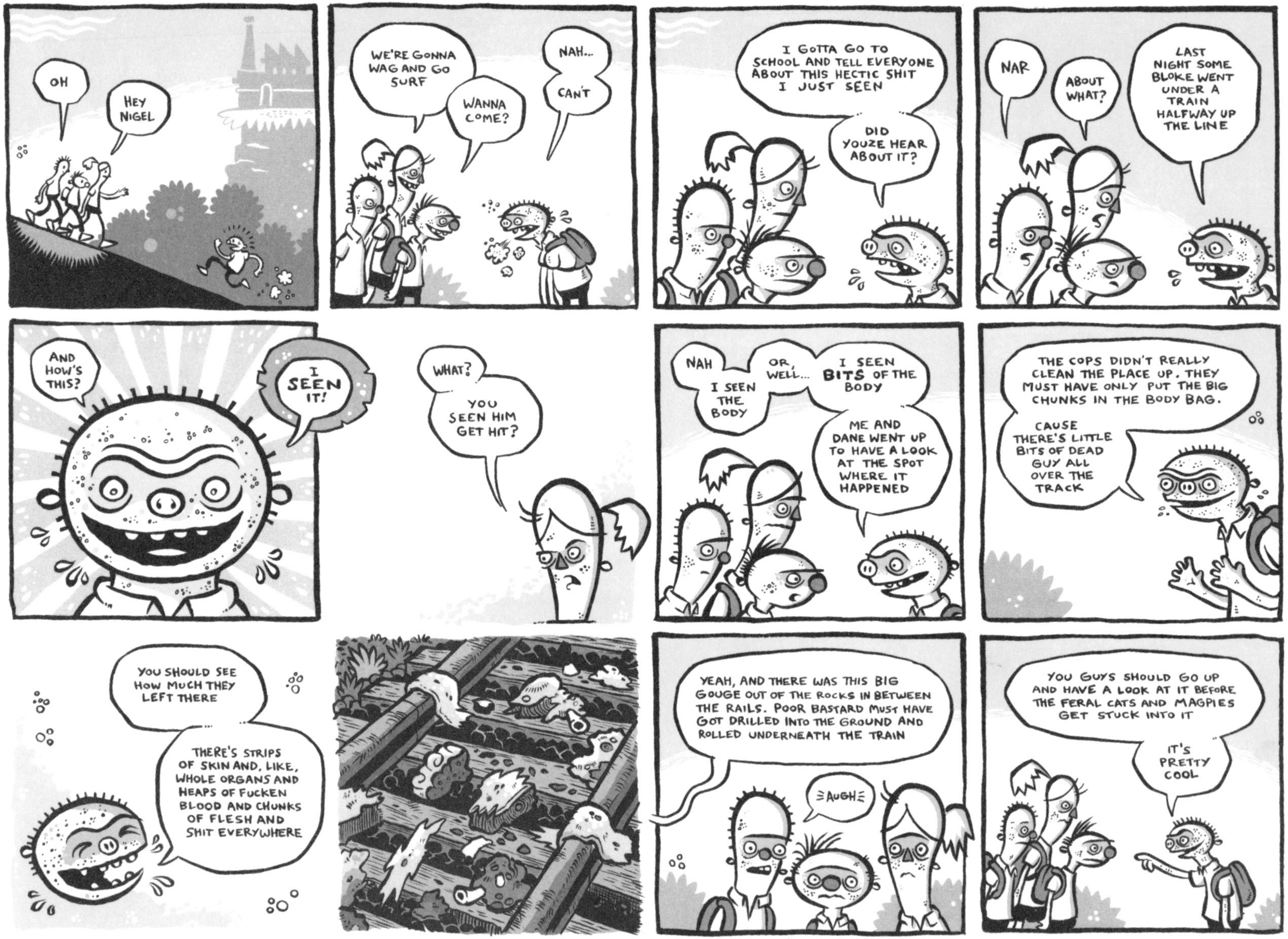
OH
HEY NIGEL
WE'RE GONNA WAG AND GO SURF
WANNA COME?
NAH...
CAN'T
I GOTTA GO TO SCHOOL AND TELL EVERYONE ABOUT THIS HECTIC SHIT I JUST SEEN
DID YOUZE HEAR ABOUT IT?
NAR
ABOUT WHAT?
LAST NIGHT SOME BLOKE WENT UNDER A TRAIN HALFWAY UP THE LINE
AND HOW'S THIS?
I SEEN IT!
WHAT?
YOU SEEN HIM GET HIT?
NAH
I SEEN THE BODY
OR, WELL...
I SEEN BITS OF THE BODY
ME AND DANE WENT UP TO HAVE A LOOK AT THE SPOT WHERE IT HAPPENED
THE COPS DIDN'T REALLY CLEAN THE PLACE UP. THEY MUST HAVE ONLY PUT THE BIG CHUNKS IN THE BODY BAG.
CAUSE THERE'S LITTLE BITS OF DEAD GUY ALL OVER THE TRACK
YOU SHOULD SEE HOW MUCH THEY LEFT THERE
THERE'S STRIPS OF SKIN AND, LIKE, WHOLE ORGANS AND HEAPS OF FUCKEN BLOOD AND CHUNKS OF FLESH AND SHIT EVERYWHERE
YEAH, AND THERE WAS THIS BIG GOUGE OUT OF THE ROCKS IN BETWEEN THE RAILS. POOR BASTARD MUST HAVE GOT DRILLED INTO THE GROUND AND ROLLED UNDERNEATH THE TRAIN
AUGH
YOU GUYS SHOULD GO UP AND HAVE A LOOK AT IT BEFORE THE FERAL CATS AND MAGPIES GET STUCK INTO IT
IT'S PRETTY COOL

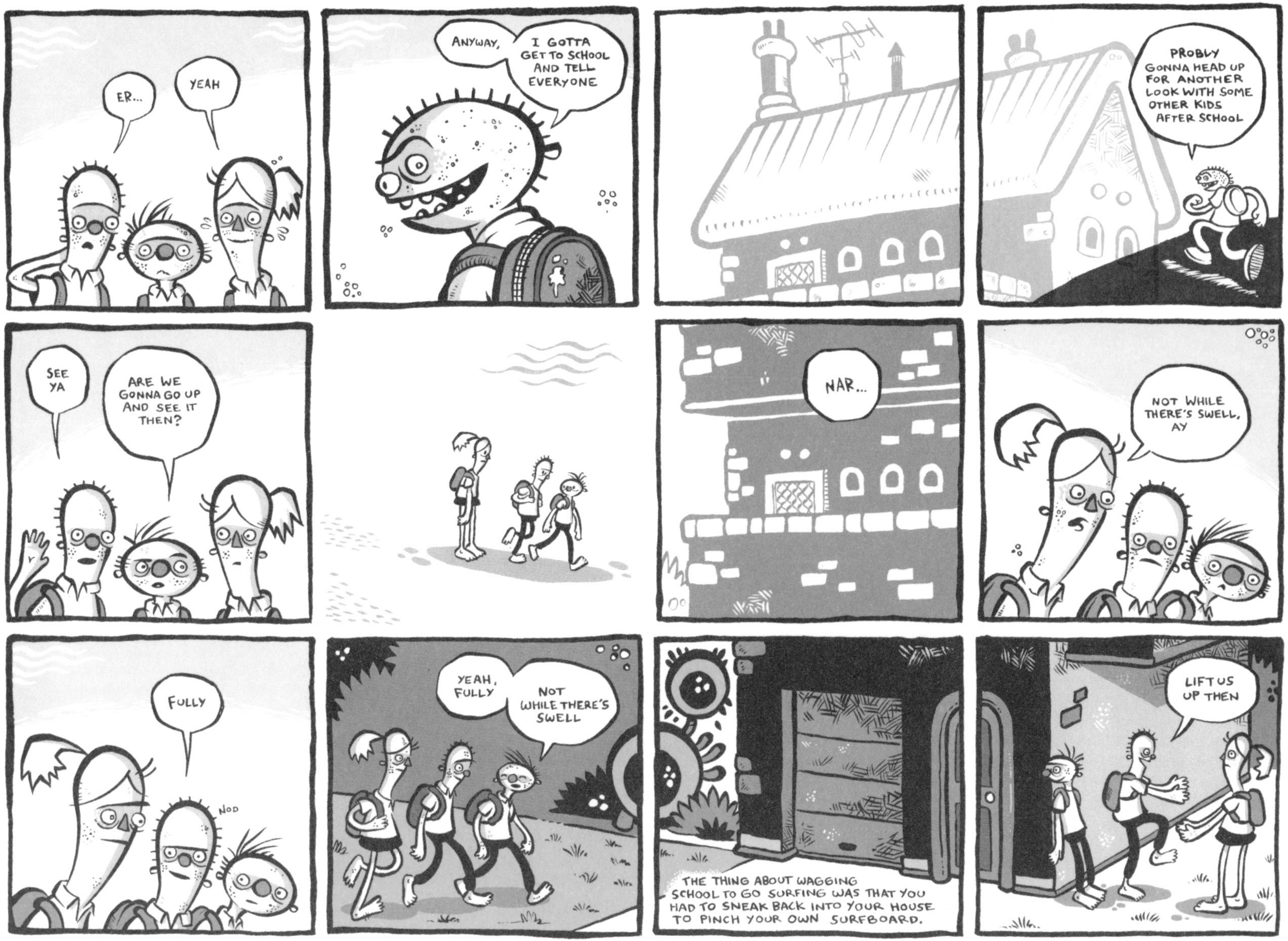
ER...
YEAH
ANYWAY,
I GOTTA GET TO SCHOOL AND TELL EVERYONE
PROBLY GONNA HEAD UP FOR ANOTHER LOOK WITH SOME OTHER KIDS AFTER SCHOOL
SEE YA
ARE WE GONNA GO UP AND SEE IT THEN?
NAR...
NOT WHILE THERE'S SWELL, AY
FULLY
NOD
YEAH, FULLY
NOT WHILE THERE'S SWELL
THE THING ABOUT WAGGING SCHOOL TO GO SURFING WAS THAT YOU HAD TO SNEAK BACK INTO YOUR HOUSE TO PINCH YOUR OWN SURFBOARD.
LIFT US UP THEN

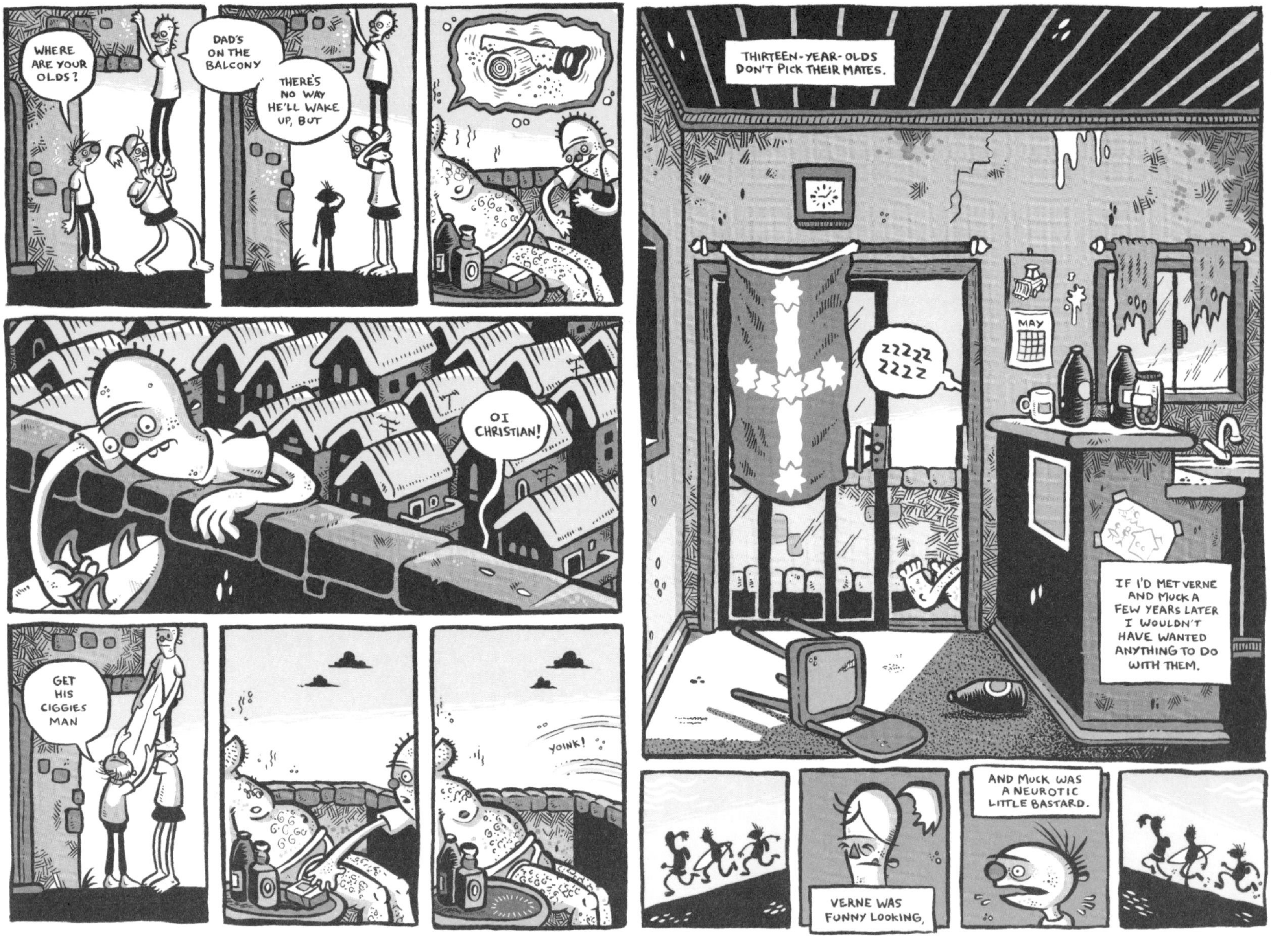
WHERE ARE YOUR OLDS?
DAD'S ON THE BALCONY
THERE'S NO WAY HE'LL WAKE UP, BUT
OI CHRISTIAN!
GET HIS CIGGIES MAN
YOINK!
THIRTEEN-YEAR-OLDS DON'T PICK THEIR MATES.
MAY
ZZZZZ ZZZZ
IF I'D MET VERNE AND MUCK A FEW YEARS LATER I WOULDN'T HAVE WANTED ANYTHING TO DO WITH THEM.
VERNE WAS FUNNY LOOKING,
AND MUCK WAS A NEUROTIC LITTLE BASTARD.

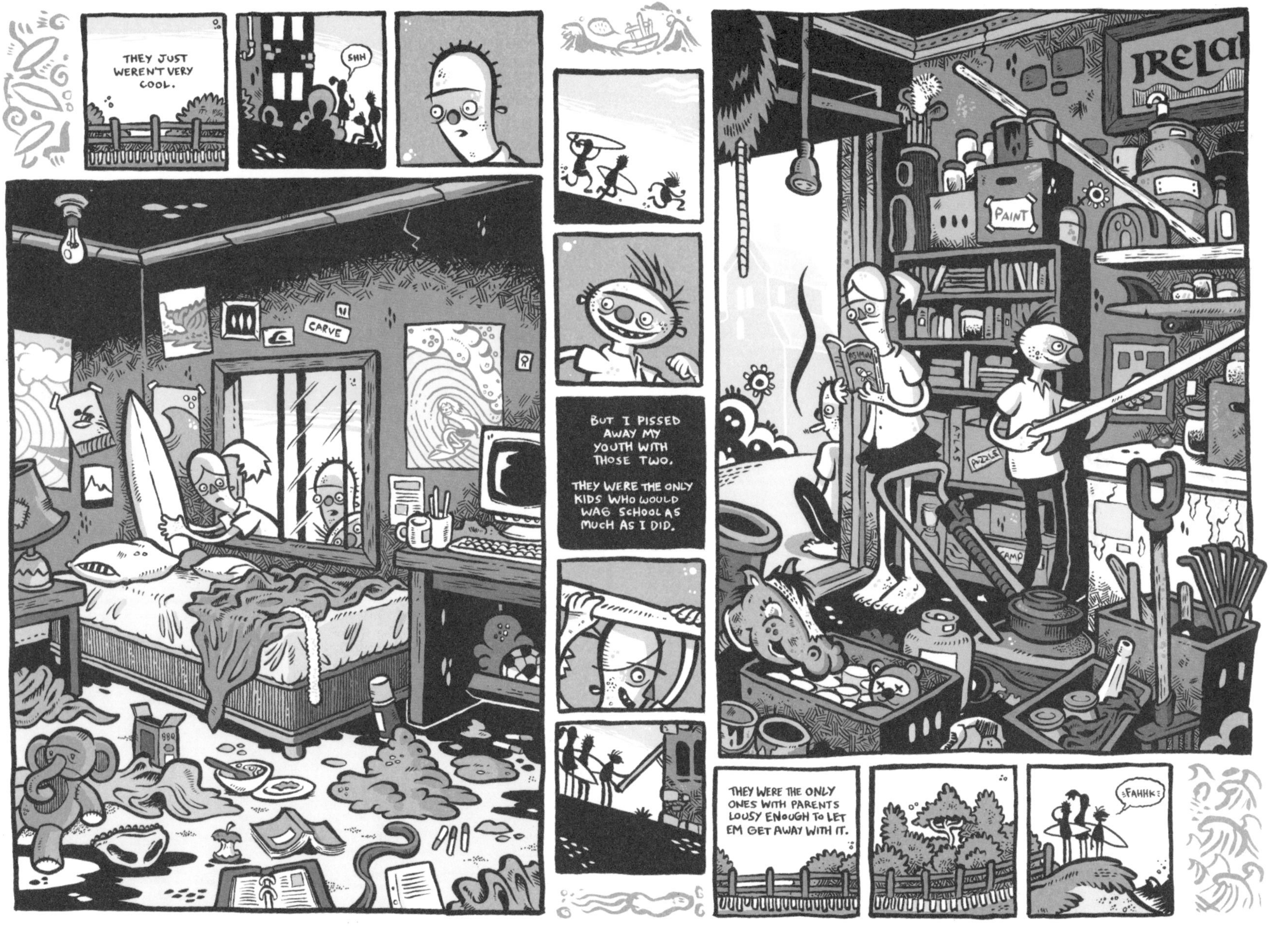
THEY JUST WEREN'T VERY COOL.
SHH
CARVE
IRELA
PAINT
BUT I PISSED AWAY MY YOUTH WITH THOSE TWO.
THEY WERE THE ONLY KIDS WHO WOULD WAG SCHOOL AS MUCH AS I DID.
ATLAS
PUZZLE
THEY WERE THE ONLY ONES WITH PARENTS LOUSY ENOUGH TO LET EM GET AWAY WITH IT.
FAHHK

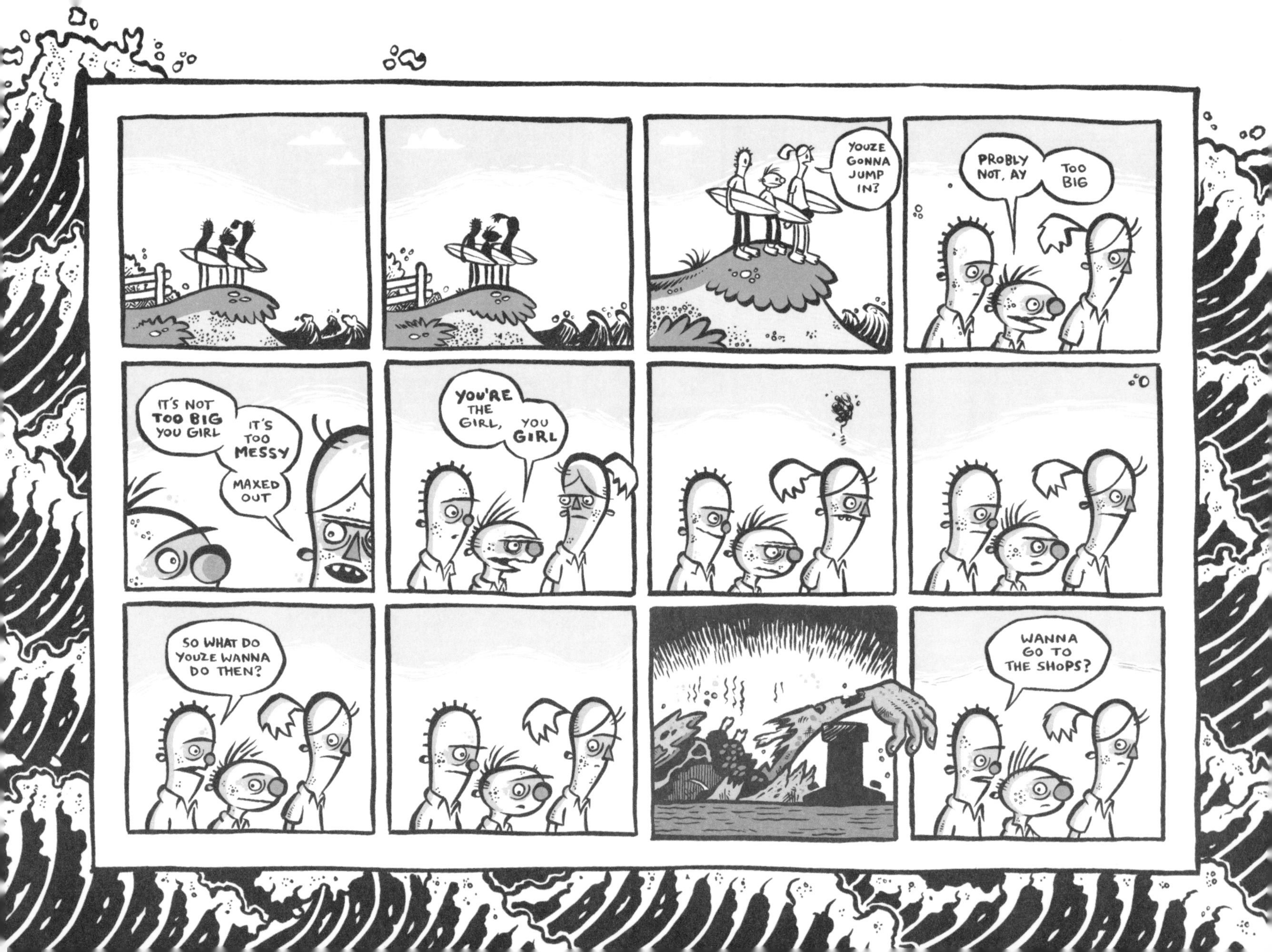
YOUZE GONNA JUMP IN?
PROBLY NOT, AY
TOO BIG
IT'S NOT TOO BIG YOU GIRL
IT'S TOO MESSY
MAXED OUT
YOU'RE THE GIRL, YOU GIRL
SO WHAT DO YOUZE WANNA DO THEN?
WANNA GO TO THE SHOPS?

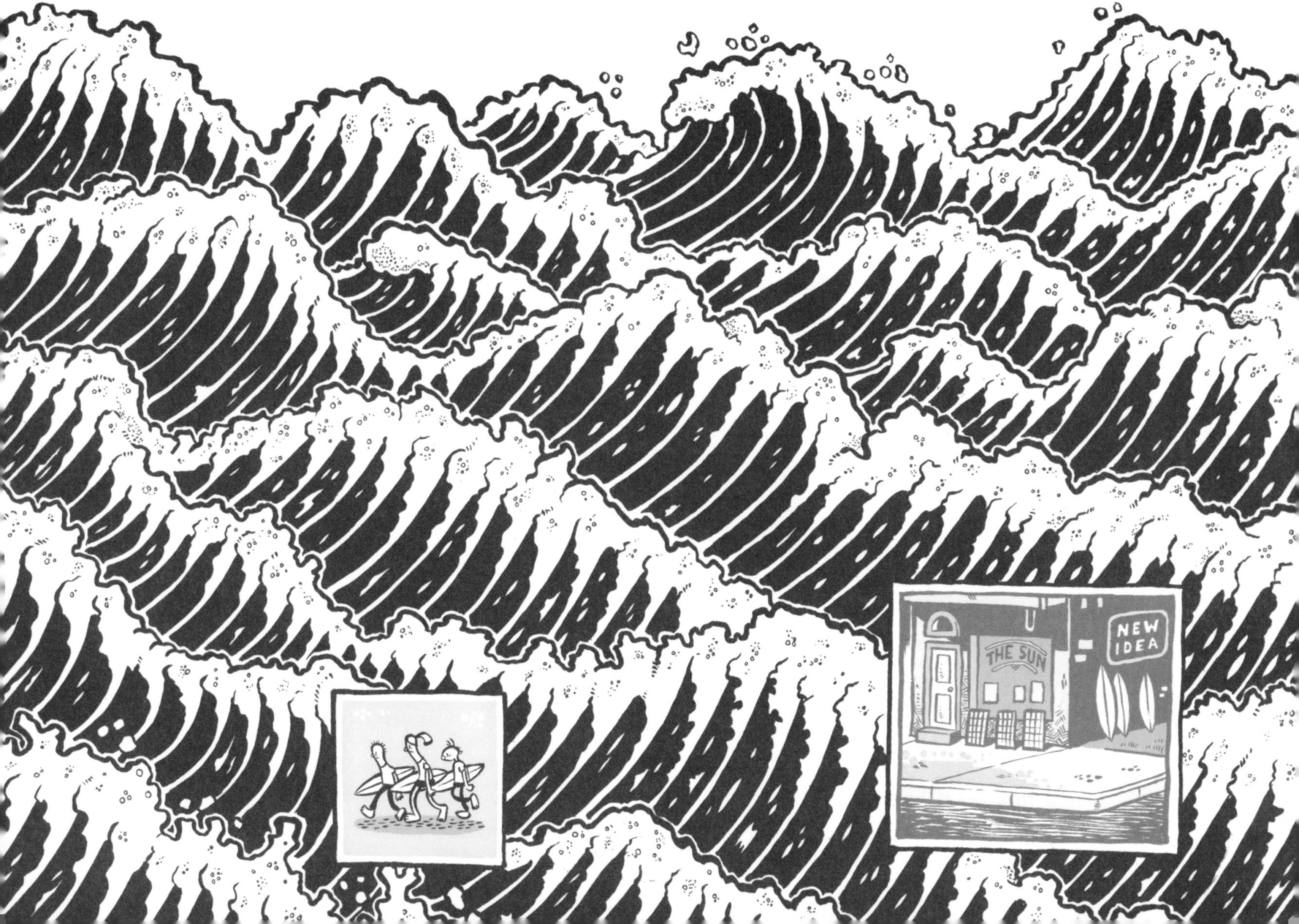
THE SUN
NEW IDEA

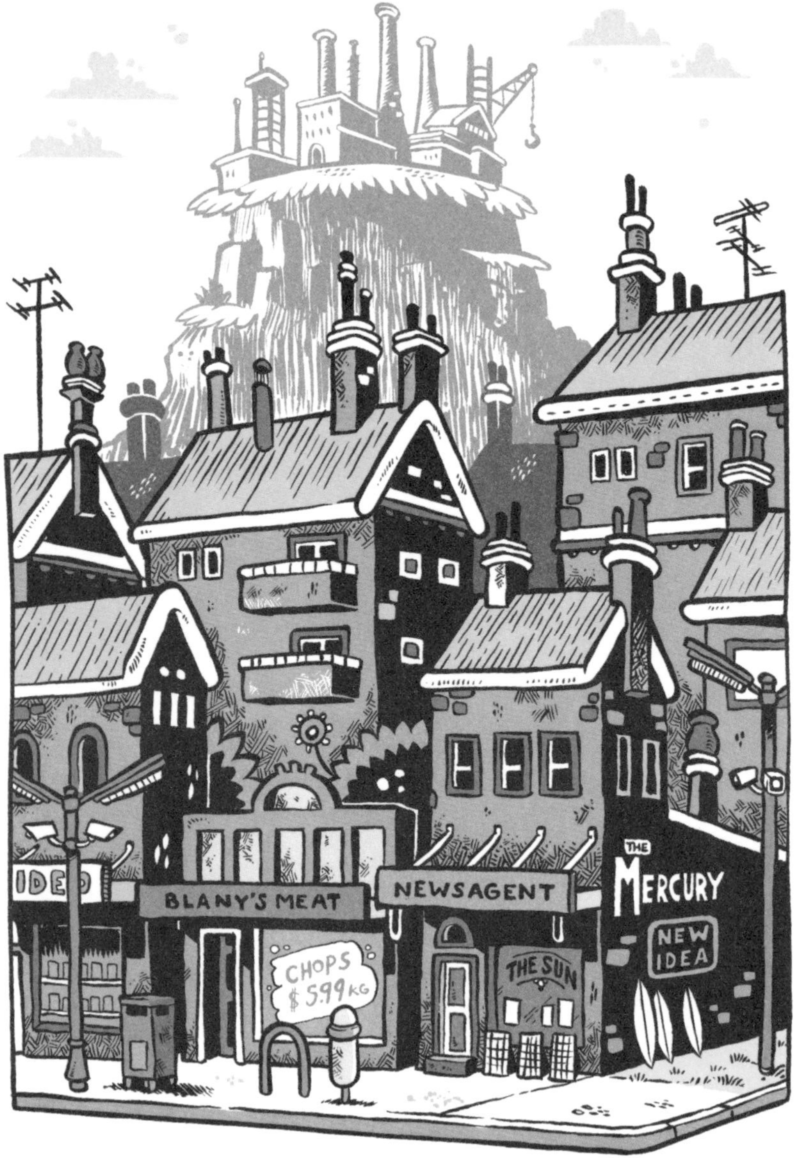
IDEO
BLANY'S MEAT
CHOPS $5.99 KG
NEWSAGENT
THE SUN
THE MERCURY
NEW IDEA

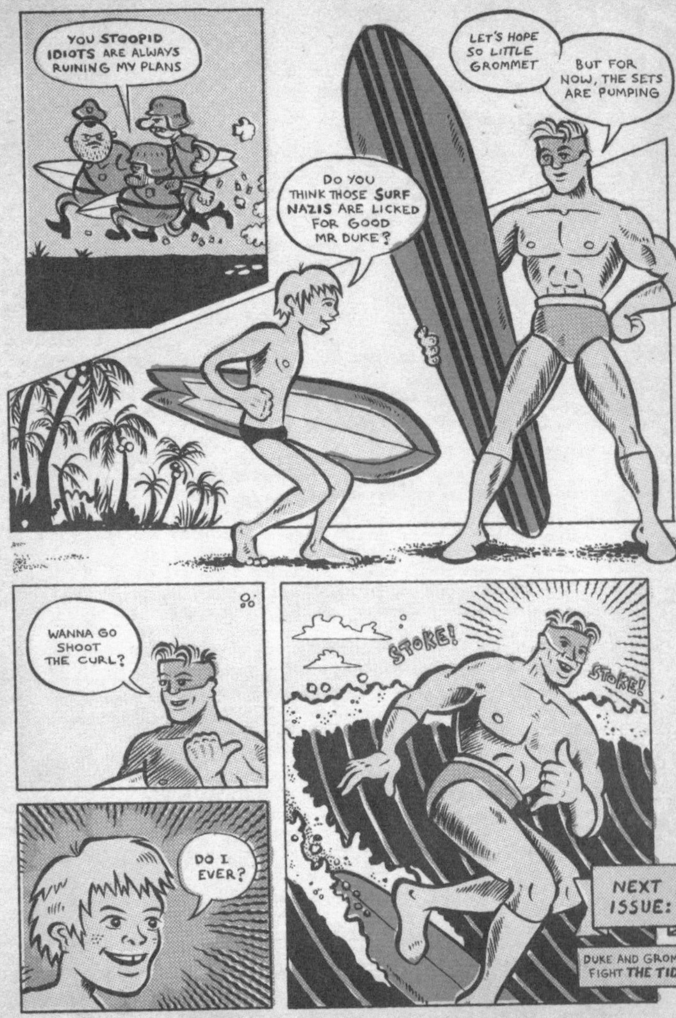
YOU STOOPID IDIOTS ARE ALWAYS RUINING MY PLANS
DO YOU THINK THOSE SURF NAZIS ARE LICKED FOR GOOD MR DUKE?
LET'S HOPE SO LITTLE GROMMET
BUT FOR NOW, THE SETS ARE PUMPING
WANNA GO SHOOT THE CURL?
DO I EVER?
STOKE!
STOKE!
NEXT ISSUE:
DUKE AND GROMMET FIGHT THE TIDE!

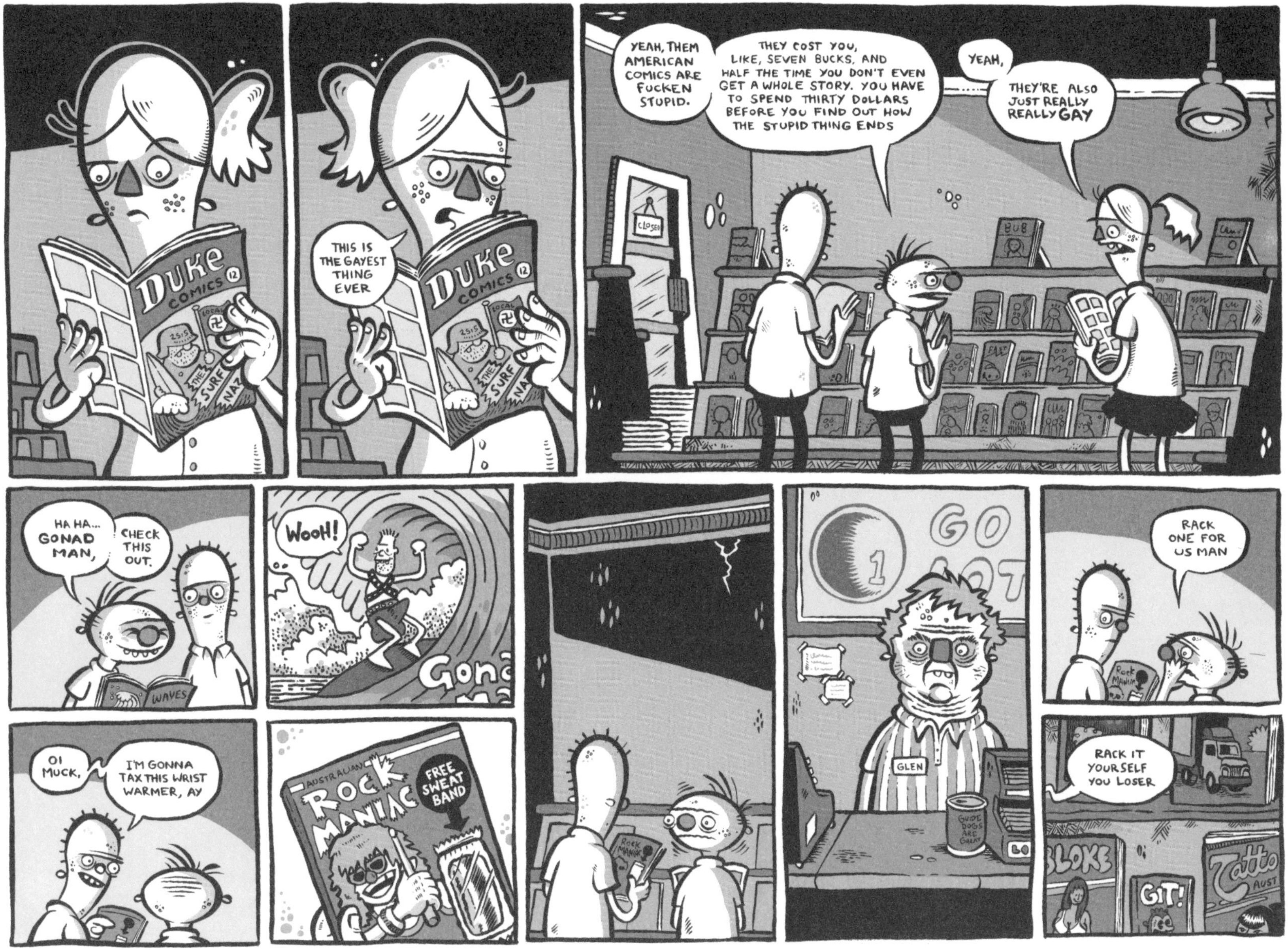
DUKE COMICS 12
THE SURF NAZ
THIS IS THE GAYEST THING EVER
YEAH, THEM AMERICAN COMICS ARE FUCKEN STUPID.
THEY COST YOU, LIKE, SEVEN BUCKS, AND HALF THE TIME YOU DON'T EVEN GET A WHOLE STORY. YOU HAVE TO SPEND THIRTY DOLLARS BEFORE YOU FIND OUT HOW THE STUPID THING ENDS
YEAH,
THEY'RE ALSO JUST REALLY REALLY GAY
CLOSED
HA HA... GONAD MAN,
CHECK THIS OUT.
WAVES
WOOH!
OI MUCK,
I'M GONNA TAX THIS WRIST WARMER, AY
AUSTRALIAN ROCK MANIAC
FREE SWEAT BAND
GO
GLEN
GUIDE DOGS ARE GREAT
RACK ONE FOR US MAN
RACK IT YOURSELF YOU LOSER
BLOKE
GIT!

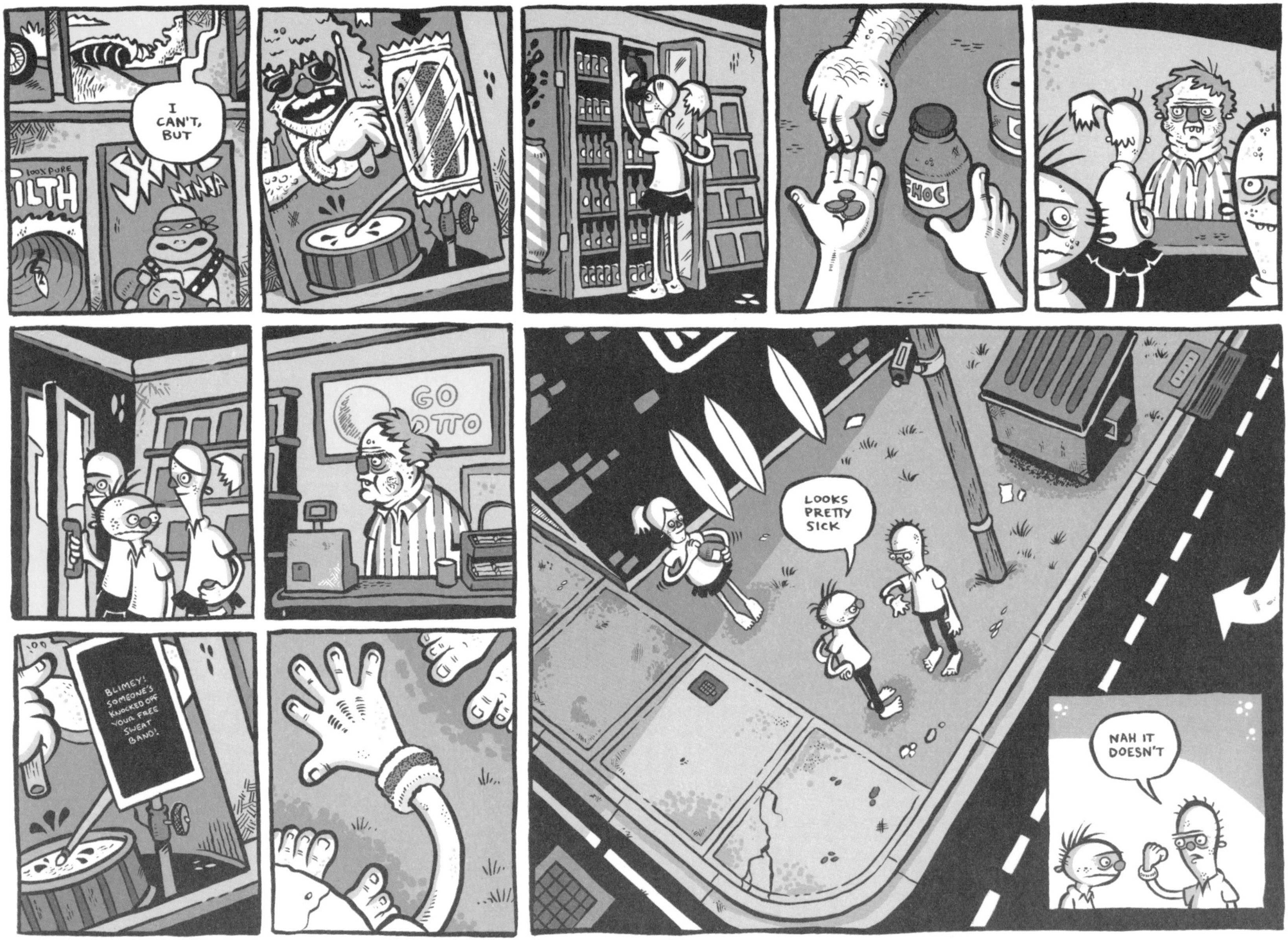
I CAN'T, BUT
100% PURE
NINJA
GO OTTO
BLIMEY! SOMEONE'S KNOCKED OFF YOUR FREE SWEAT BAND!
LOOKS PRETTY SICK
NAH IT DOESN'T

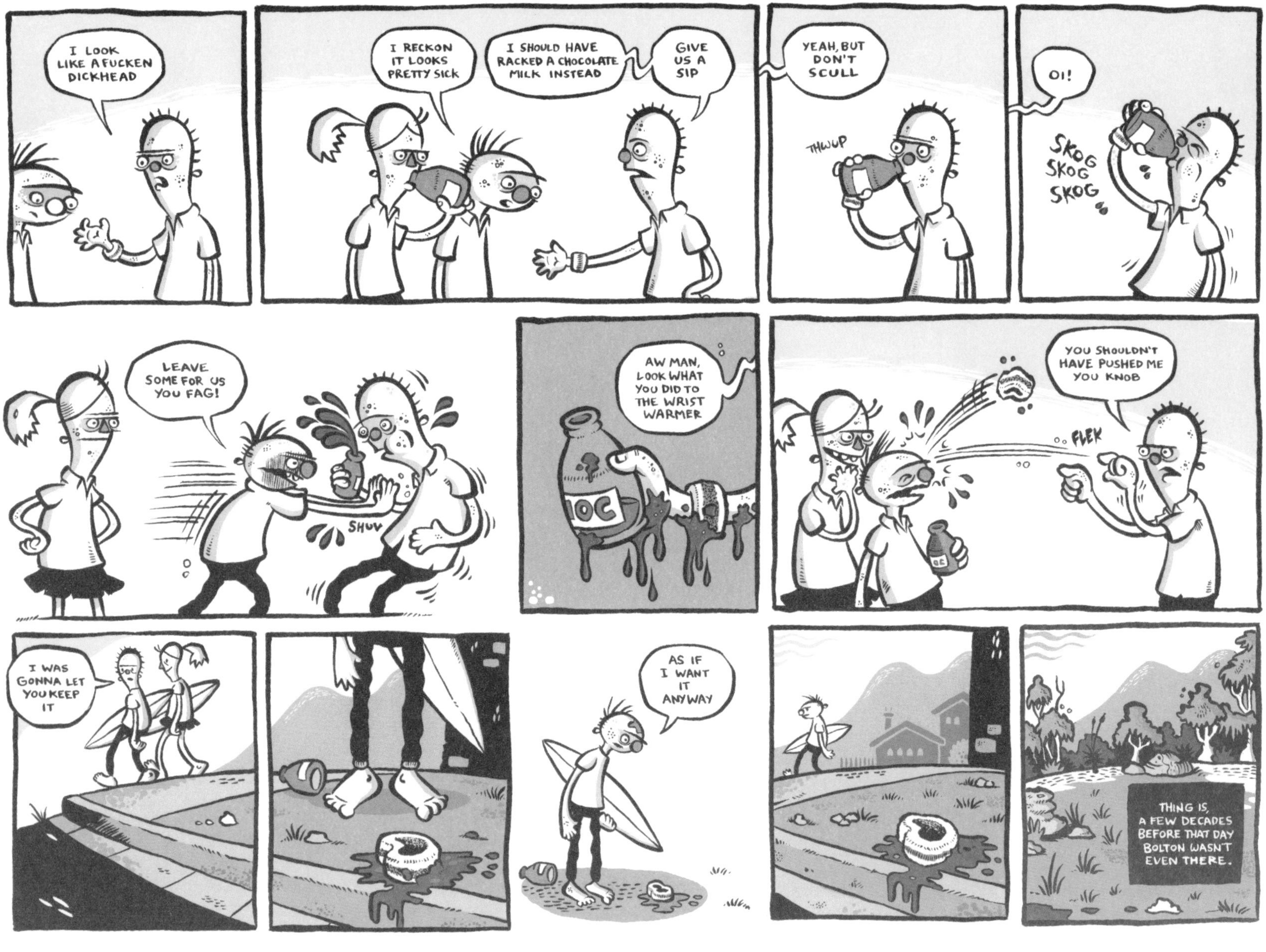
I LOOK LIKE A FUCKEN DICKHEAD
I RECKON IT LOOKS PRETTY SICK
I SHOULD HAVE RACKED A CHOCOLATE MILK INSTEAD
GIVE US A SIP
YEAH, BUT DON'T SCULL
THWUP
OI!
SKOG SKOG SKOG
LEAVE SOME FOR US YOU FAG!
SHUV
AW MAN, LOOK WHAT YOU DID TO THE WRIST WARMER
IOC
YOU SHOULDN'T HAVE PUSHED ME YOU KNOB
FLEK
I WAS GONNA LET YOU KEEP IT
AS IF I WANT IT ANYWAY
THING IS, A FEW DECADES BEFORE THAT DAY BOLTON WASN'T EVEN THERE.

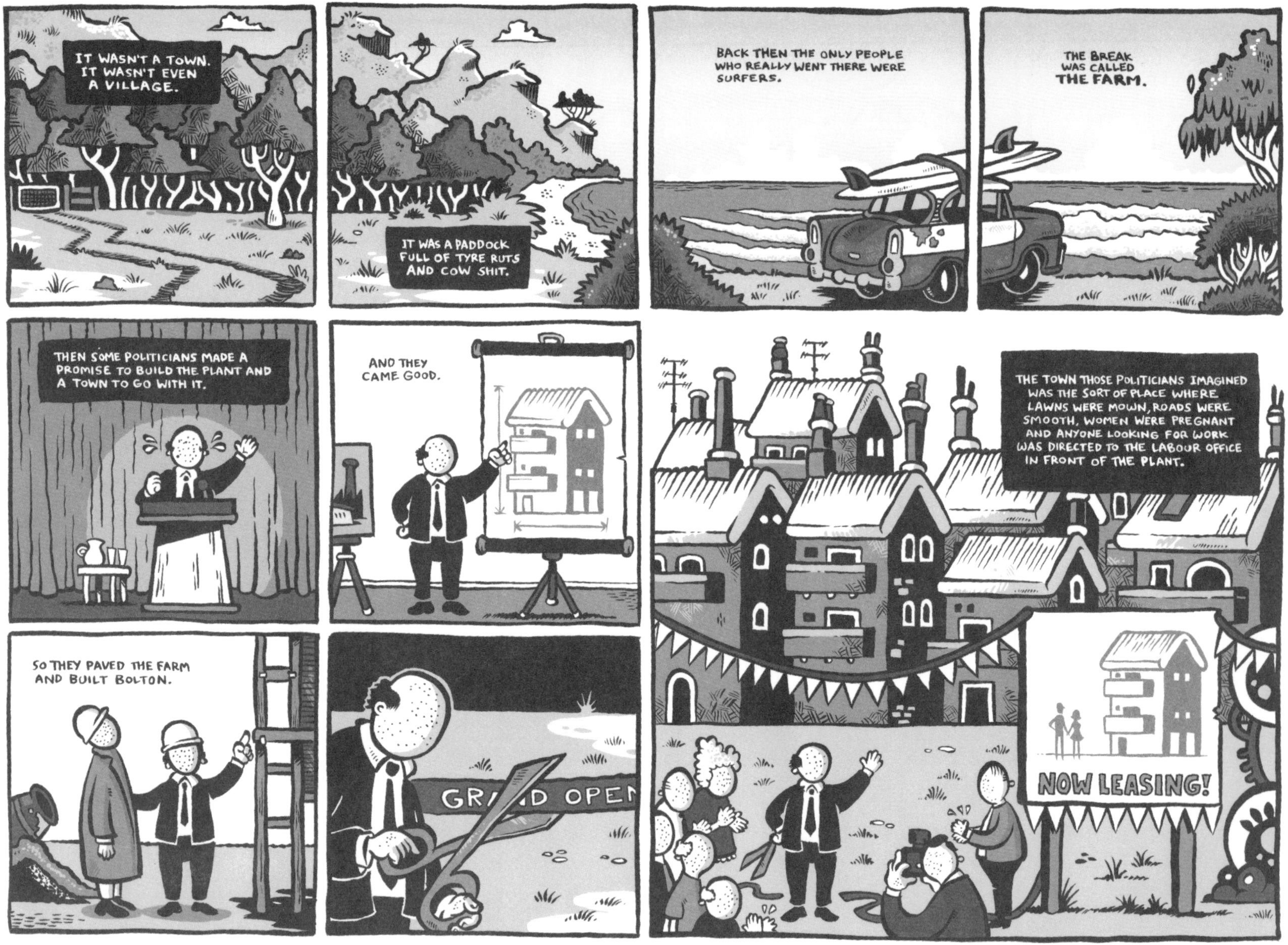
IT WASN'T A TOWN. IT WASN'T EVEN A VILLAGE.
IT WAS A PADDOCK FULL OF TYRE RUTS AND COW SHIT.
BACK THEN THE ONLY PEOPLE WHO REALLY WENT THERE WERE SURFERS.
THE BREAK WAS CALLED THE FARM.
THEN SOME POLITICIANS MADE A PROMISE TO BUILD THE PLANT AND A TOWN TO GO WITH IT.
AND THEY CAME GOOD.
THE TOWN THOSE POLITICIANS IMAGINED WAS THE SORT OF PLACE WHERE LAWNS WERE MOWN, ROADS WERE SMOOTH, WOMEN WERE PREGNANT AND ANYONE LOOKING FOR WORK WAS DIRECTED TO THE LABOUR OFFICE IN FRONT OF THE PLANT.
SO THEY PAVED THE FARM AND BUILT BOLTON.
GRAND OPEN
NOW LEASING!

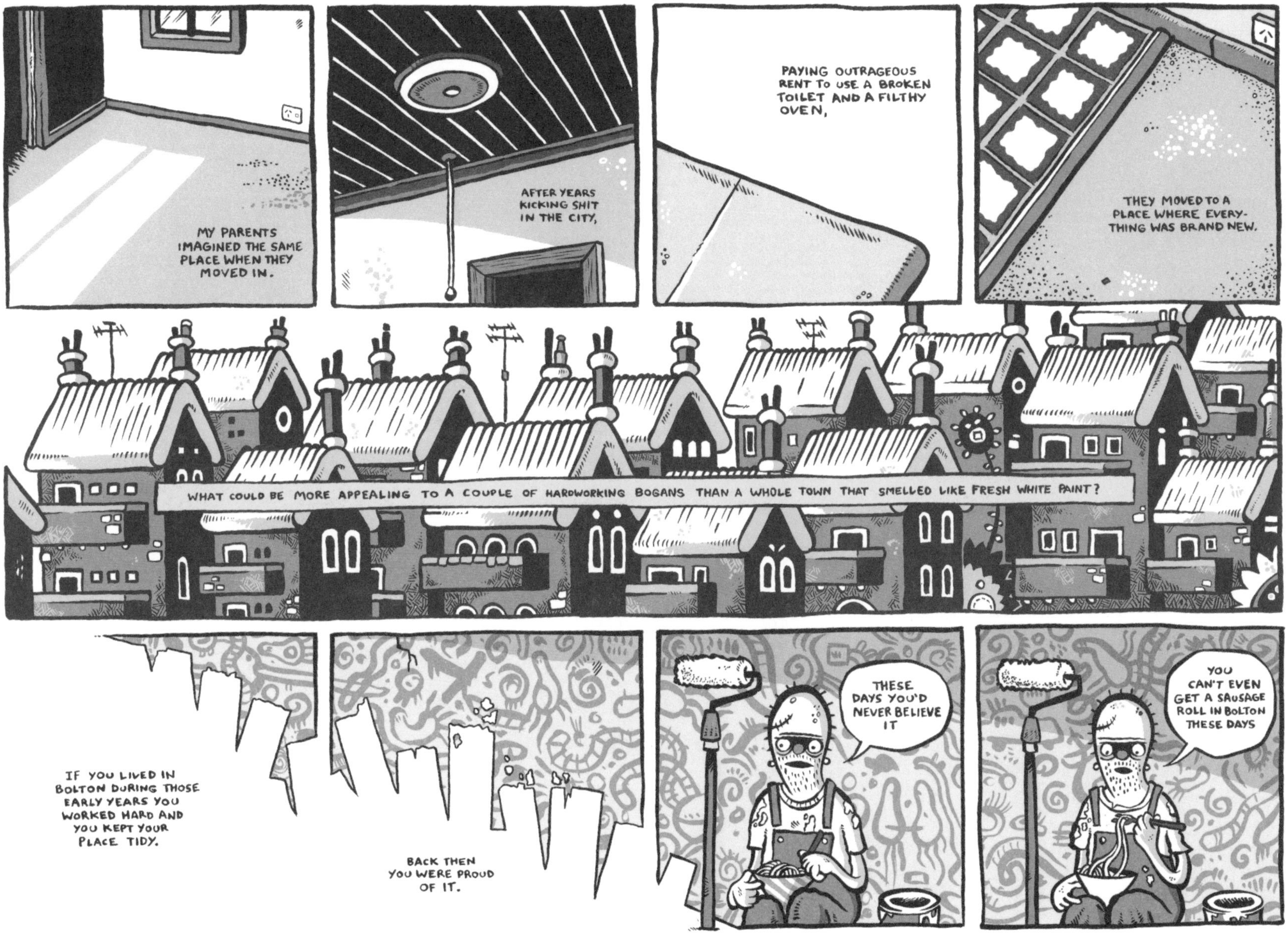
MY PARENTS IMAGINED THE SAME PLACE WHEN THEY MOVED IN.
AFTER YEARS KICKING SHIT IN THE CITY,
PAYING OUTRAGEOUS RENT TO USE A BROKEN TOILET AND A FILTHY OVEN,
THEY MOVED TO A PLACE WHERE EVERY-THING WAS BRAND NEW.
WHAT COULD BE MORE APPEALING TO A COUPLE OF HARDWORKING BOGANS THAN A WHOLE TOWN THAT SMELLED LIKE FRESH WHITE PAINT?
IF YOU LIVED IN BOLTON DURING THOSE EARLY YEARS YOU WORKED HARD AND YOU KEPT YOUR PLACE TIDY.
BACK THEN YOU WERE PROUD OF IT.
THESE DAYS YOU'D NEVER BELIEVE IT
YOU CAN'T EVEN GET A SAUSAGE ROLL IN BOLTON THESE DAYS

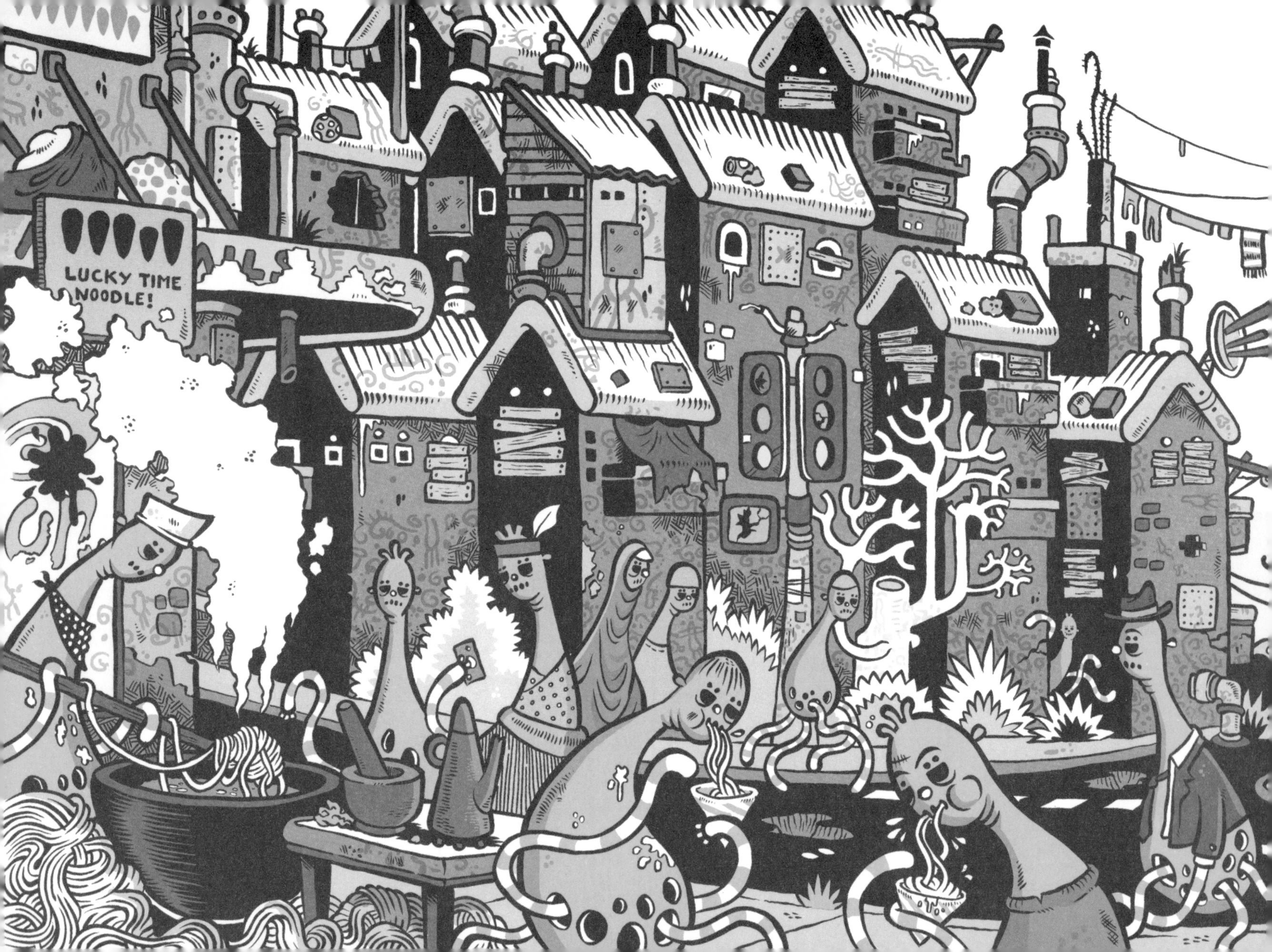
LUCKY TIME NOODLE!

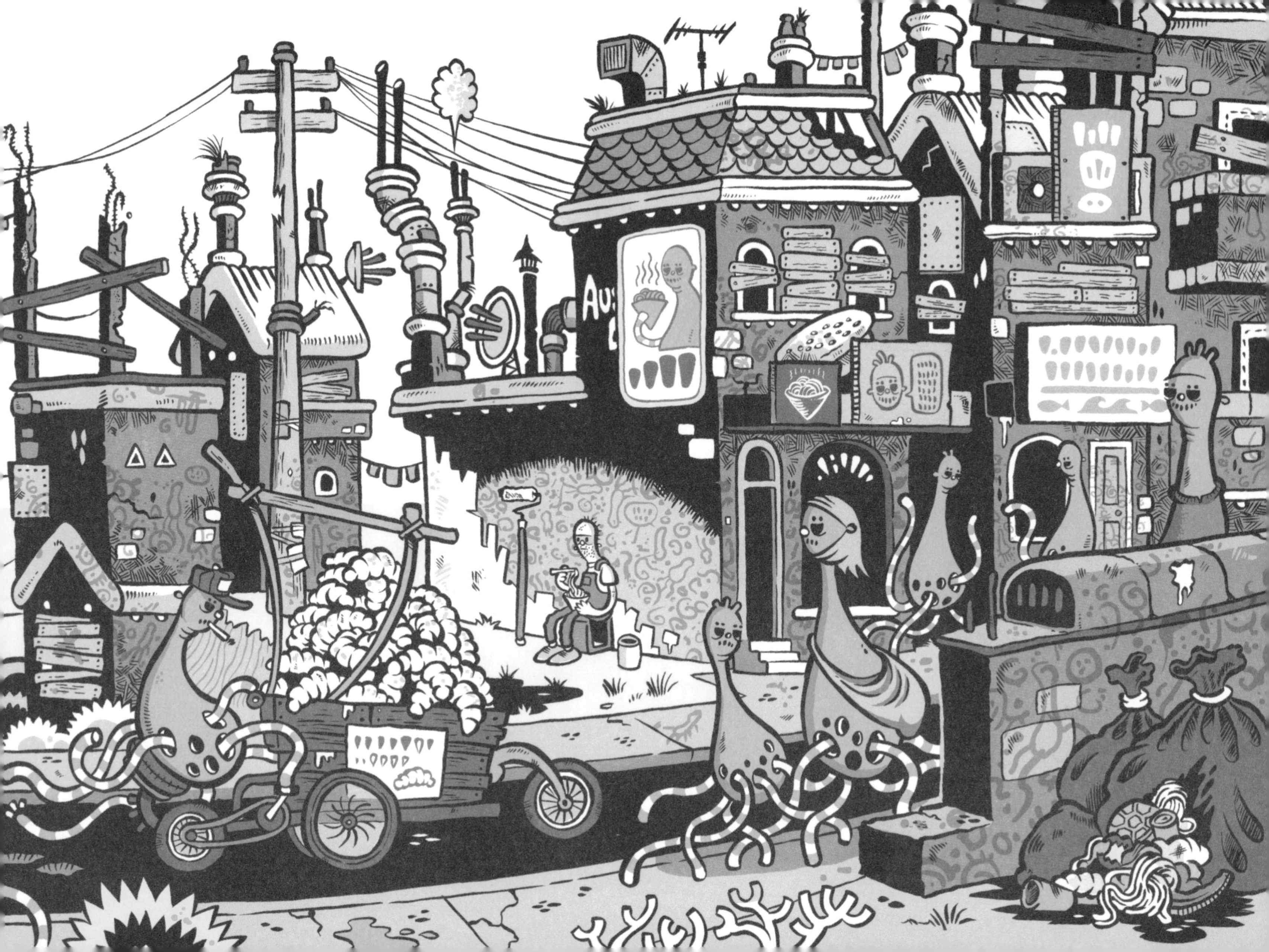

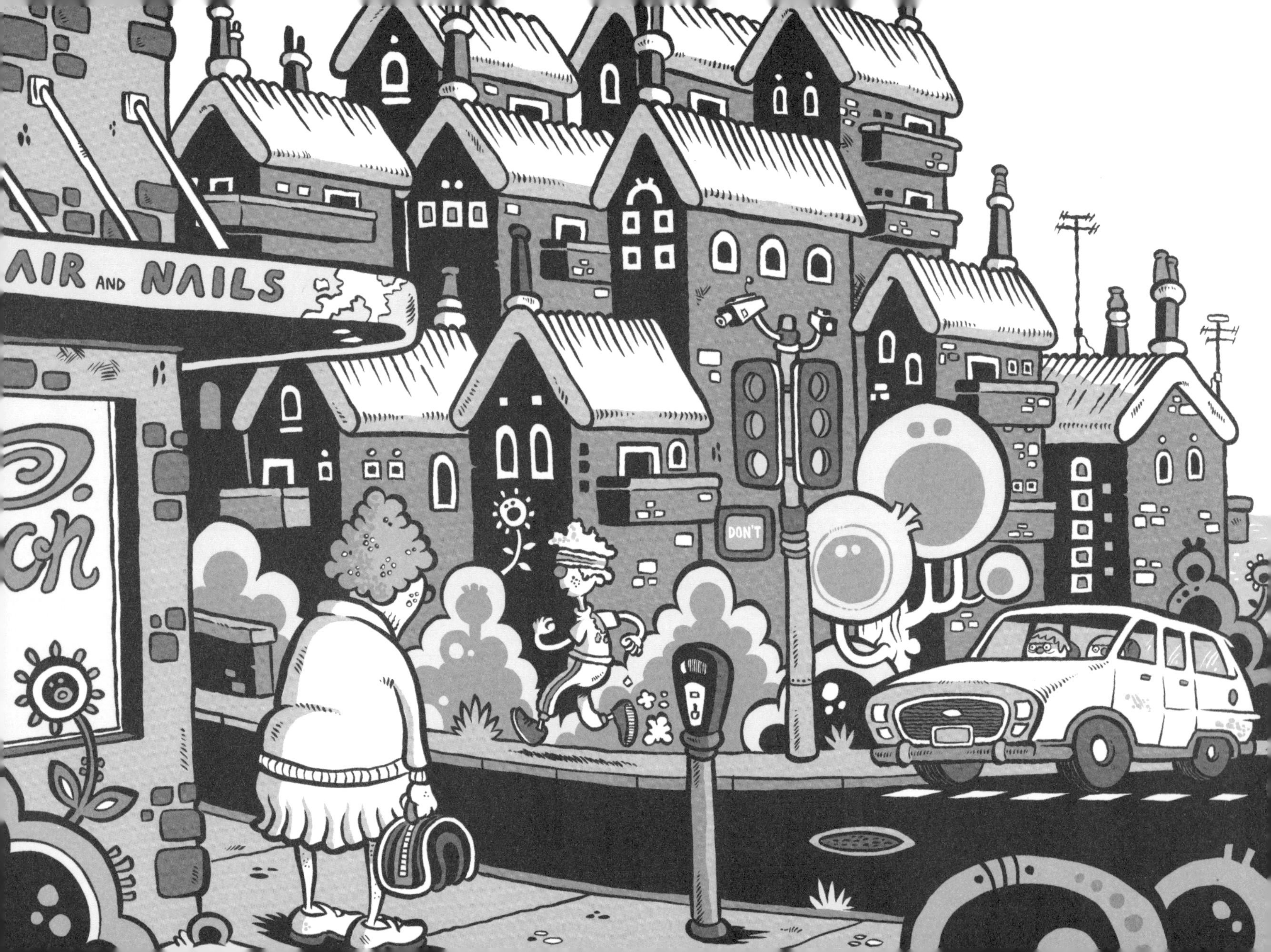
AIR AND NAILS
DON'T

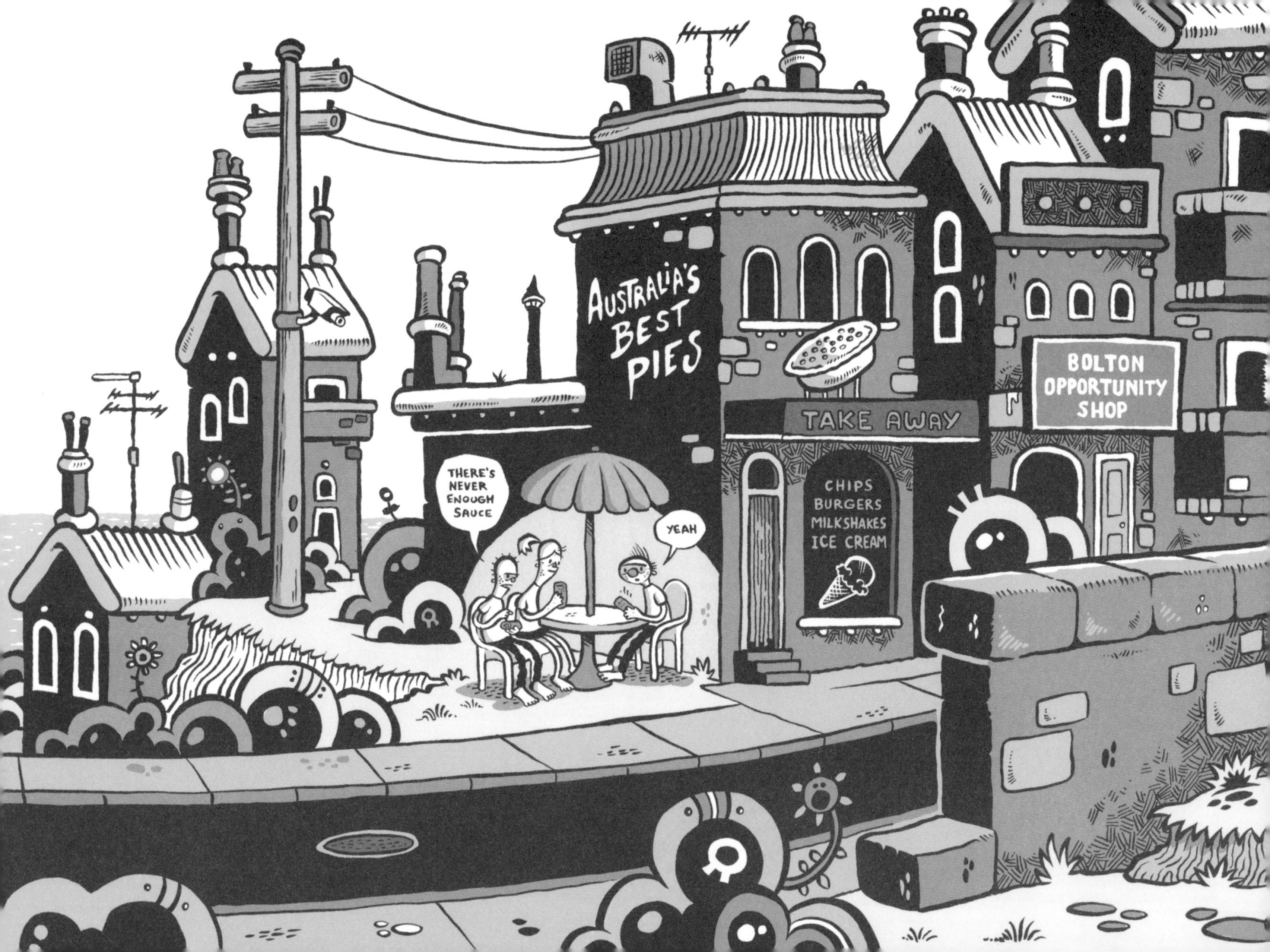
AUSTRALIA'S BEST PIES
TAKE AWAY
BOLTON OPPORTUNITY SHOP
THERE'S NEVER ENOUGH SAUCE
YEAH
CHIPS BURGERS MILKSHAKES ICE CREAM

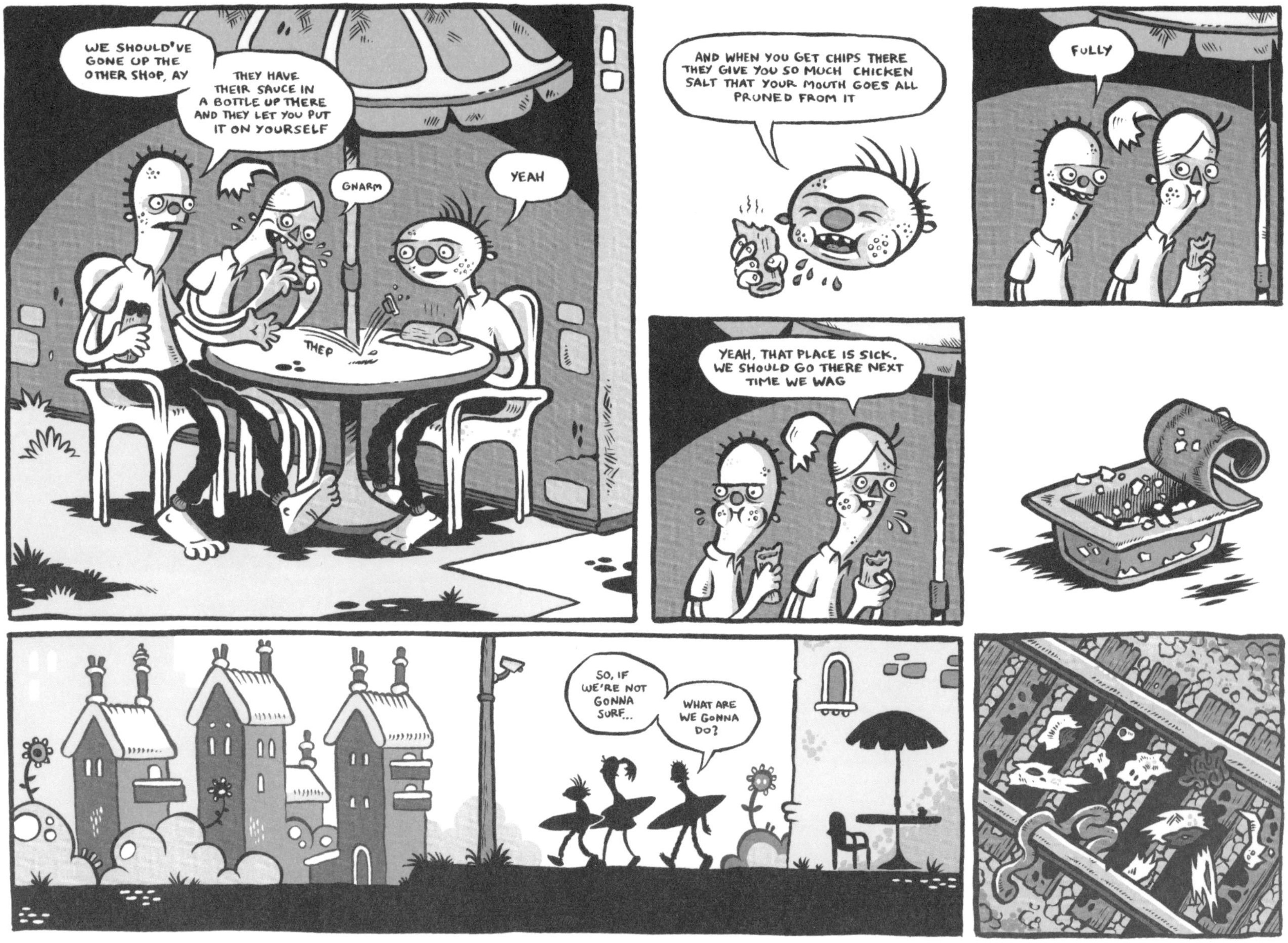

WE SHOULD'VE GONE UP THE OTHER SHOP, AY
THEY HAVE THEIR SAUCE IN A BOTTLE UP THERE AND THEY LET YOU PUT IT ON YOURSELF
GNARM
THEP
YEAH
AND WHEN YOU GET CHIPS THERE THEY GIVE YOU SO MUCH CHICKEN SALT THAT YOUR MOUTH GOES ALL PRUNED FROM IT
FULLY
YEAH, THAT PLACE IS SICK. WE SHOULD GO THERE NEXT TIME WE WAG
SO, IF WE'RE NOT GONNA SURF...
WHAT ARE WE GONNA DO?

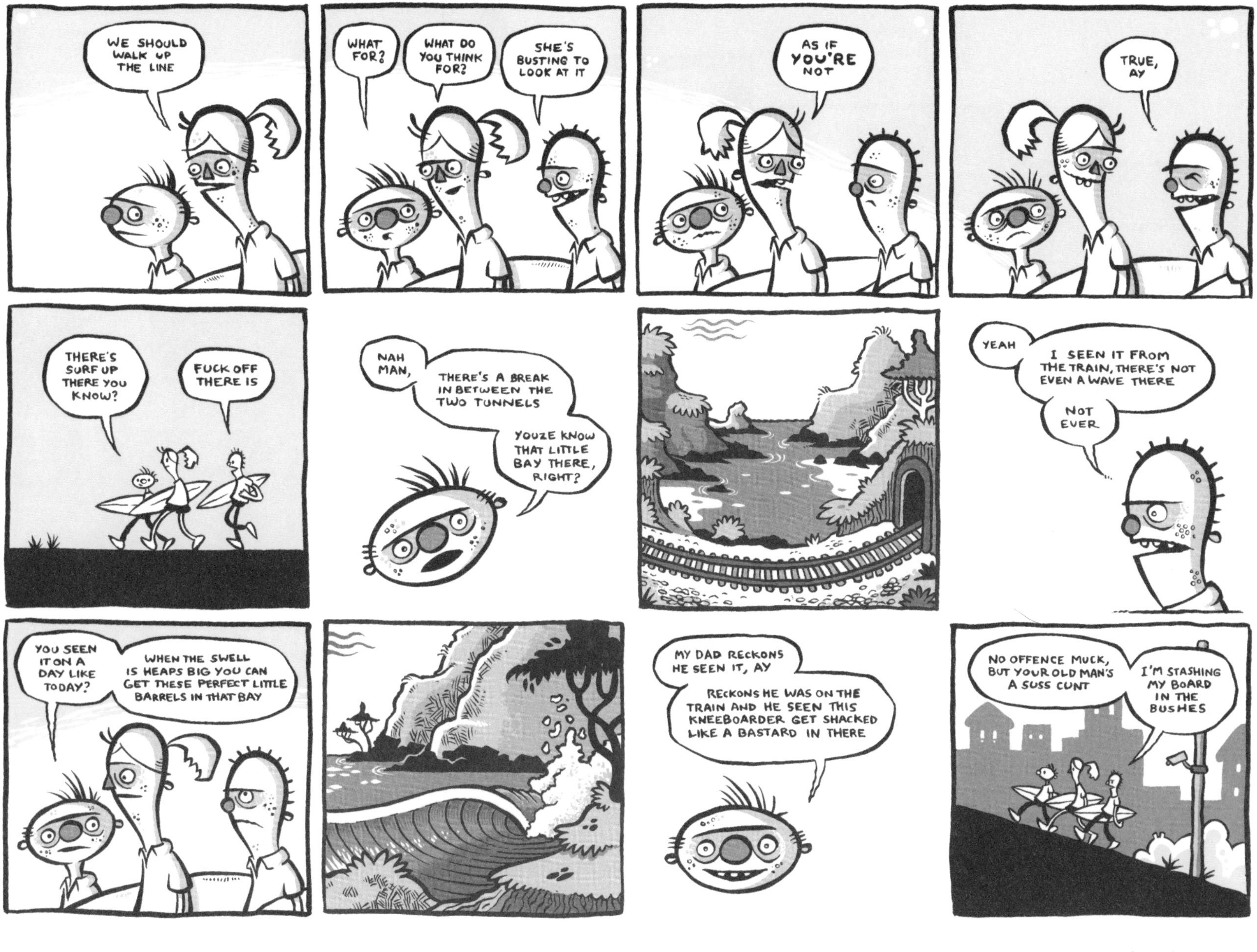
WE SHOULD WALK UP THE LINE
WHAT FOR?
WHAT DO YOU THINK FOR?
SHE'S BUSTING TO LOOK AT IT
AS IF YOU'RE NOT
TRUE, AY
THERE'S SURF UP THERE YOU KNOW?
FUCK OFF THERE IS
NAH MAN,
THERE'S A BREAK IN BETWEEN THE TWO TUNNELS
YOUZE KNOW THAT LITTLE BAY THERE, RIGHT?
YEAH
I SEEN IT FROM THE TRAIN, THERE'S NOT EVEN A WAVE THERE
NOT EVER
YOU SEEN IT ON A DAY LIKE TODAY?
WHEN THE SWELL IS HEAPS BIG YOU CAN GET THESE PERFECT LITTLE BARRELS IN THAT BAY
MY DAD RECKONS HE SEEN IT, AY
RECKONS HE WAS ON THE TRAIN AND HE SEEN THIS KNEEBOARDER GET SHACKED LIKE A BASTARD IN THERE
NO OFFENCE MUCK, BUT YOUR OLD MAN'S A SUSS CUNT
I'M STASHING MY BOARD IN THE BUSHES

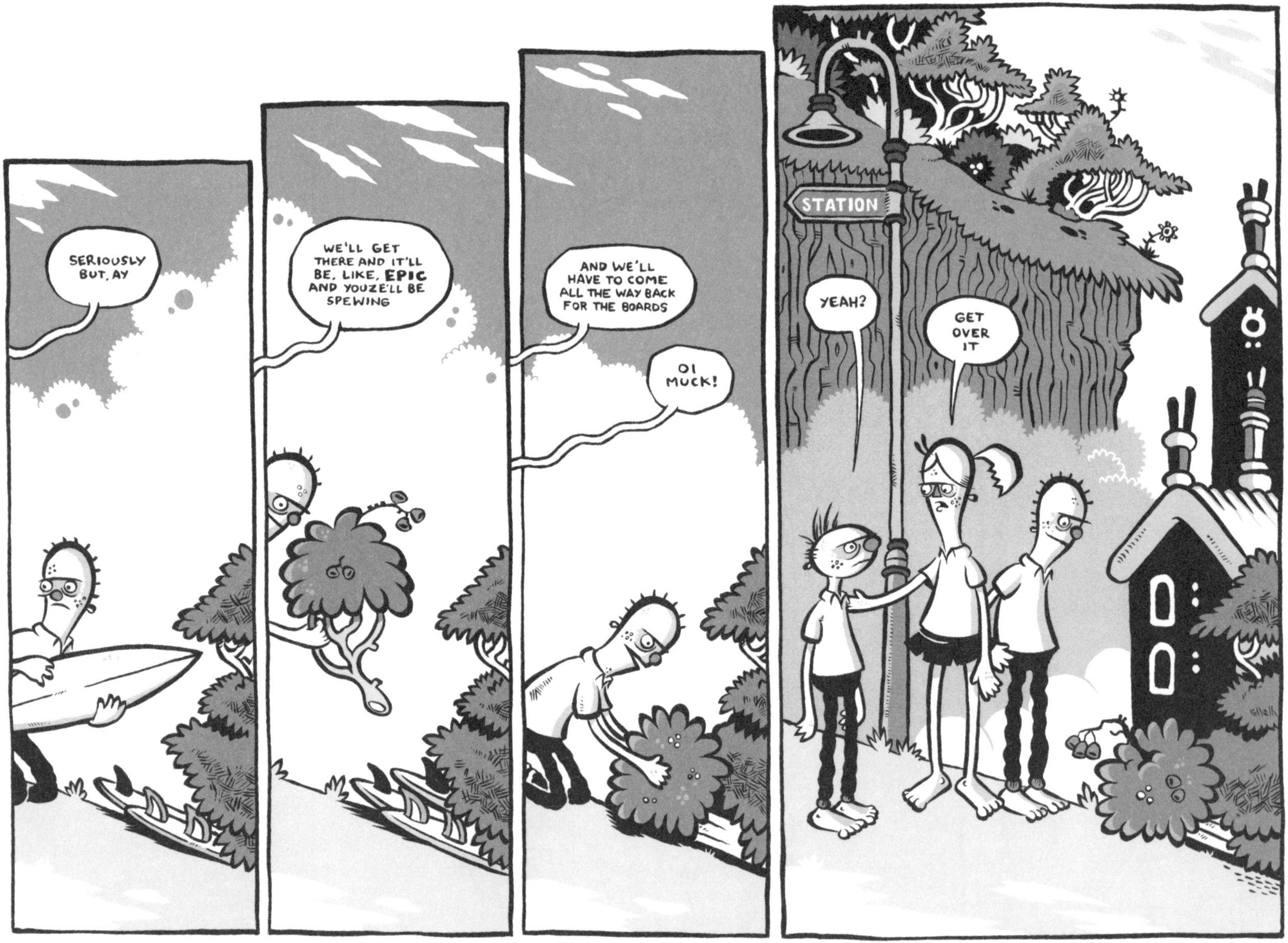
SERIOUSLY BUT, AY
WE'LL GET THERE AND IT'LL BE, LIKE, EPIC AND YOUZE'LL BE SPEWING
AND WE'LL HAVE TO COME ALL THE WAY BACK FOR THE BOARDS
OI MUCK!
STATION
YEAH?
GET OVER IT

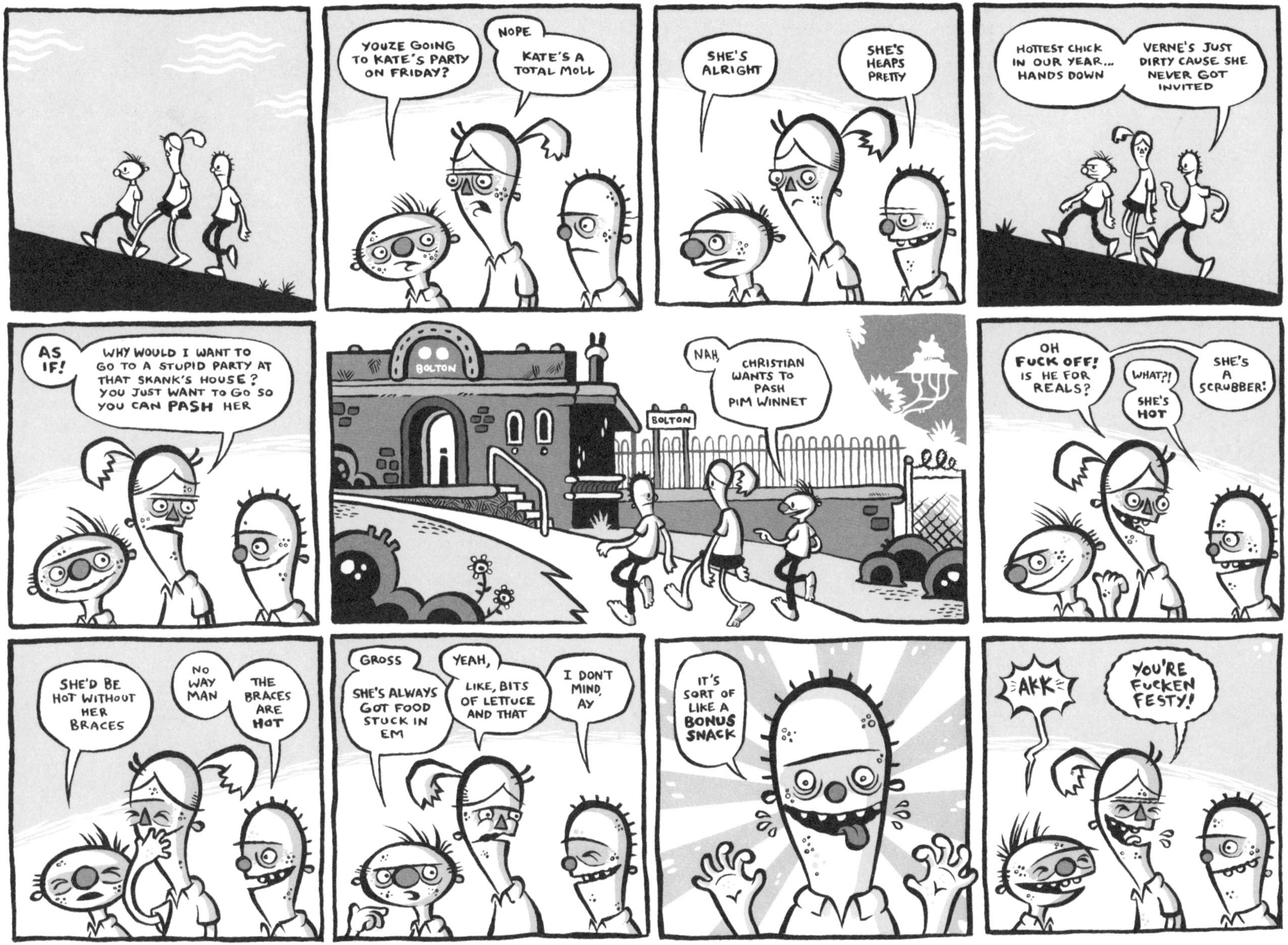

YOUZE GOING TO KATE'S PARTY ON FRIDAY?
NOPE
KATE'S A TOTAL MOLL
SHE'S ALRIGHT
SHE'S HEAPS PRETTY
HOTTEST CHICK IN OUR YEAR... HANDS DOWN
VERNE'S JUST DIRTY CAUSE SHE NEVER GOT INVITED
AS IF!
WHY WOULD I WANT TO GO TO A STUPID PARTY AT THAT SKANK'S HOUSE? YOU JUST WANT TO GO SO YOU CAN PASH HER
BOLTON
BOLTON
NAH,
CHRISTIAN WANTS TO PASH PIM WINNET
OH FUCK OFF! IS HE FOR REALS?
WHAT?!
SHE'S HOT
SHE'S A SCRUBBER!
SHE'D BE HOT WITHOUT HER BRACES
NO WAY MAN
THE BRACES ARE HOT
GROSS
SHE'S ALWAYS GOT FOOD STUCK IN EM
YEAH,
LIKE, BITS OF LETTUCE AND THAT
I DON'T MIND, AY
IT'S SORT OF LIKE A BONUS SNACK
AKK
YOU'RE FUCKEN FESTY!

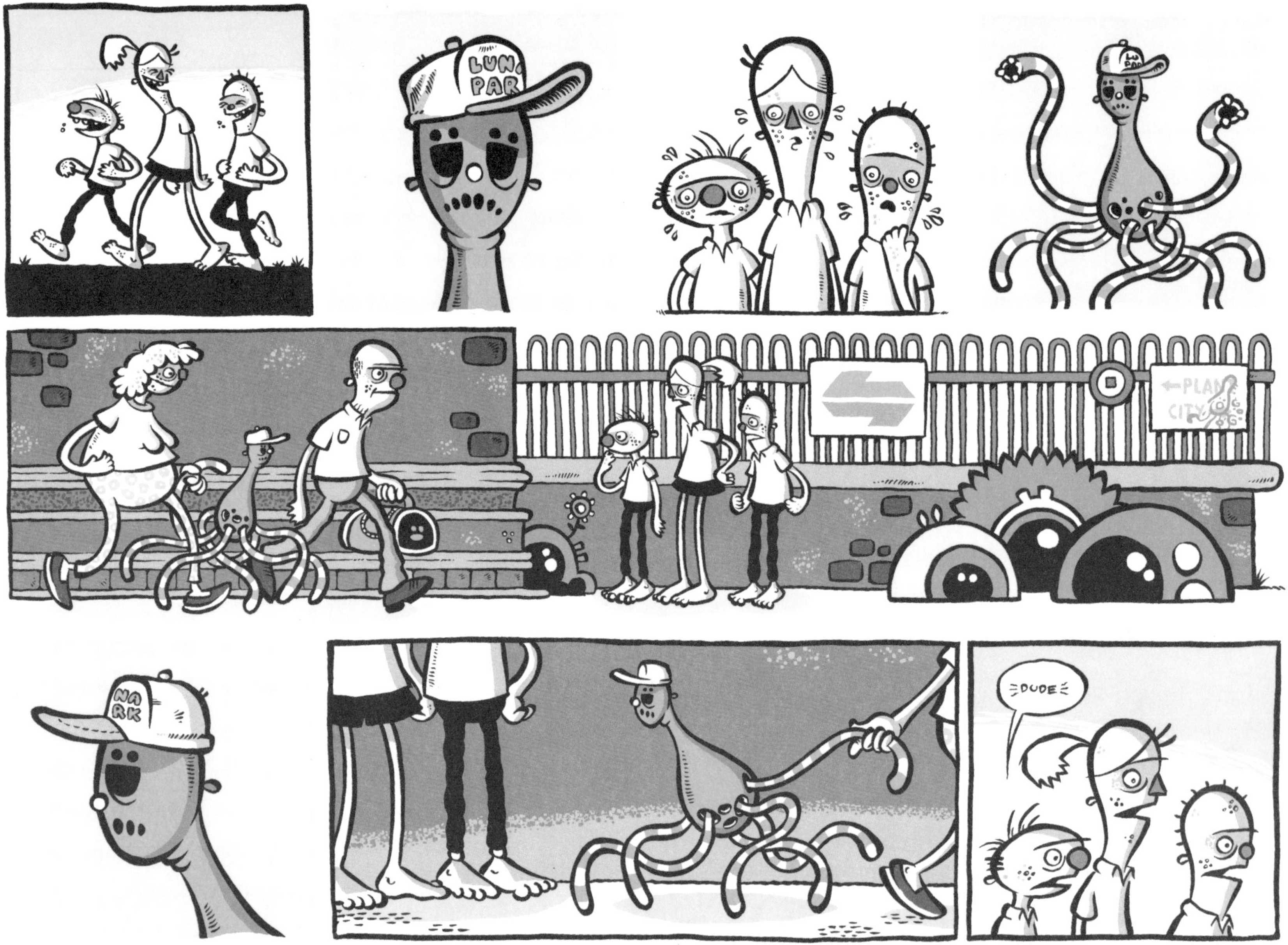
LUN PAR
←PLAN CITY
NA RK
DUDE

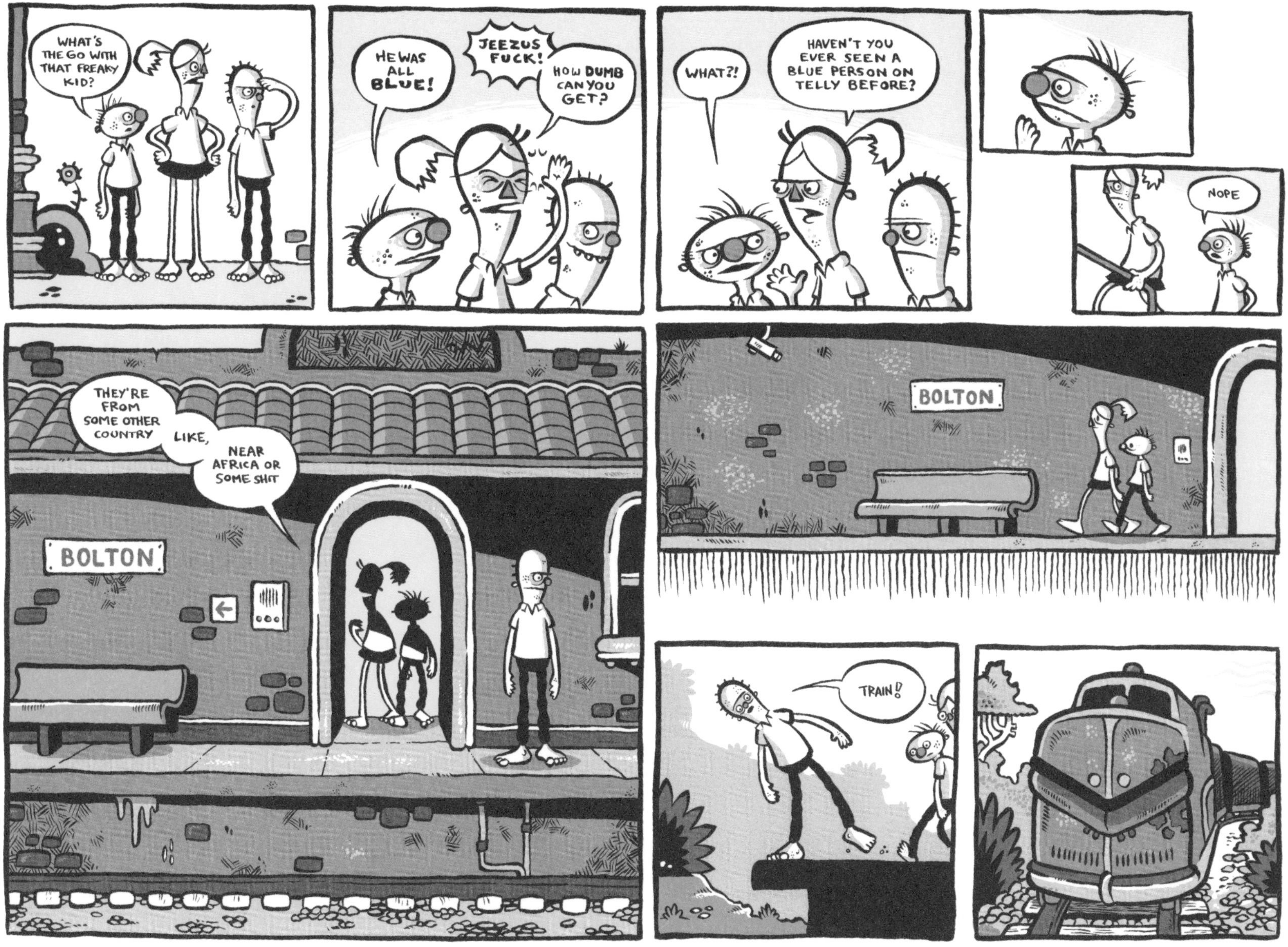
WHAT'S THE GO WITH THAT FREAKY KID?
HE WAS ALL BLUE!
JEEZUS FUCK!
HOW DUMB CAN YOU GET?
WHAT?!
HAVEN'T YOU EVER SEEN A BLUE PERSON ON TELLY BEFORE?
NOPE
THEY'RE FROM SOME OTHER COUNTRY
LIKE,
NEAR AFRICA OR SOME SHIT
BOLTON
BOLTON
TRAIN!

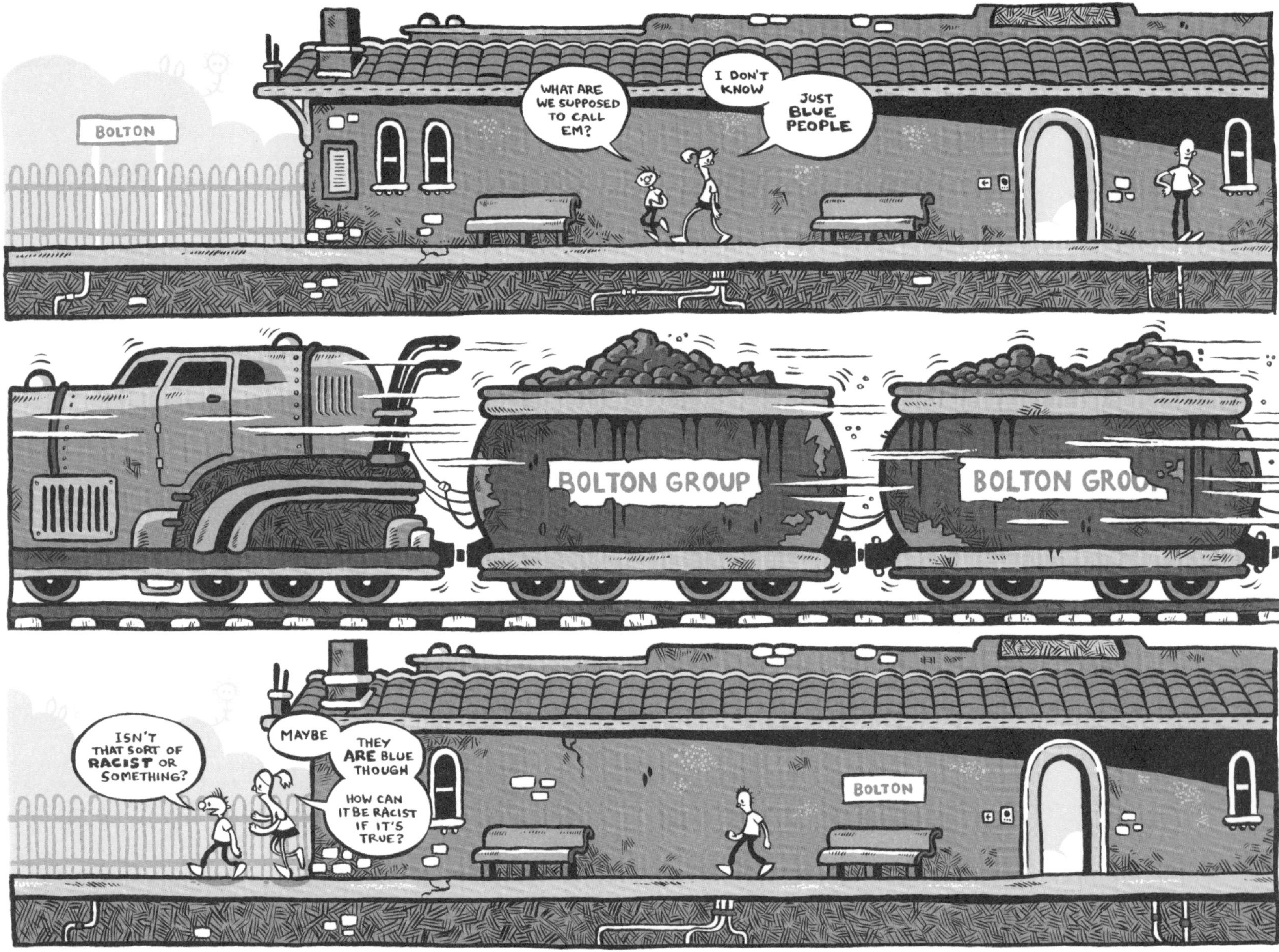
BOLTON
WHAT ARE WE SUPPOSED TO CALL EM?
I DON'T KNOW
JUST BLUE PEOPLE
BOLTON GROUP
BOLTON GROU
ISN'T THAT SORT OF RACIST OR SOMETHING?
MAYBE
THEY ARE BLUE THOUGH
HOW CAN IT BE RACIST IF IT'S TRUE?
BOLTON

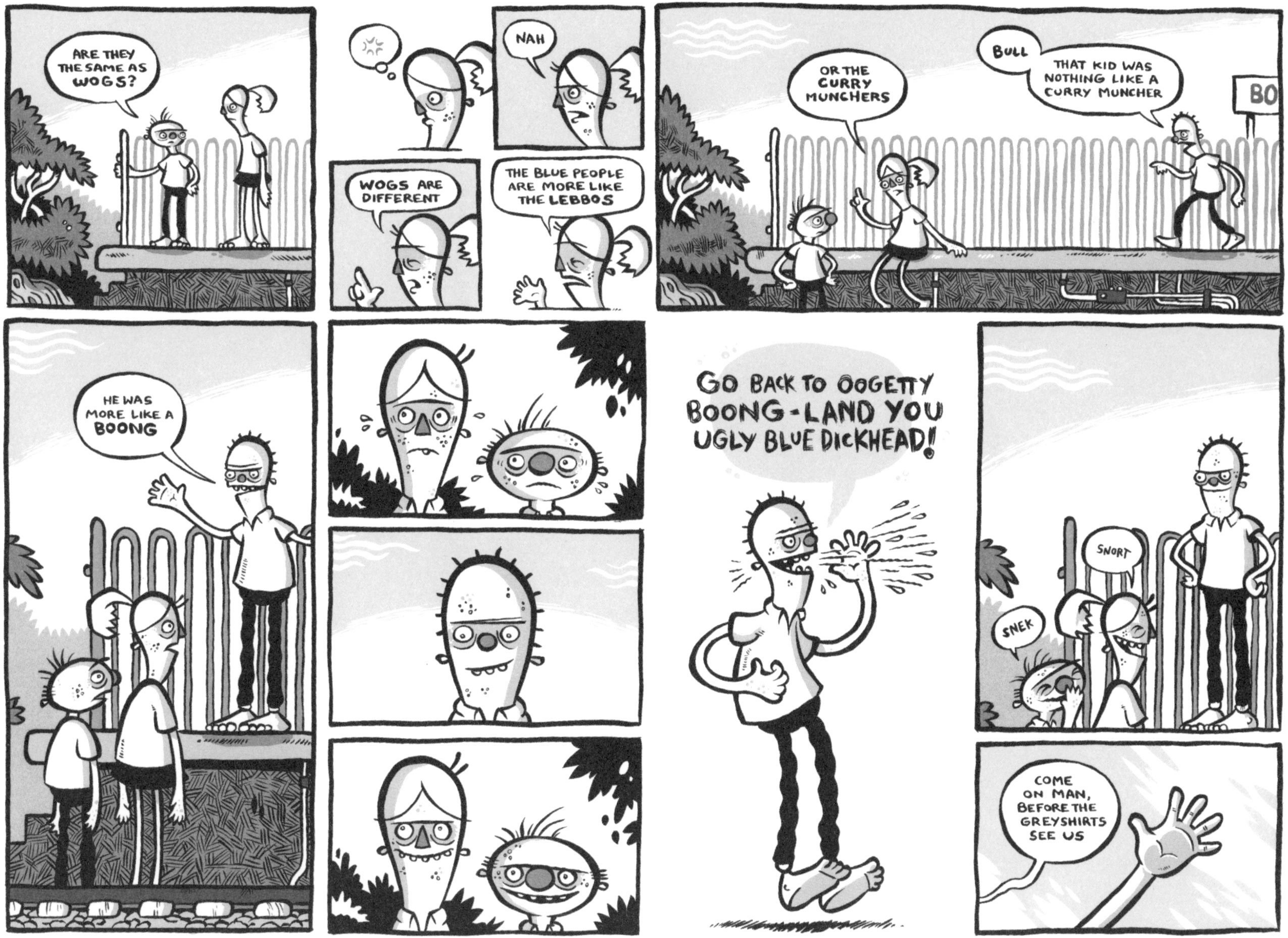
ARE THEY THE SAME AS WOGS?
NAH
WOGS ARE DIFFERENT
THE BLUE PEOPLE ARE MORE LIKE THE LEBBOS
OR THE CURRY MUNCHERS
BULL
THAT KID WAS NOTHING LIKE A CURRY MUNCHER
BO
HE WAS MORE LIKE A BOONG
GO BACK TO OOGETTY BOONG-LAND YOU UGLY BLUE DICKHEAD!
SNORT
SNEK
COME ON MAN, BEFORE THE GREYSHIRTS SEE US

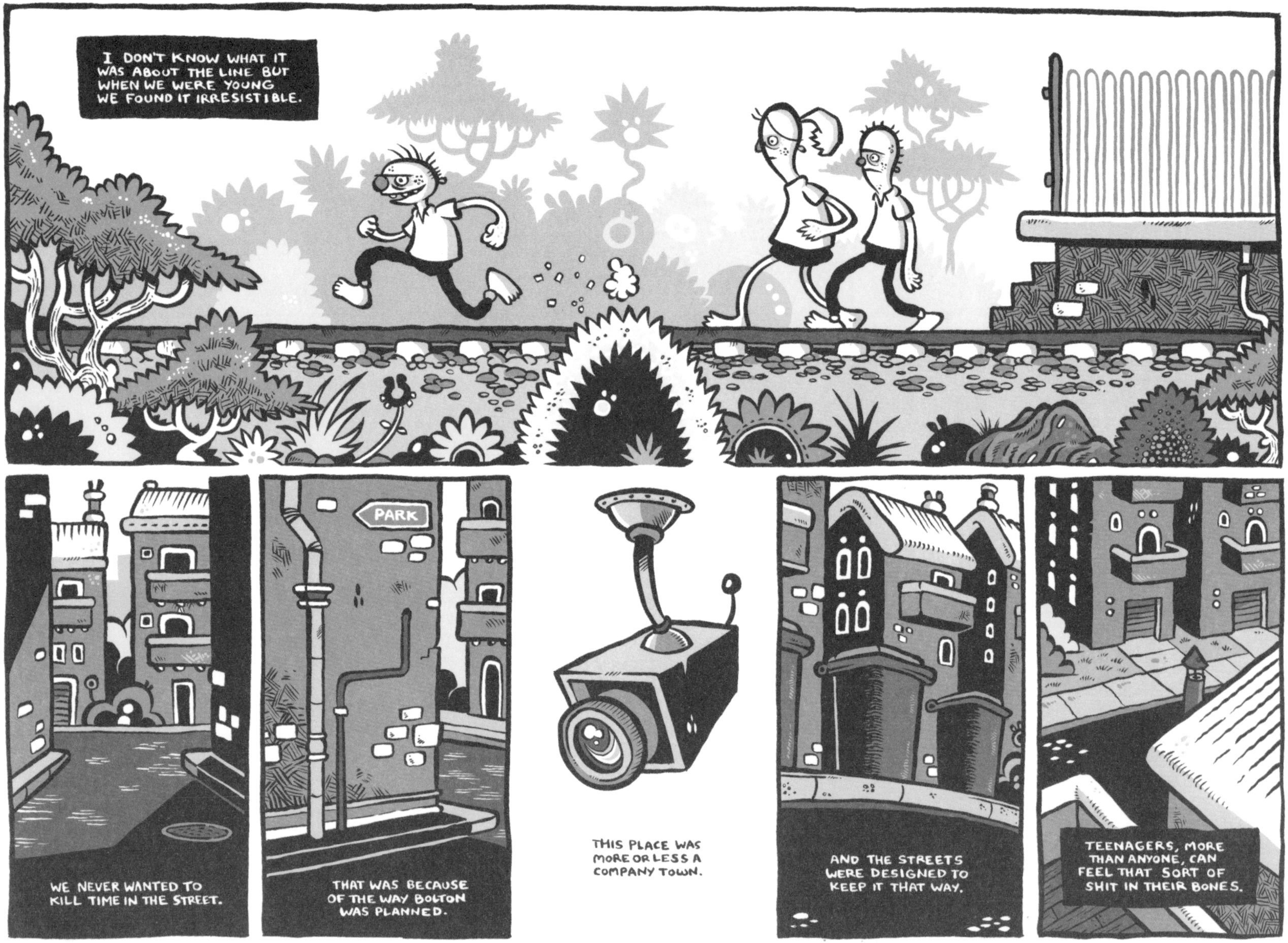
I DON'T KNOW WHAT IT WAS ABOUT THE LINE BUT WHEN WE WERE YOUNG WE FOUND IT IRRESISTIBLE.
WE NEVER WANTED TO KILL TIME IN THE STREET.
PARK
THAT WAS BECAUSE OF THE WAY BOLTON WAS PLANNED.
THIS PLACE WAS MORE OR LESS A COMPANY TOWN.
AND THE STREETS WERE DESIGNED TO KEEP IT THAT WAY.
TEENAGERS, MORE THAN ANYONE, CAN FEEL THAT SORT OF SHIT IN THEIR BONES.

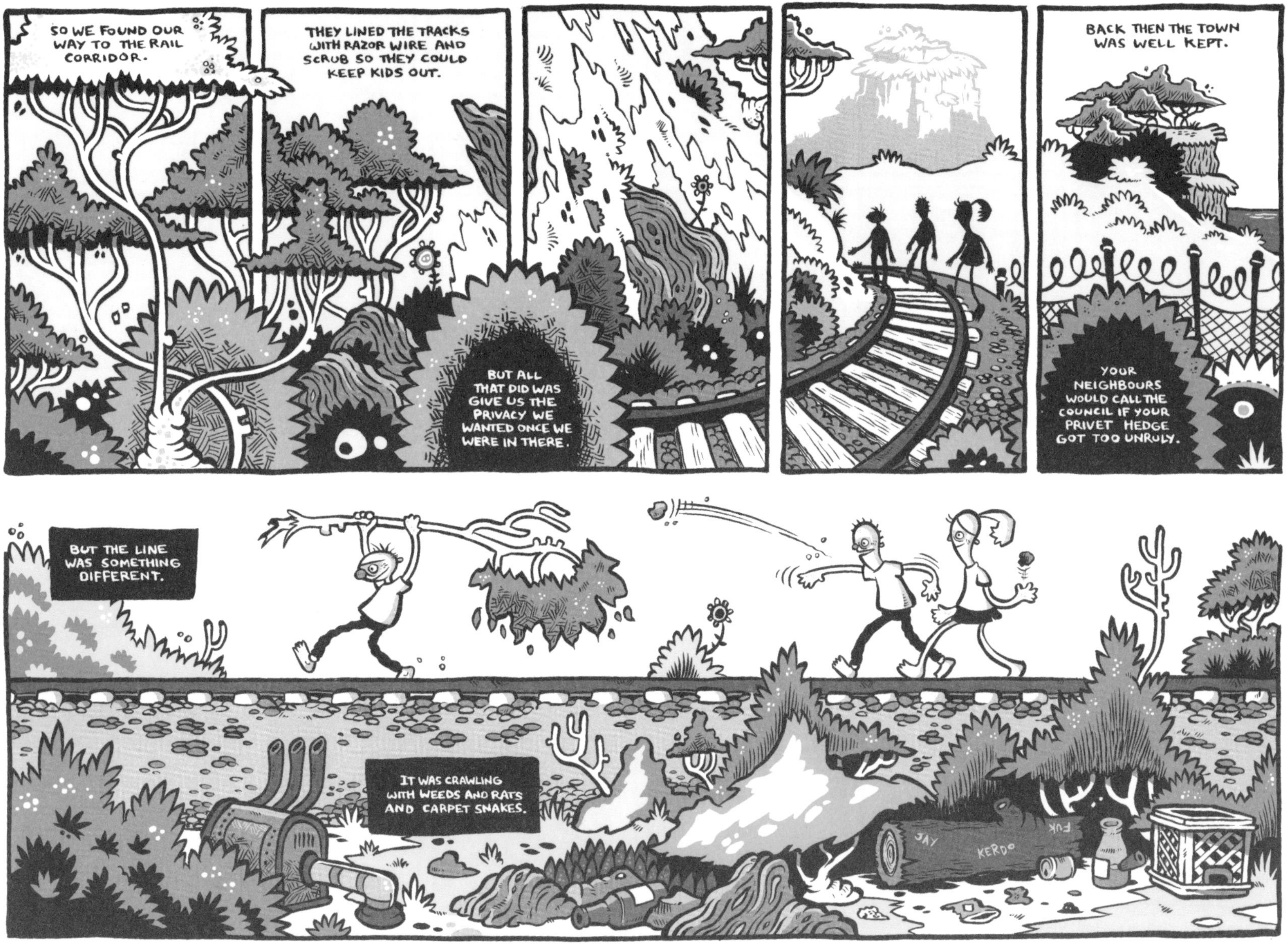
SO WE FOUND OUR WAY TO THE RAIL CORRIDOR.
THEY LINED THE TRACKS WITH RAZOR WIRE AND SCRUB SO THEY COULD KEEP KIDS OUT.
BUT ALL THAT DID WAS GIVE US THE PRIVACY WE WANTED ONCE WE WERE IN THERE.
BACK THEN THE TOWN WAS WELL KEPT.
YOUR NEIGHBOURS WOULD CALL THE COUNCIL IF YOUR PRIVET HEDGE GOT TOO UNRULY.
BUT THE LINE WAS SOMETHING DIFFERENT.
IT WAS CRAWLING WITH WEEDS AND RATS AND CARPET SNAKES.
JAY
KERDO
FUK

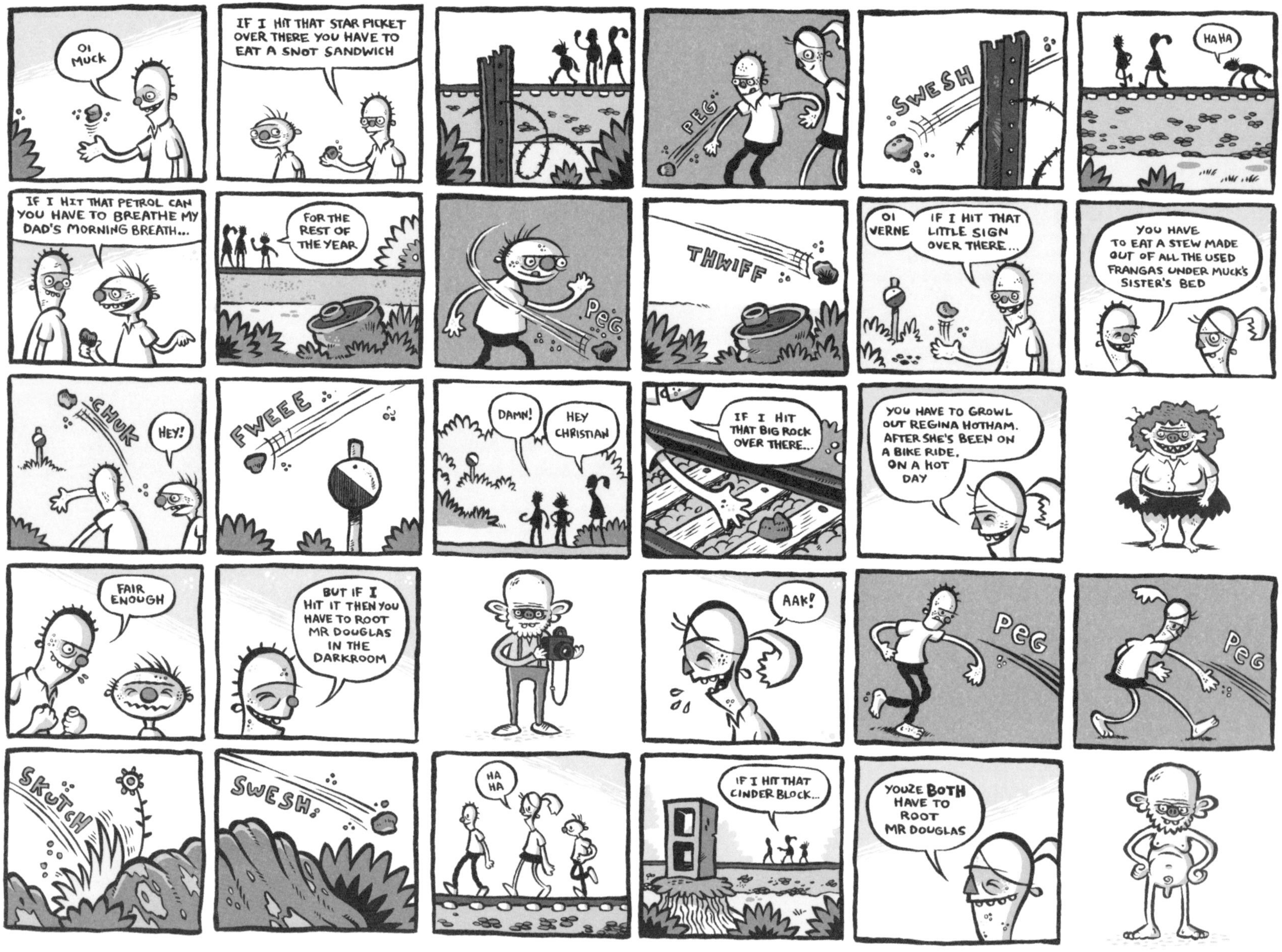
OI MUCK
IF I HIT THAT STAR PICKET OVER THERE YOU HAVE TO EAT A SNOT SANDWICH
PEG
SWESH
HA HA
IF I HIT THAT PETROL CAN YOU HAVE TO BREATHE MY DAD'S MORNING BREATH...
FOR THE REST OF THE YEAR
PEG
THWIFF
OI VERNE
IF I HIT THAT LITTLE SIGN OVER THERE...
YOU HAVE TO EAT A STEW MADE OUT OF ALL THE USED FRANGAS UNDER MUCK'S SISTER'S BED
CHUK
HEY!
FWEEE
DAMN!
HEY CHRISTIAN
IF I HIT THAT BIG ROCK OVER THERE...
YOU HAVE TO GROWL OUT REGINA HOTHAM. AFTER SHE'S BEEN ON A BIKE RIDE. ON A HOT DAY
FAIR ENOUGH
BUT IF I HIT IT THEN YOU HAVE TO ROOT MR DOUGLAS IN THE DARKROOM
AAK!
PEG
PEG
SKUTCH
SWESH
HA HA
IF I HIT THAT CINDER BLOCK...
YOUZE BOTH HAVE TO ROOT MR DOUGLAS

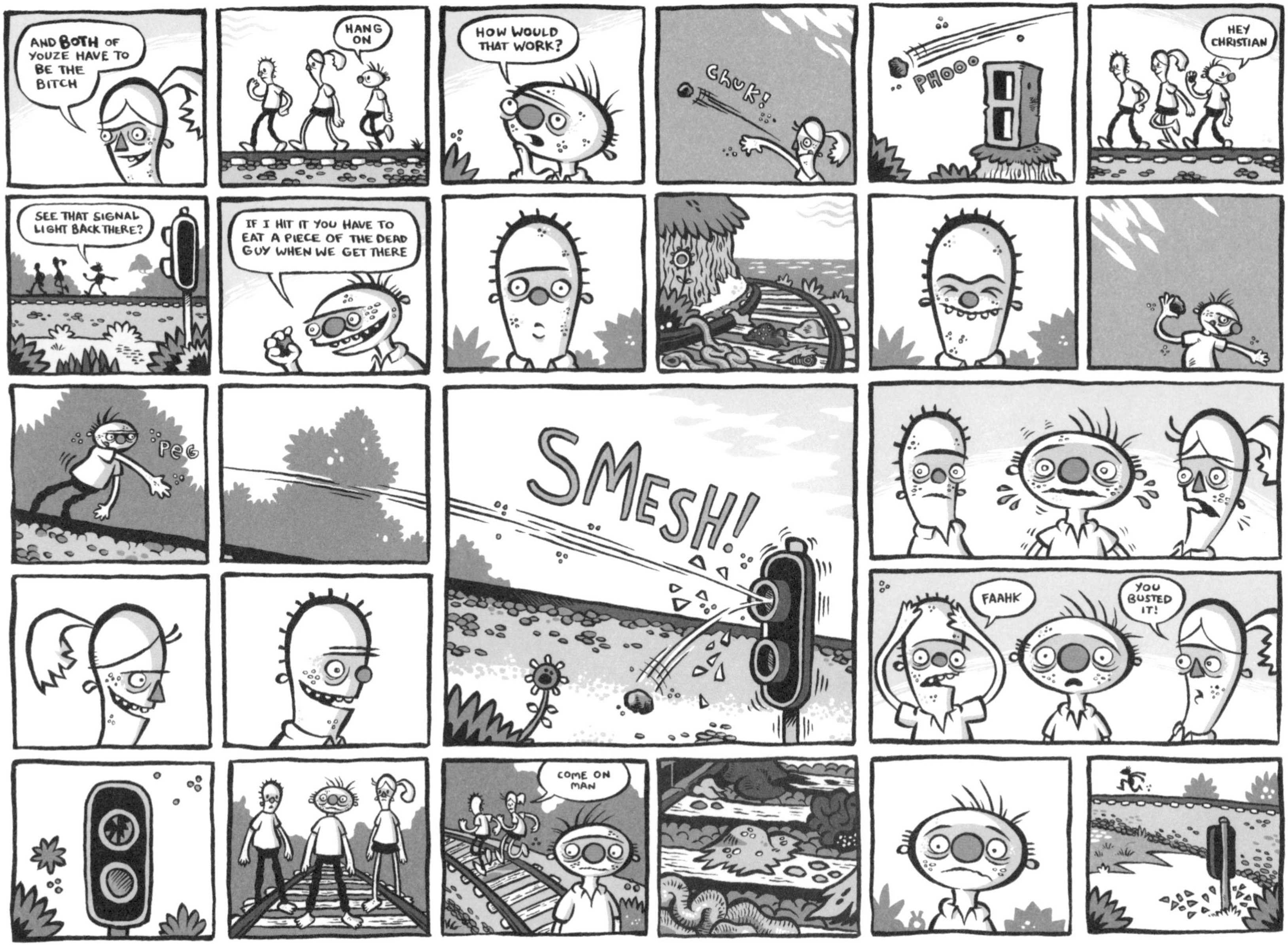
AND BOTH OF YOUZE HAVE TO BE THE BITCH
HANG ON
HOW WOULD THAT WORK?
CHUK!
PHOOO
HEY CHRISTIAN
SEE THAT SIGNAL LIGHT BACK THERE?
IF I HIT IT YOU HAVE TO EAT A PIECE OF THE DEAD GUY WHEN WE GET THERE
PEG
SMESH!
FAAHK
YOU BUSTED IT!
COME ON MAN

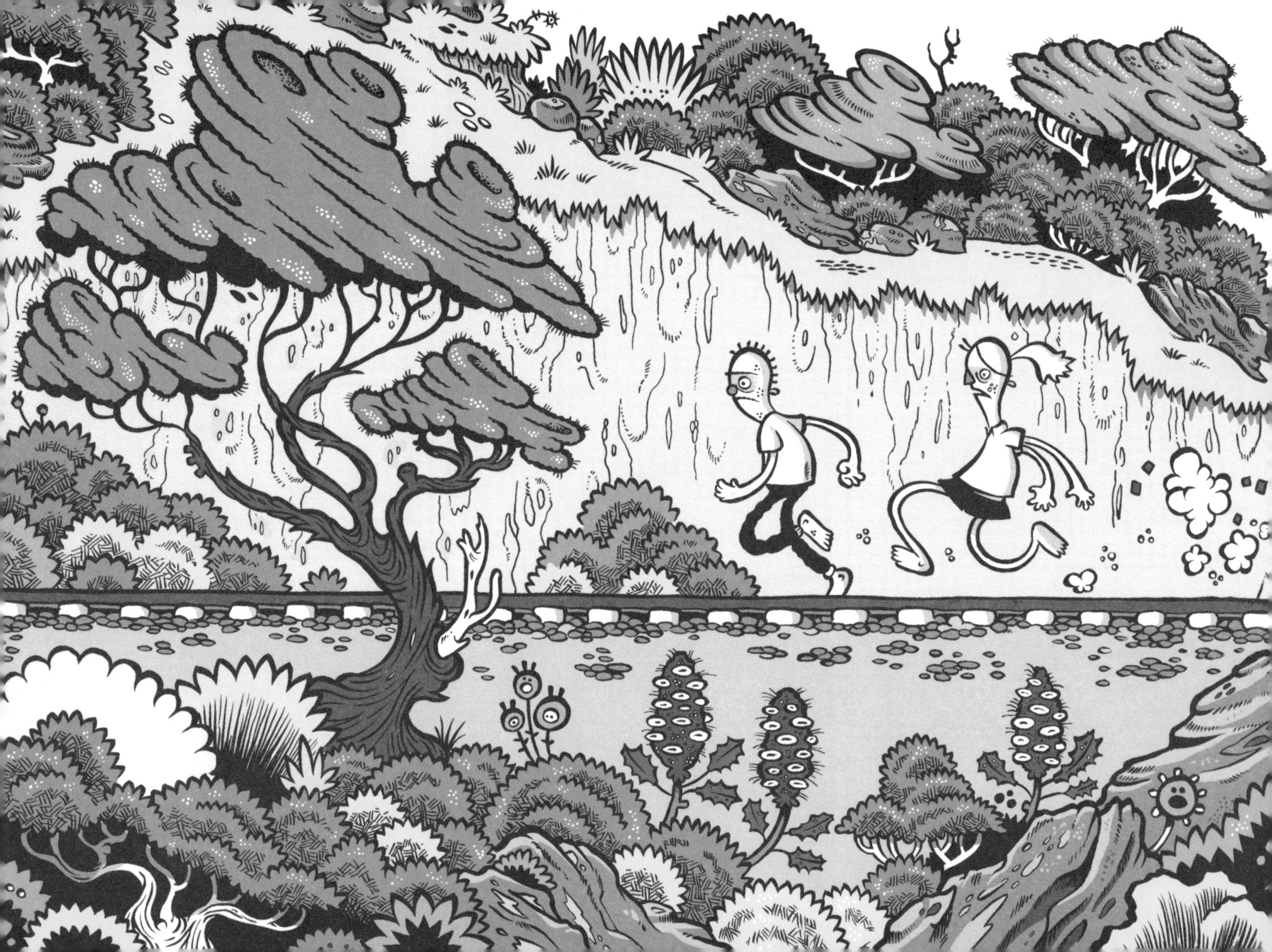

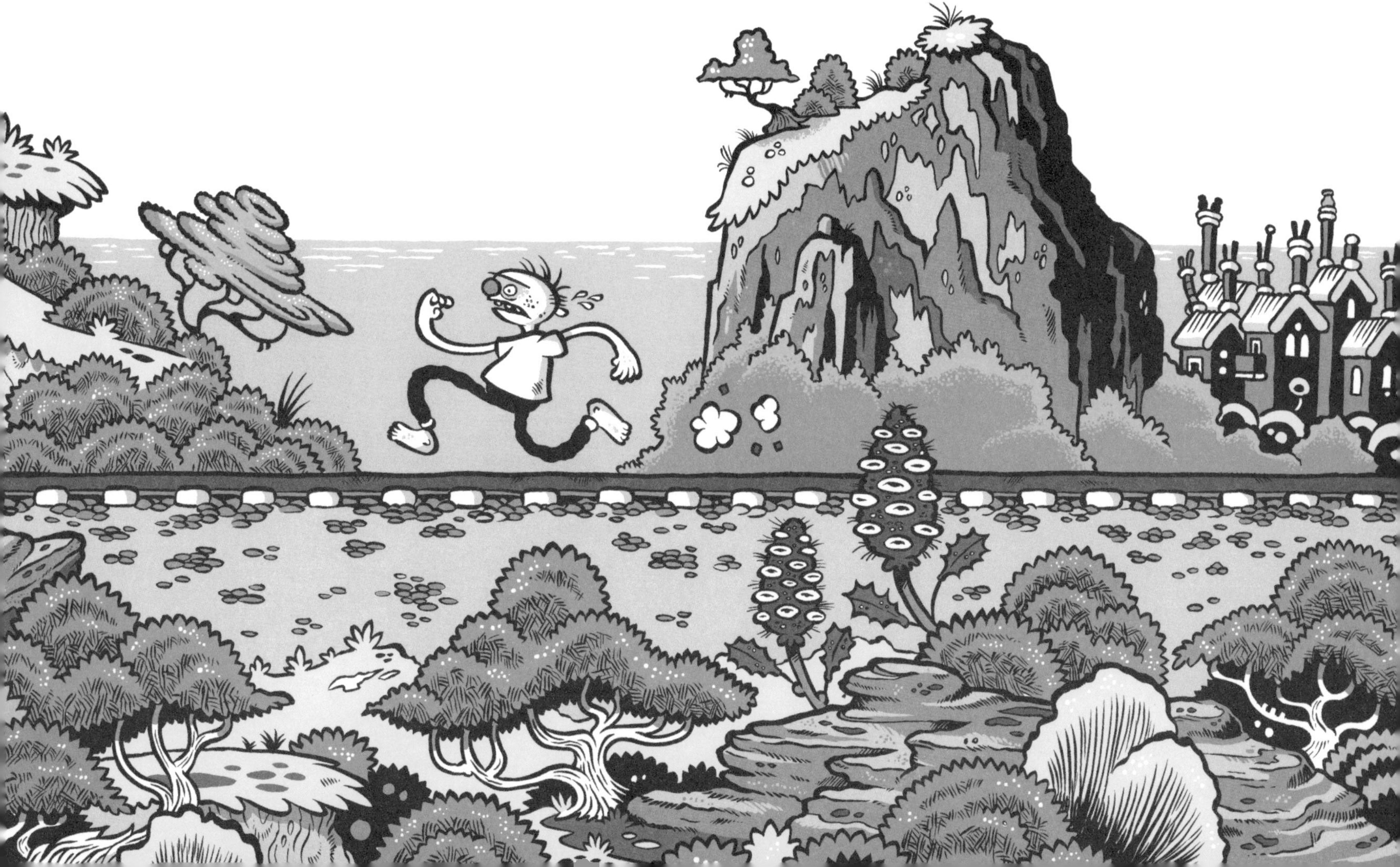

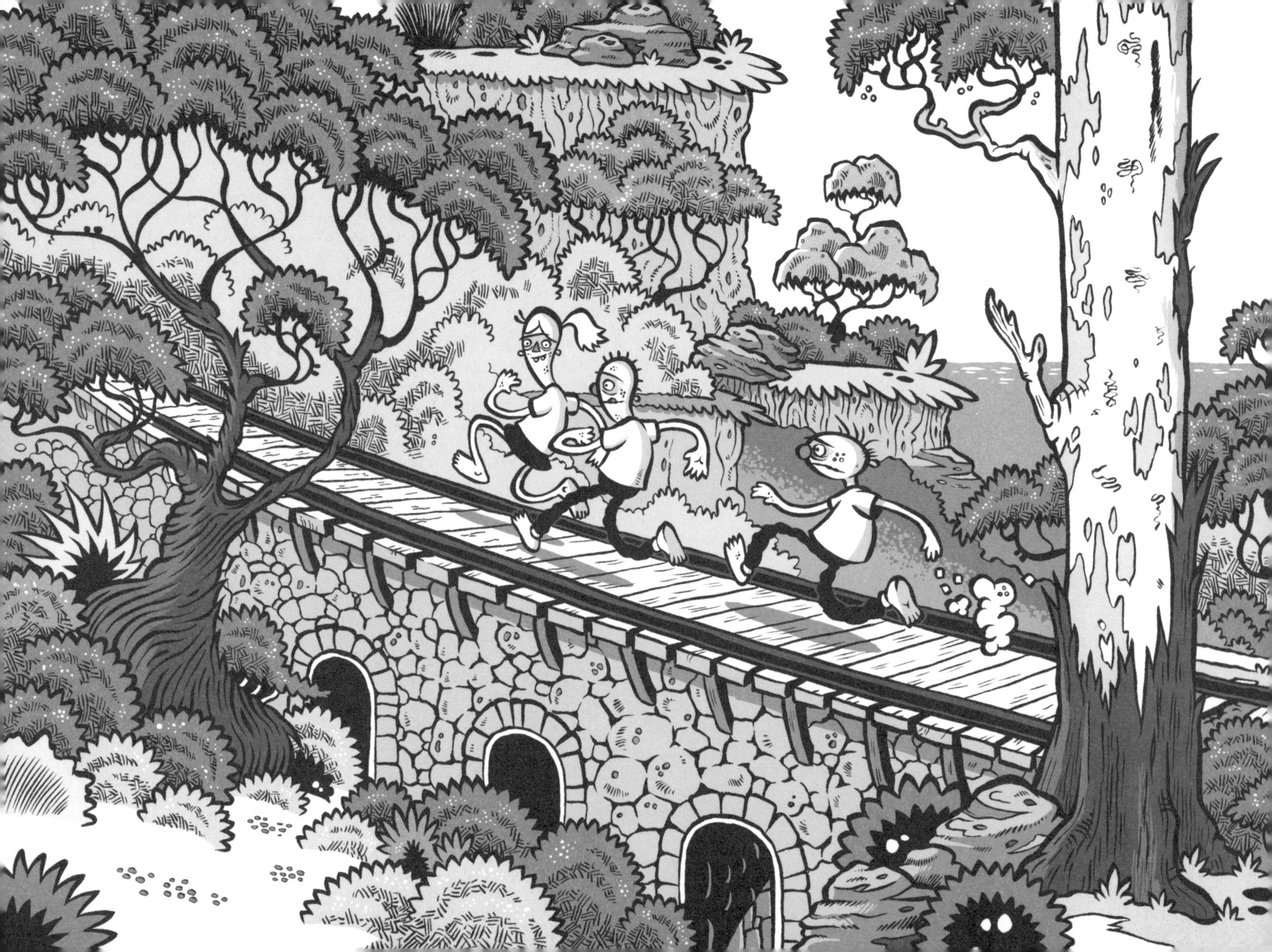

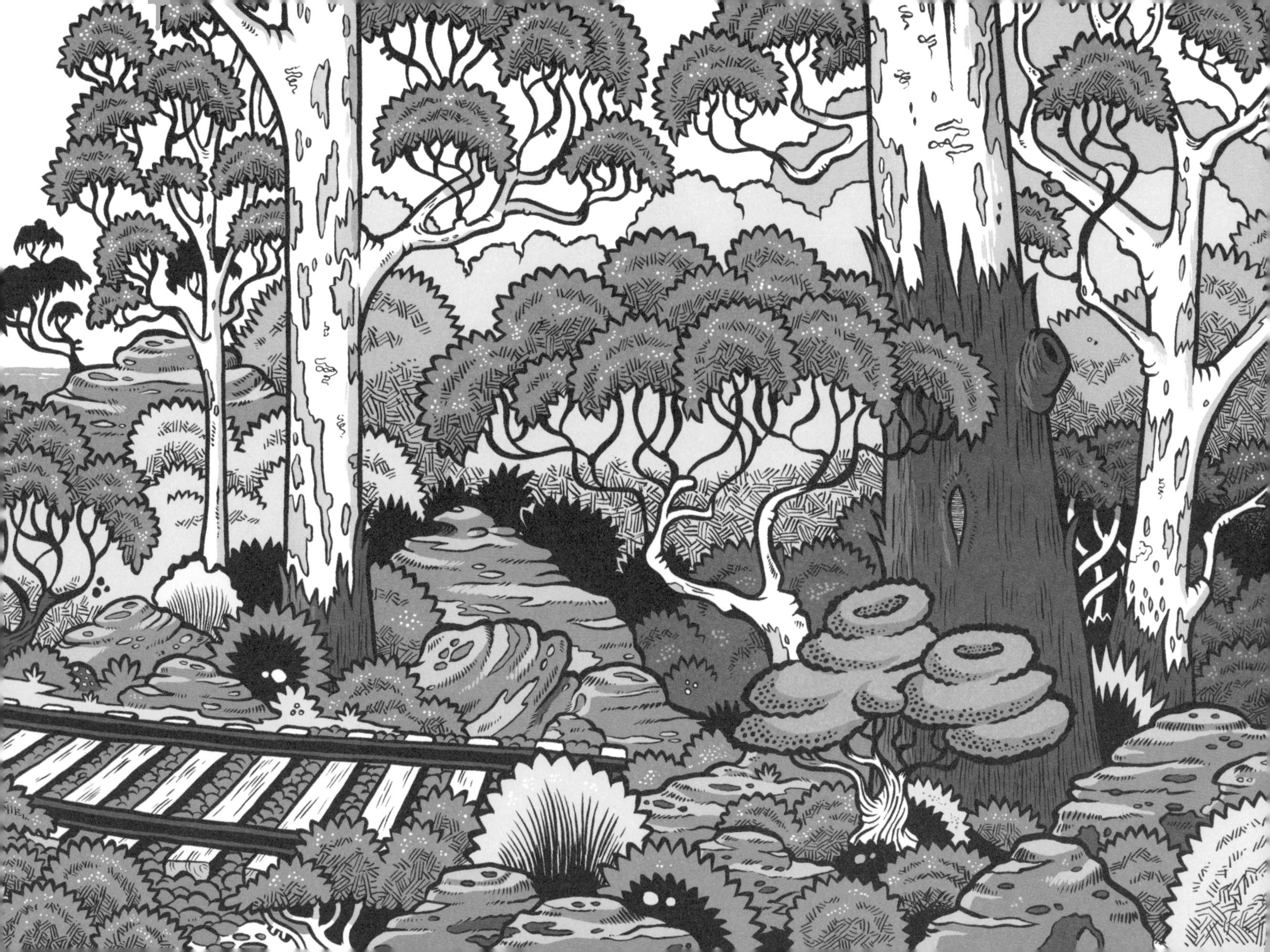

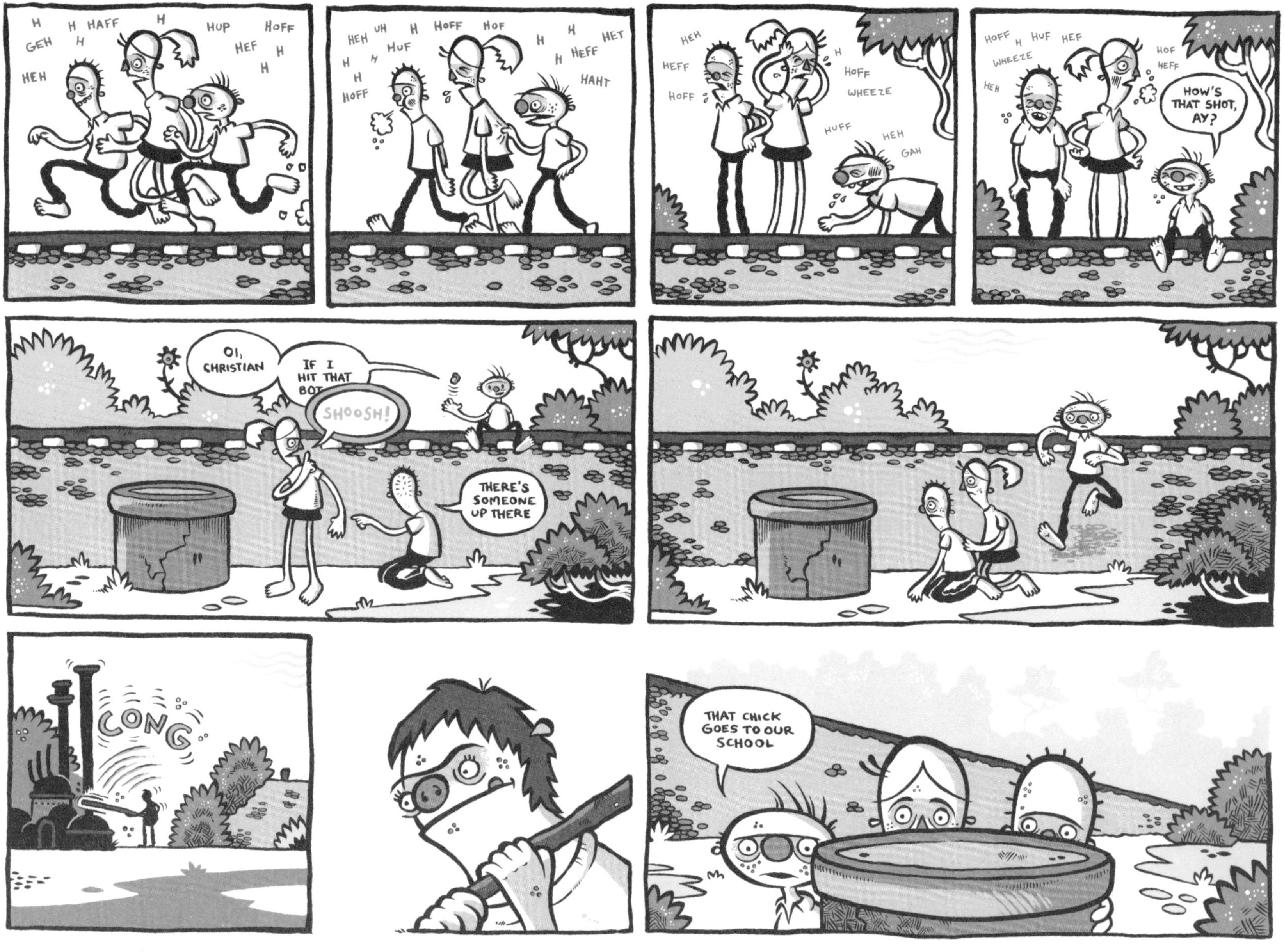

H H HAFF H HUP HOFF
GEH H HEF H
HEH H
HEH UH H HOFF HOF H H HET
H H HUF H HEFF
H HAHT
HOFF
HEH
HEFF H
HOFF HOFF
WHEEZE
HUFF HEH
GAH
HOFF H HUF HEF
WHEEZE HOF
HEH HEFF
HOW'S THAT SHOT, AY?
OI, CHRISTIAN
IF I HIT THAT BOT
SHOOSH!
THERE'S SOMEONE UP THERE
CONG
THAT CHICK GOES TO OUR SCHOOL

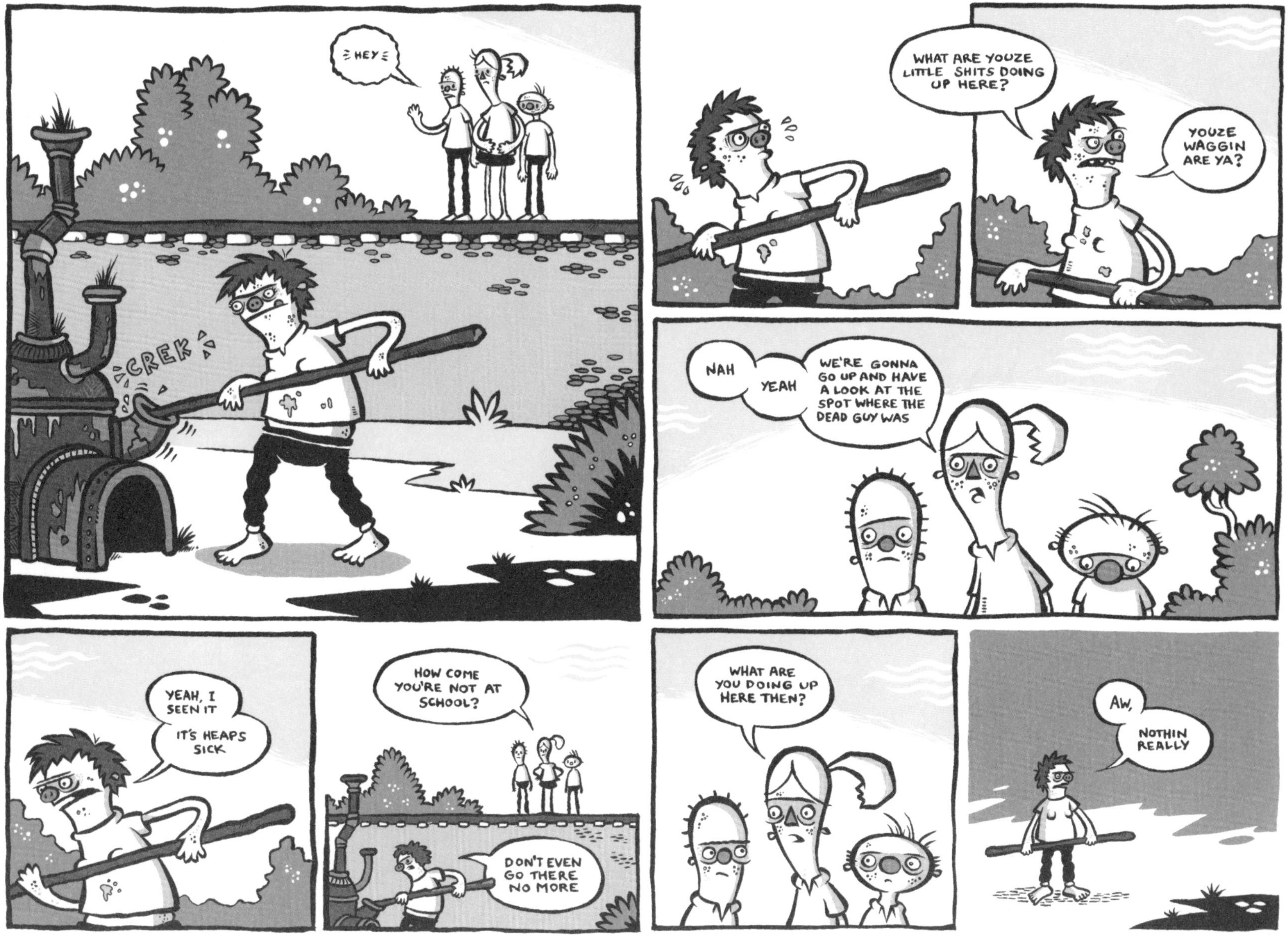
HEY
CREK
WHAT ARE YOUZE LITTLE SHITS DOING UP HERE?
YOUZE WAGGIN ARE YA?
NAH
YEAH
WE'RE GONNA GO UP AND HAVE A LOOK AT THE SPOT WHERE THE DEAD GUY WAS
YEAH, I SEEN IT
IT'S HEAPS SICK
HOW COME YOU'RE NOT AT SCHOOL?
DON'T EVEN GO THERE NO MORE
WHAT ARE YOU DOING UP HERE THEN?
AW,
NOTHIN REALLY

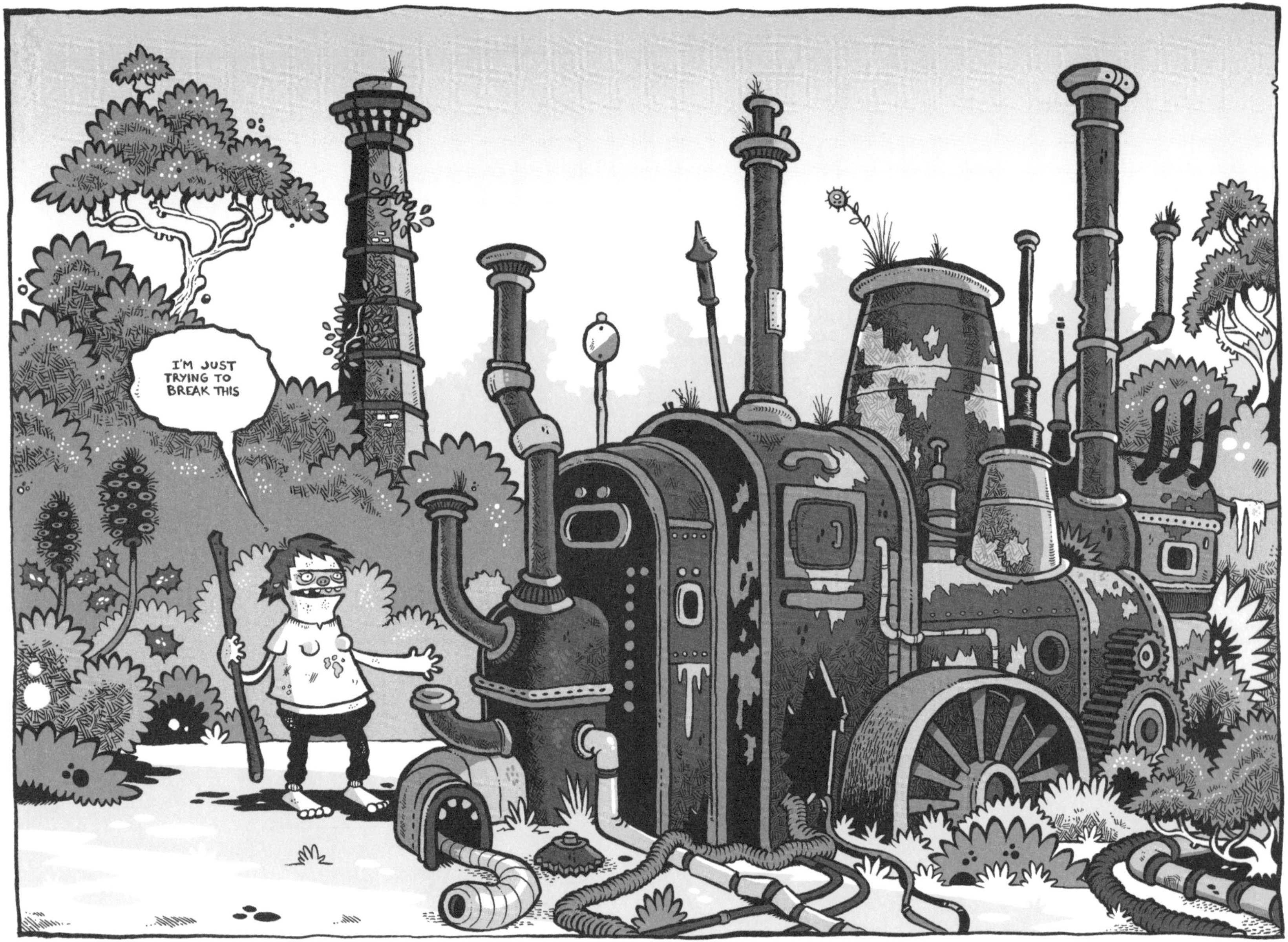
I'M JUST TRYING TO BREAK THIS

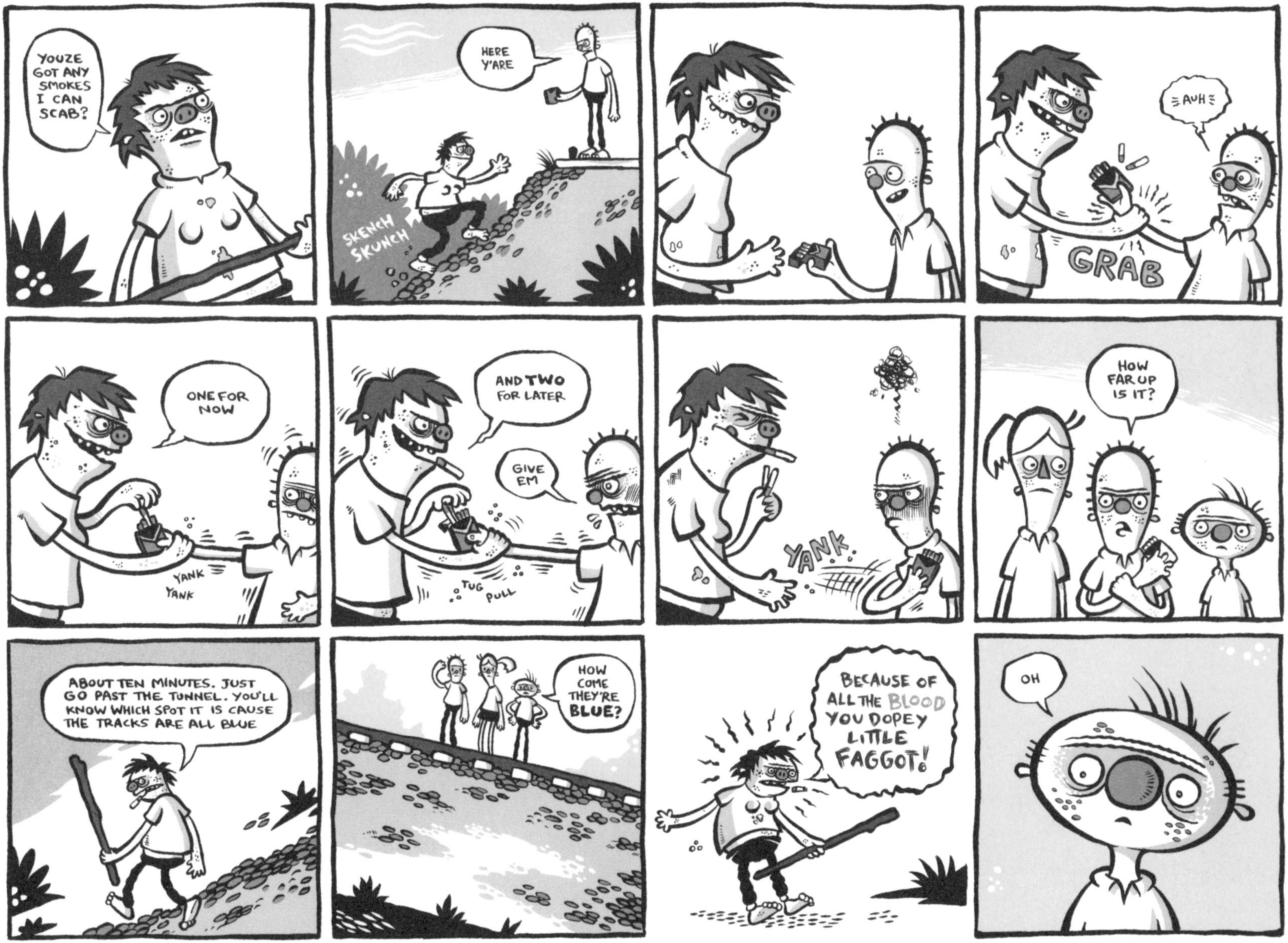
YOUZE GOT ANY SMOKES I CAN SCAB?
HERE Y'ARE
SKENCH SKUNCH
AUH
GRAB
ONE FOR NOW
YANK
YANK
AND TWO FOR LATER
GIVE EM
TUG
PULL
YANK
HOW FAR UP IS IT?
ABOUT TEN MINUTES. JUST GO PAST THE TUNNEL. YOU'LL KNOW WHICH SPOT IT IS CAUSE THE TRACKS ARE ALL BLUE
HOW COME THEY'RE BLUE?
BECAUSE OF ALL THE BLOOD YOU DOPEY LITTLE FAGGOT!
OH

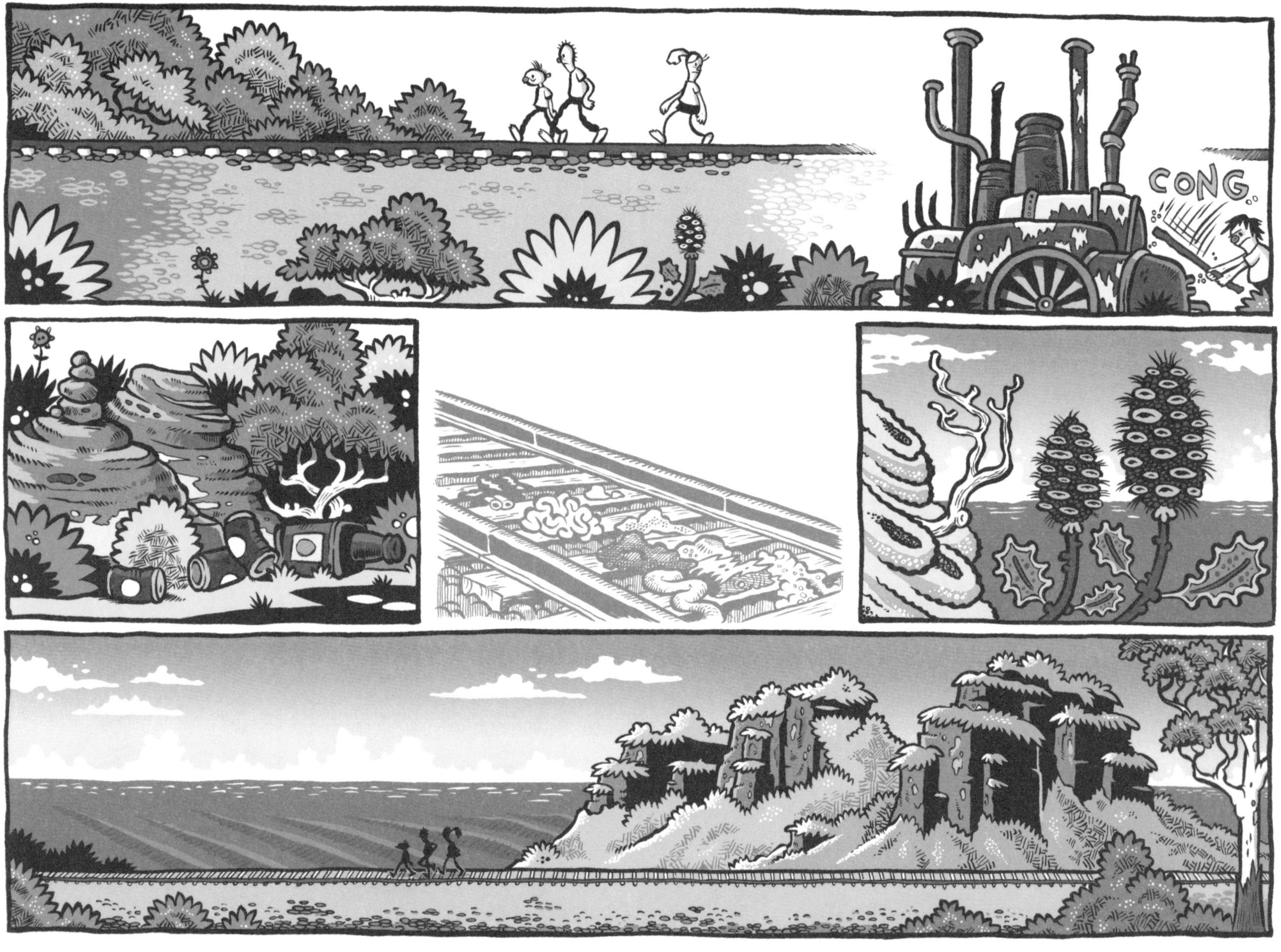
CONG

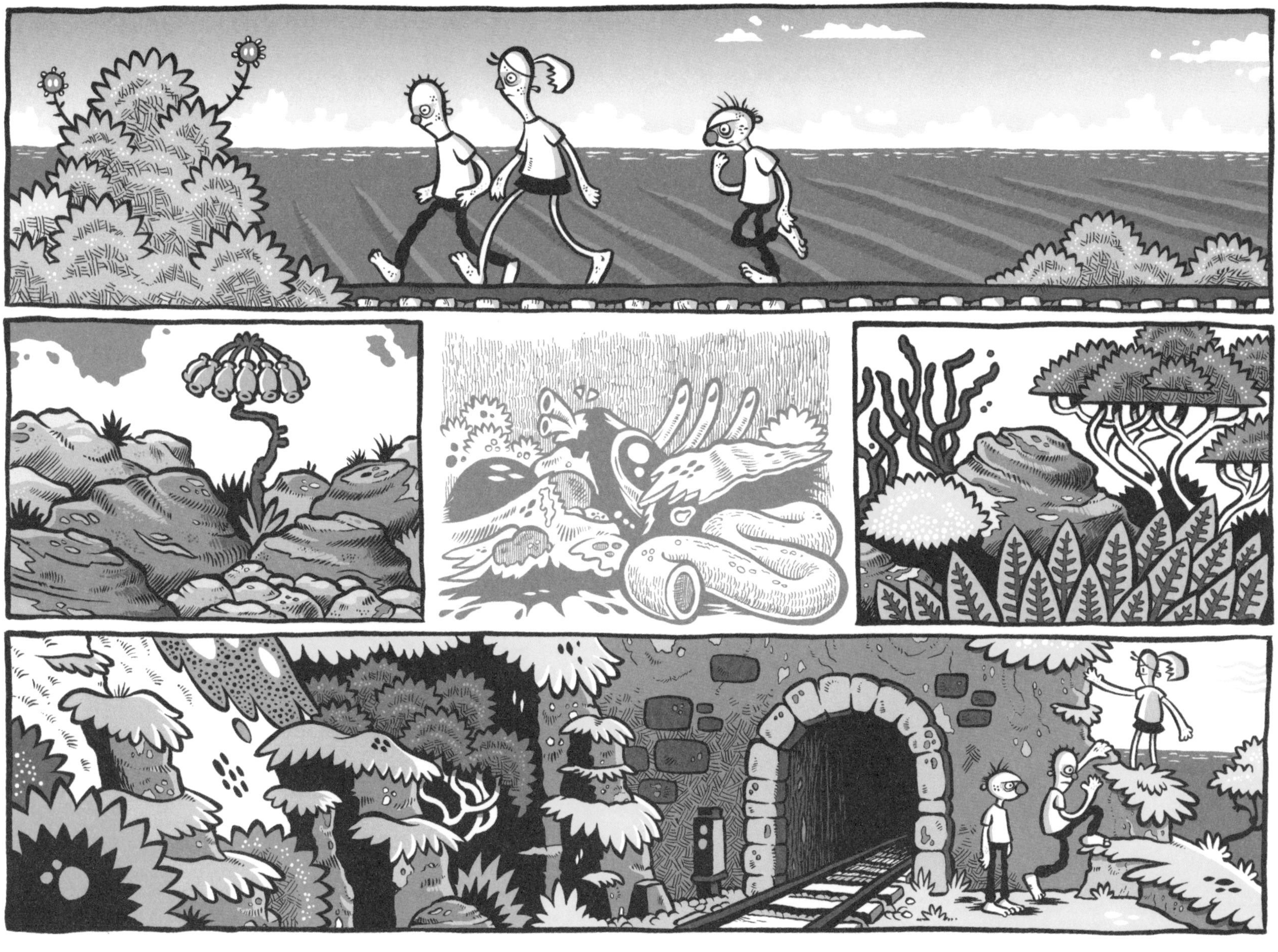

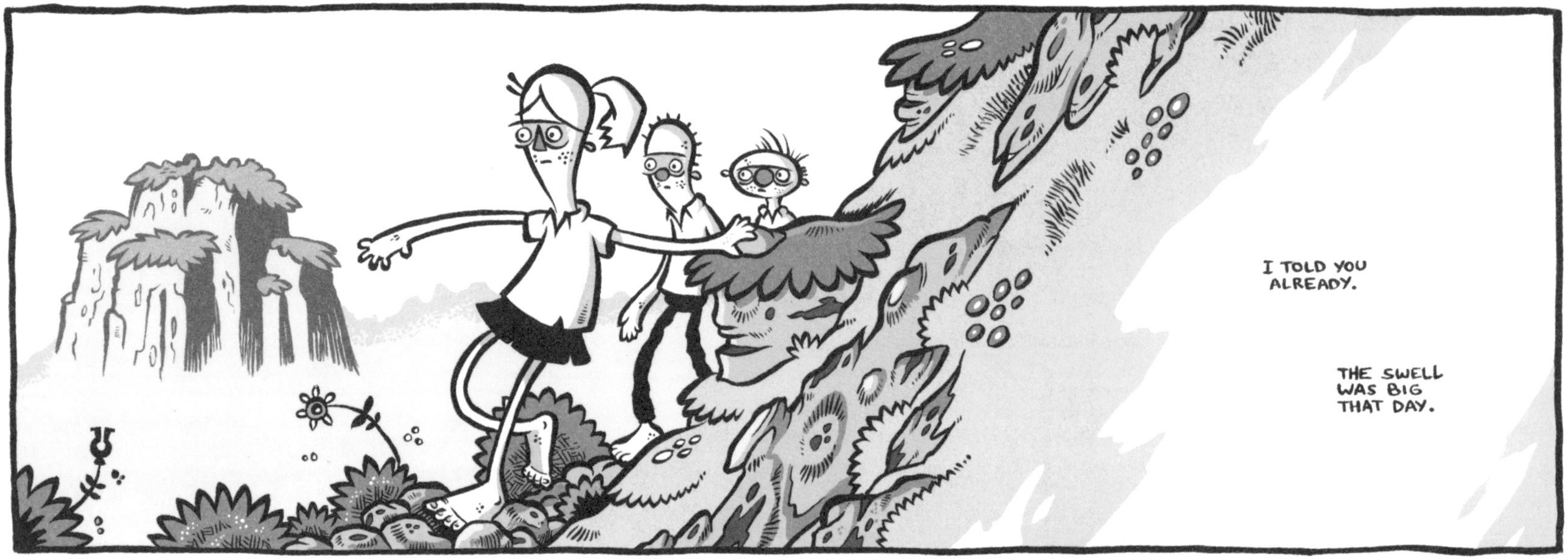
I TOLD YOU ALREADY.
THE SWELL WAS BIG THAT DAY.

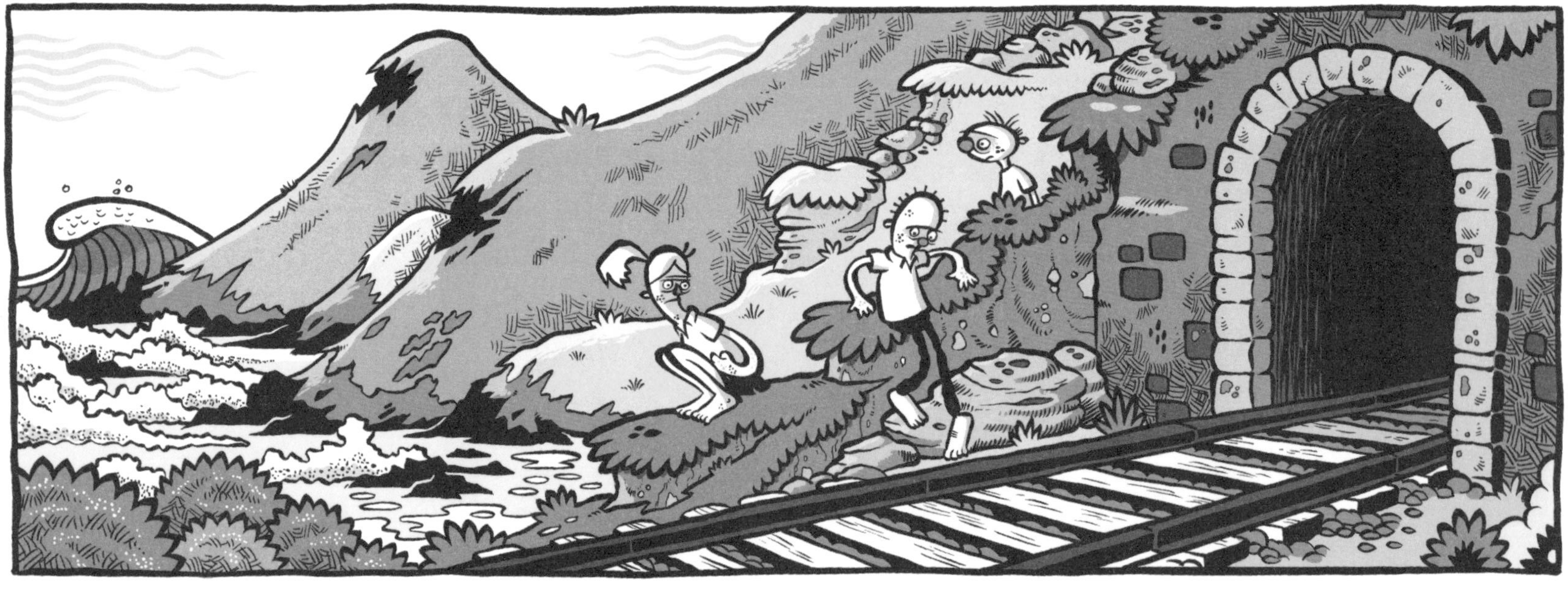

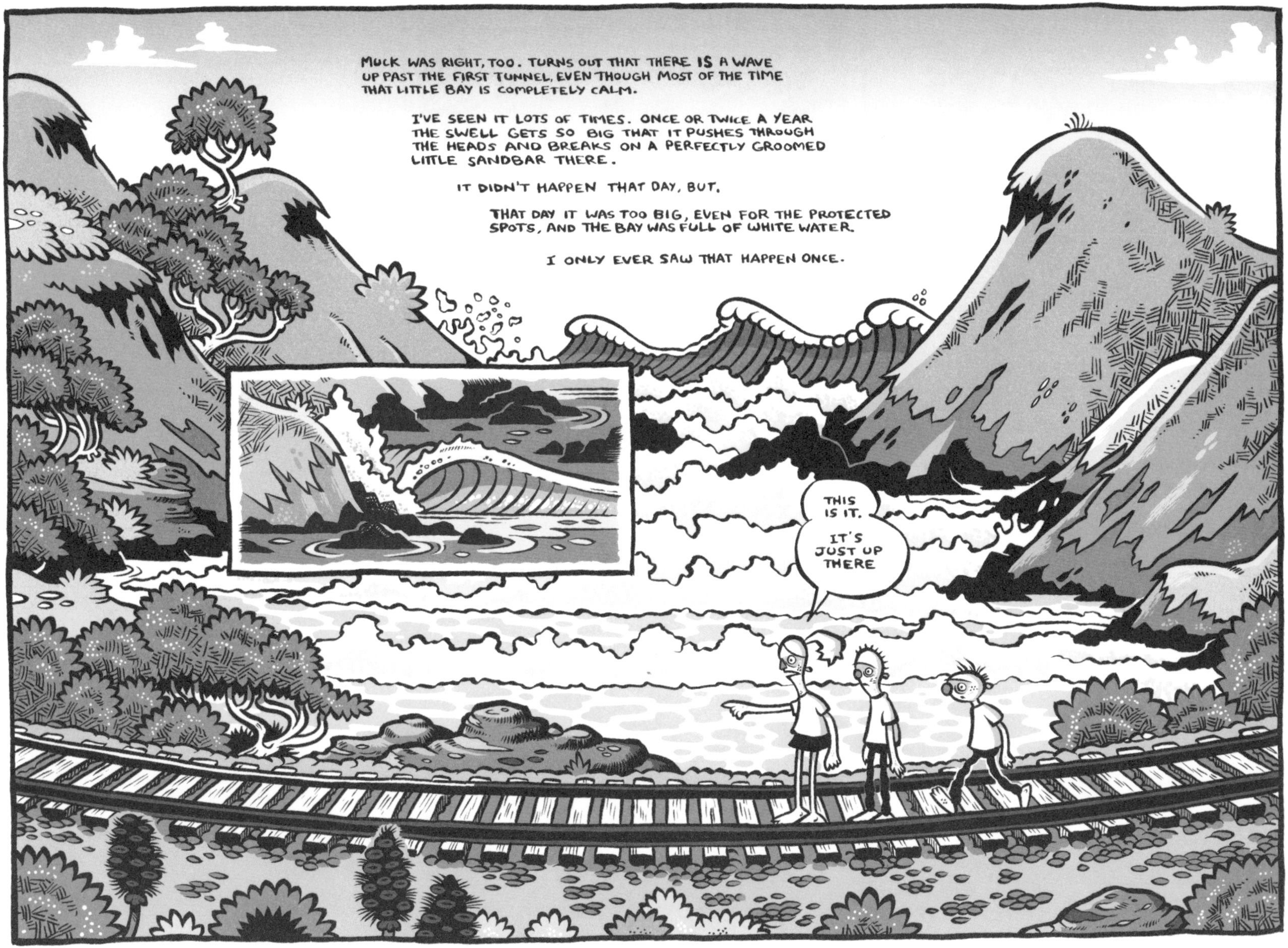
MUCK WAS RIGHT, TOO. TURNS OUT THAT THERE IS A WAVE UP PAST THE FIRST TUNNEL, EVEN THOUGH MOST OF THE TIME THAT LITTLE BAY IS COMPLETELY CALM.
I'VE SEEN IT LOTS OF TIMES. ONCE OR TWICE A YEAR THE SWELL GETS SO BIG THAT IT PUSHES THROUGH THE HEADS AND BREAKS ON A PERFECTLY GROOMED LITTLE SANDBAR THERE.
IT DIDN'T HAPPEN THAT DAY, BUT.
THAT DAY IT WAS TOO BIG, EVEN FOR THE PROTECTED SPOTS, AND THE BAY WAS FULL OF WHITE WATER.
I ONLY EVER SAW THAT HAPPEN ONCE.
THIS IS IT.
IT'S JUST UP THERE

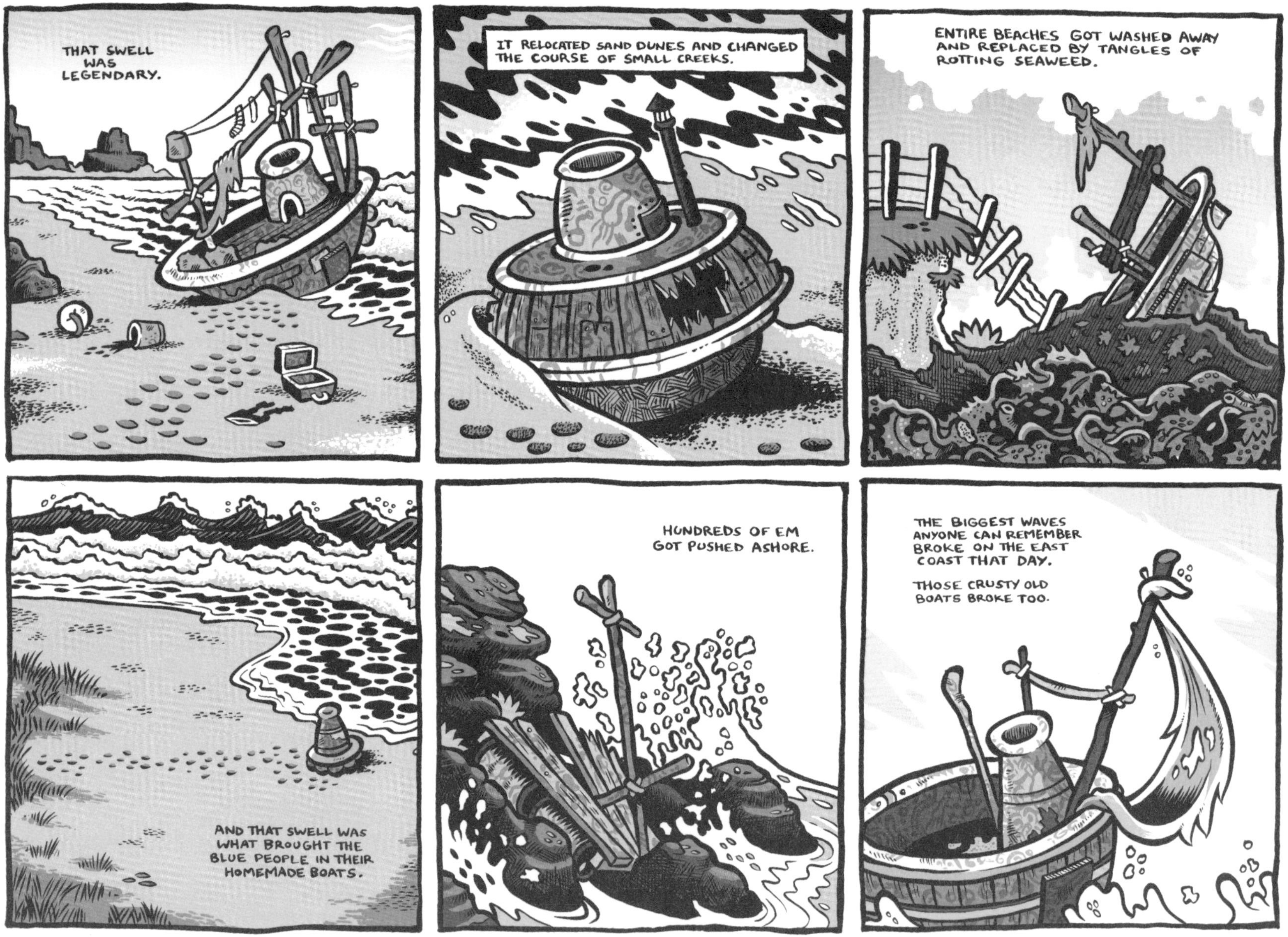
THAT SWELL WAS LEGENDARY.
IT RELOCATED SAND DUNES AND CHANGED THE COURSE OF SMALL CREEKS.
ENTIRE BEACHES GOT WASHED AWAY AND REPLACED BY TANGLES OF ROTTING SEAWEED.
AND THAT SWELL WAS WHAT BROUGHT THE BLUE PEOPLE IN THEIR HOMEMADE BOATS.
HUNDREDS OF EM GOT PUSHED ASHORE.
THE BIGGEST WAVES ANYONE CAN REMEMBER BROKE ON THE EAST COAST THAT DAY.
THOSE CRUSTY OLD BOATS BROKE TOO.

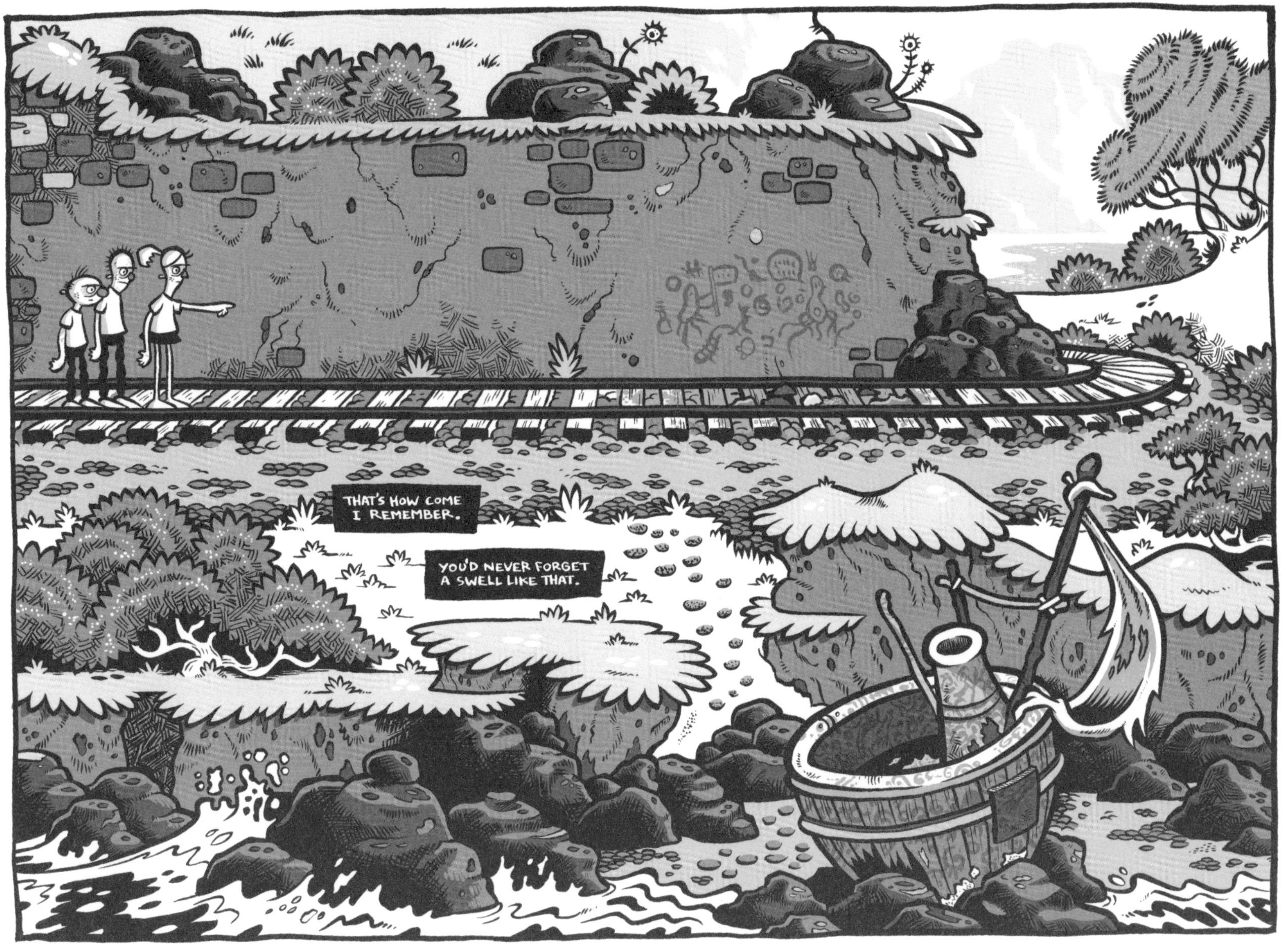
THAT'S HOW COME I REMEMBER.
YOU'D NEVER FORGET A SWELL LIKE THAT.

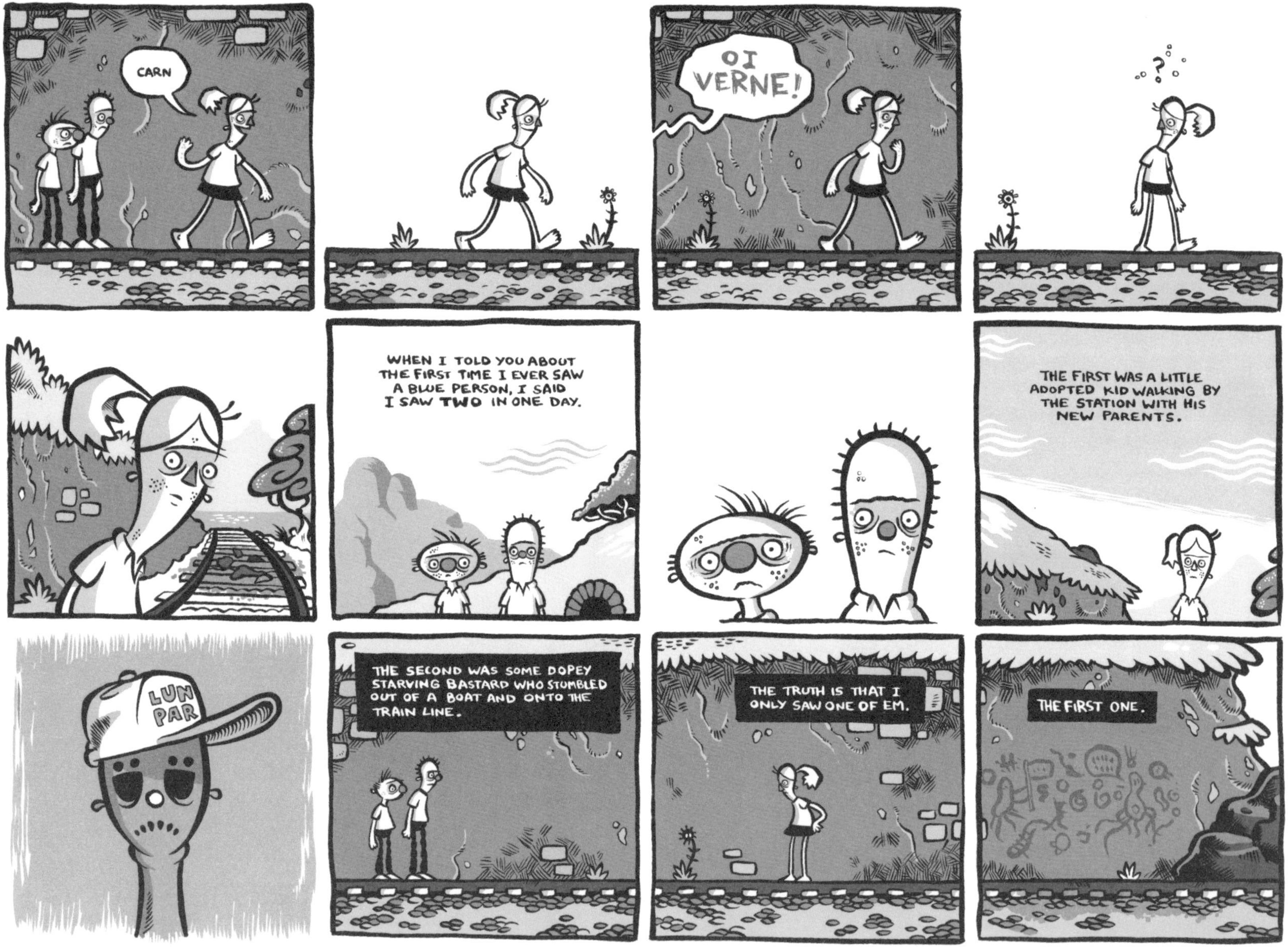
CARN
OI VERNE!
?
WHEN I TOLD YOU ABOUT THE FIRST TIME I EVER SAW A BLUE PERSON, I SAID I SAW TWO IN ONE DAY.
THE FIRST WAS A LITTLE ADOPTED KID WALKING BY THE STATION WITH HIS NEW PARENTS.
LUN PAR
THE SECOND WAS SOME DOPEY STARVING BASTARD WHO STUMBLED OUT OF A BOAT AND ONTO THE TRAIN LINE.
THE TRUTH IS THAT I ONLY SAW ONE OF EM.
THE FIRST ONE.

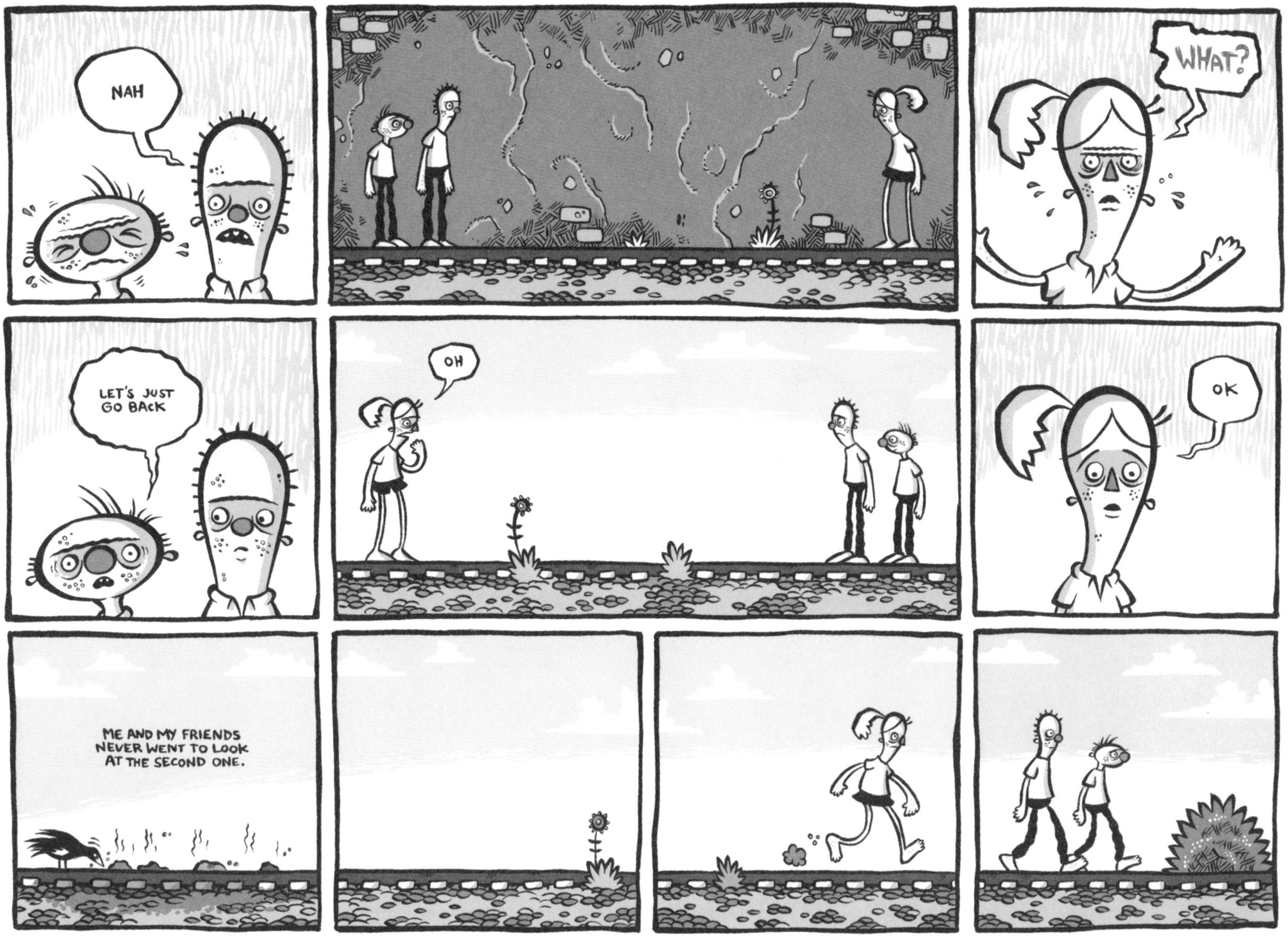
NAH
WHAT?
LET'S JUST GO BACK
OH
OK
ME AND MY FRIENDS NEVER WENT TO LOOK AT THE SECOND ONE.

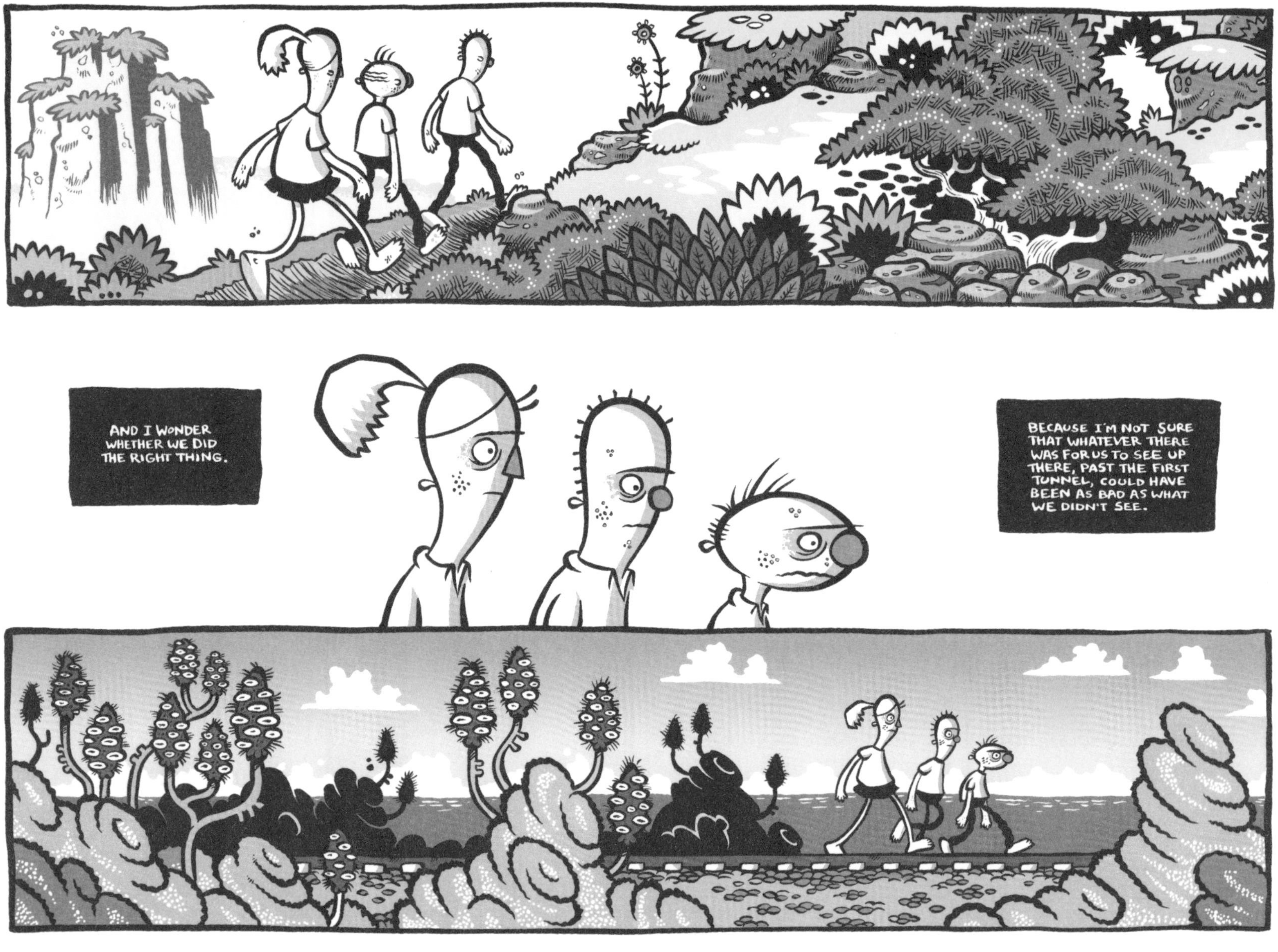
AND I WONDER WHETHER WE DID THE RIGHT THING.
BECAUSE I'M NOT SURE THAT WHATEVER THERE WAS FOR US TO SEE UP THERE, PAST THE FIRST TUNNEL, COULD HAVE BEEN AS BAD AS WHAT WE DIDN'T SEE.

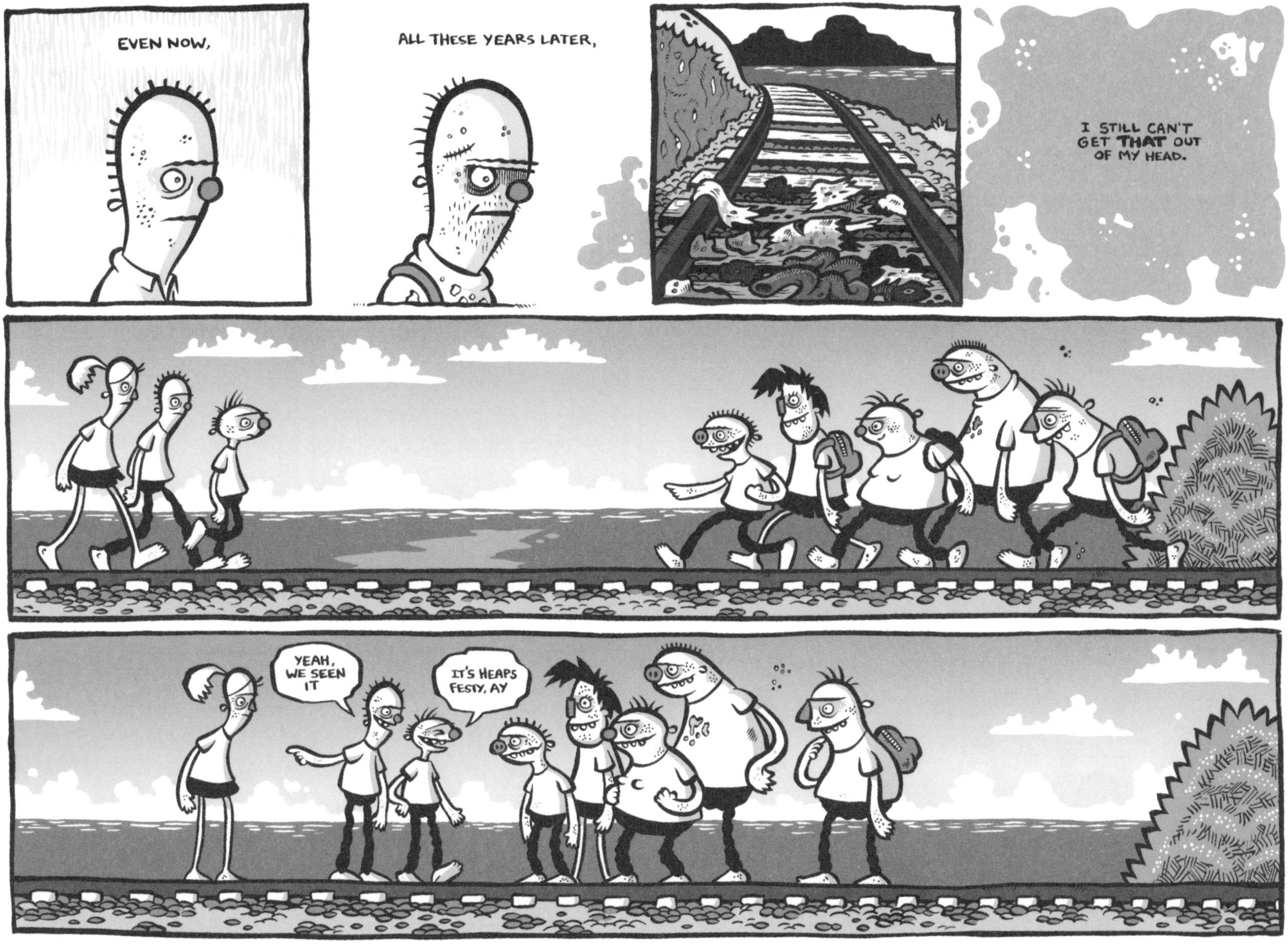
EVEN NOW,
ALL THESE YEARS LATER,
I STILL CAN'T GET THAT OUT OF MY HEAD.
YEAH, WE SEEN IT
IT'S HEAPS FESTY, AY

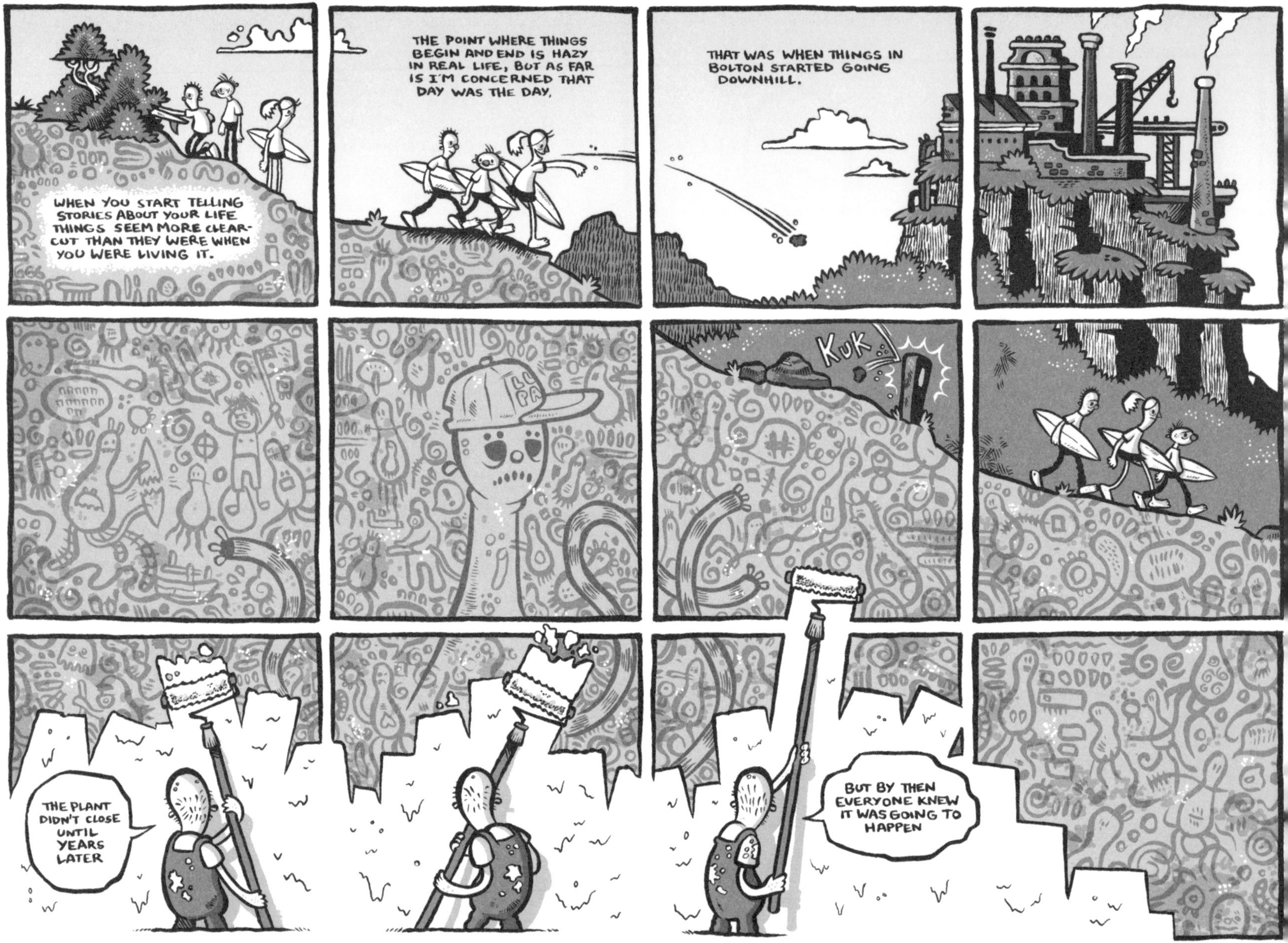
WHEN YOU START TELLING STORIES ABOUT YOUR LIFE THINGS SEEM MORE CLEAR-CUT THAN THEY WERE WHEN YOU WERE LIVING IT.
THE POINT WHERE THINGS BEGIN AND END IS HAZY IN REAL LIFE, BUT AS FAR IS I'M CONCERNED THAT DAY WAS THE DAY.
THAT WAS WHEN THINGS IN BOLTON STARTED GOING DOWNHILL.
KUK
THE PLANT DIDN'T CLOSE UNTIL YEARS LATER
BUT BY THEN EVERYONE KNEW IT WAS GOING TO HAPPEN

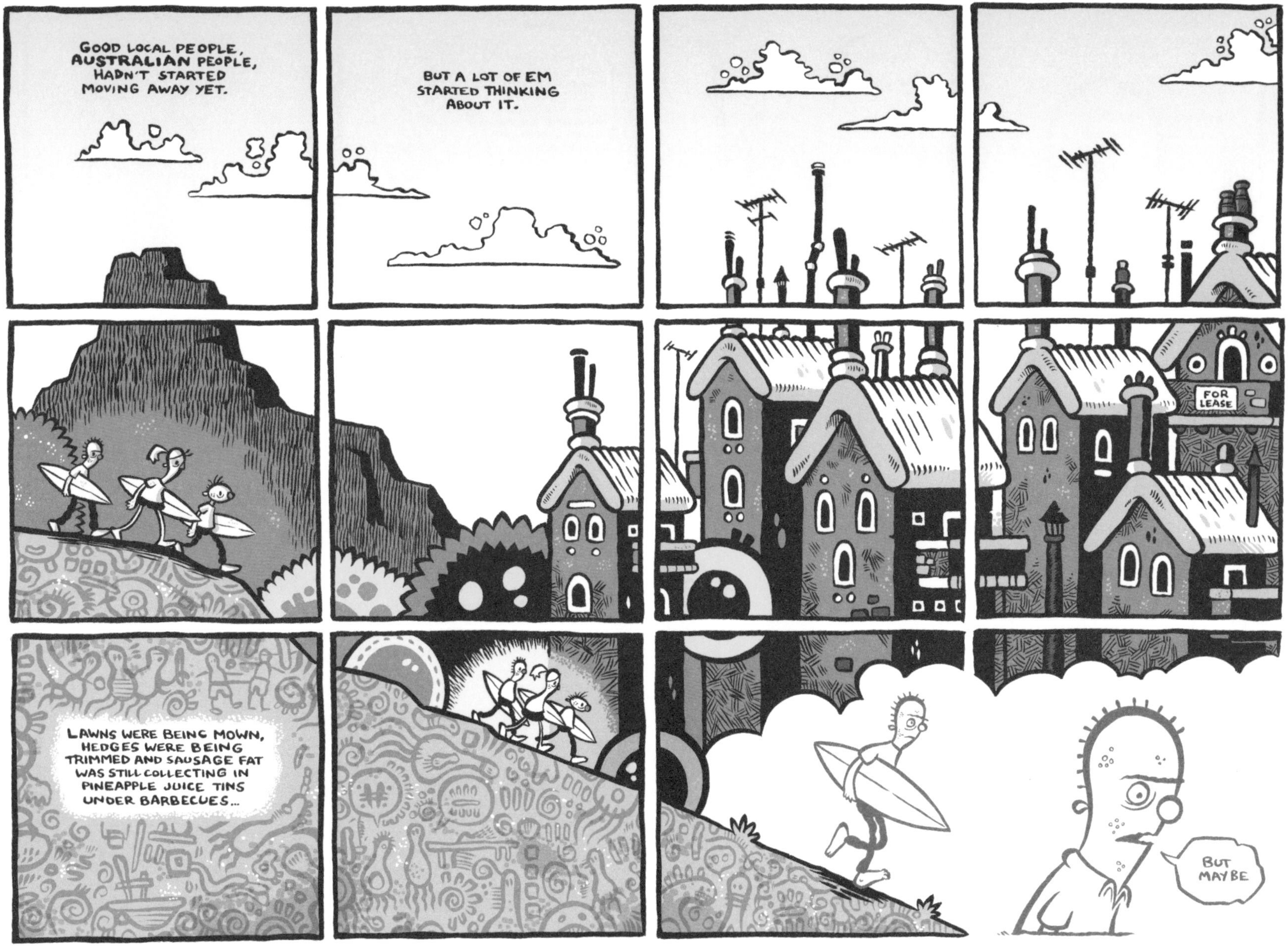
GOOD LOCAL PEOPLE, AUSTRALIAN PEOPLE, HADN'T STARTED MOVING AWAY YET.
BUT A LOT OF EM STARTED THINKING ABOUT IT.
FOR LEASE
LAWNS WERE BEING MOWN, HEDGES WERE BEING TRIMMED AND SAUSAGE FAT WAS STILL COLLECTING IN PINEAPPLE JUICE TINS UNDER BARBECUES...
BUT MAYBE

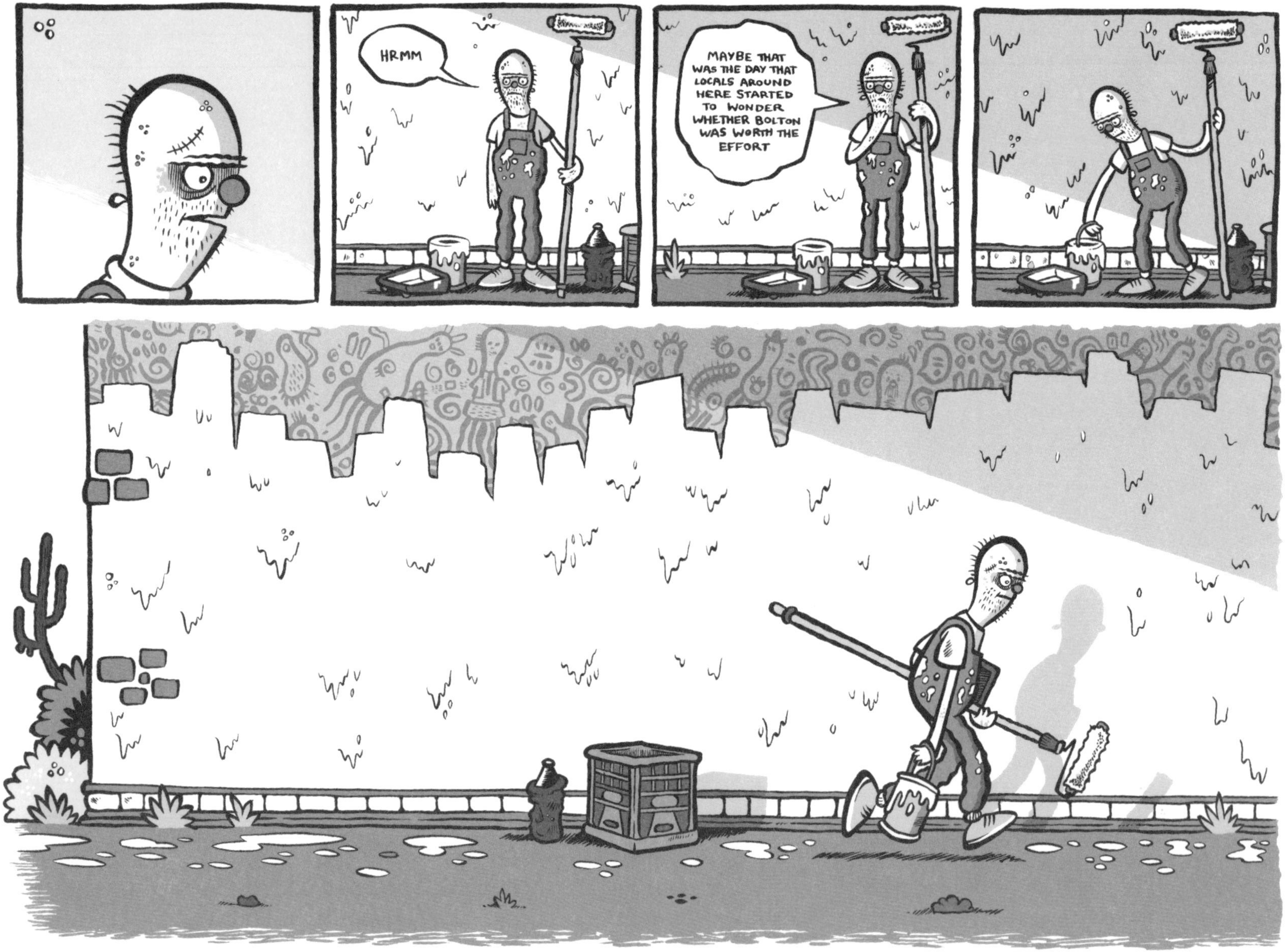

HRMM
MAYBE THAT WAS THE DAY THAT LOCALS AROUND HERE STARTED TO WONDER WHETHER BOLTON WAS WORTH THE EFFORT

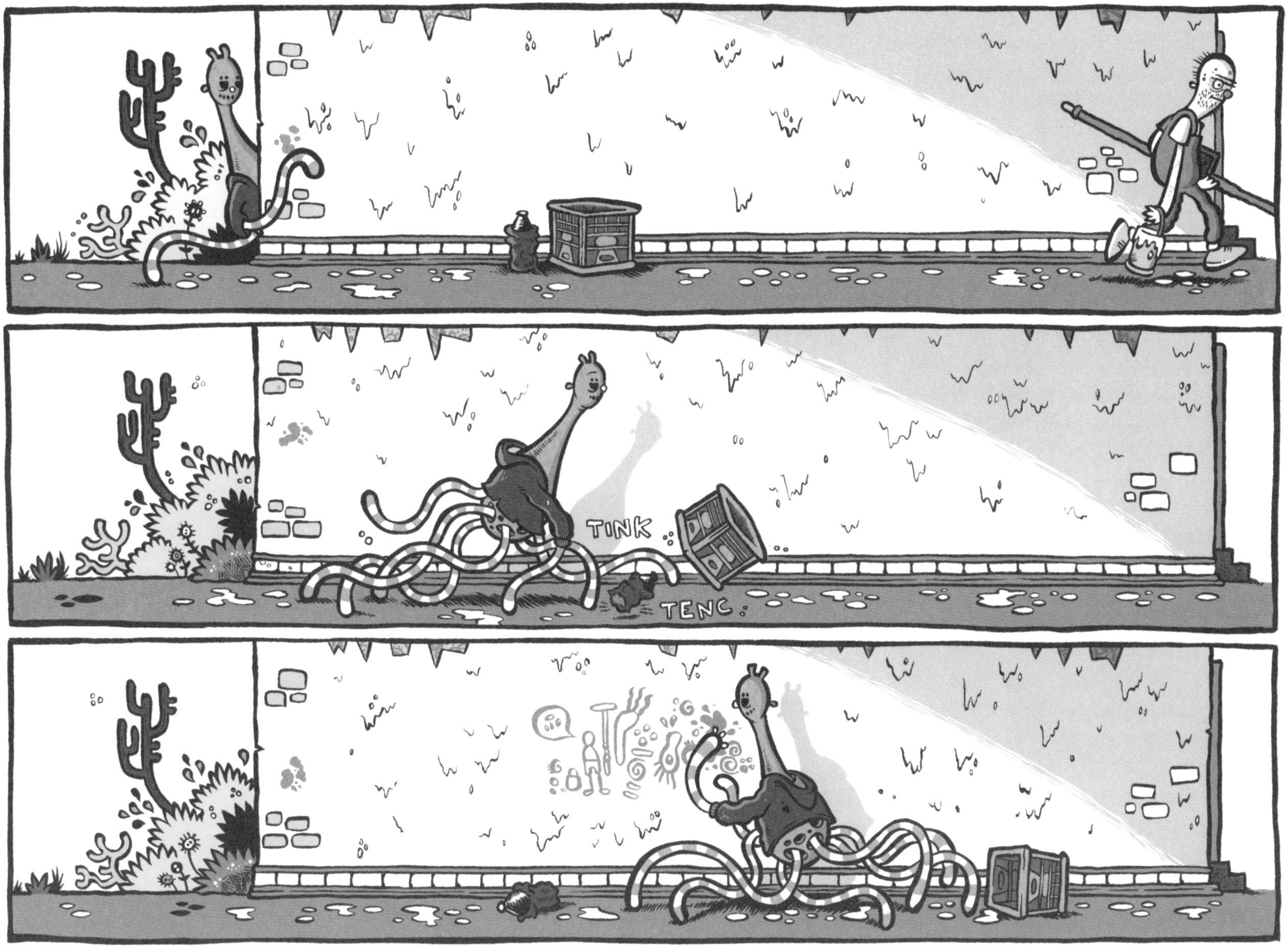
TINK
TENC

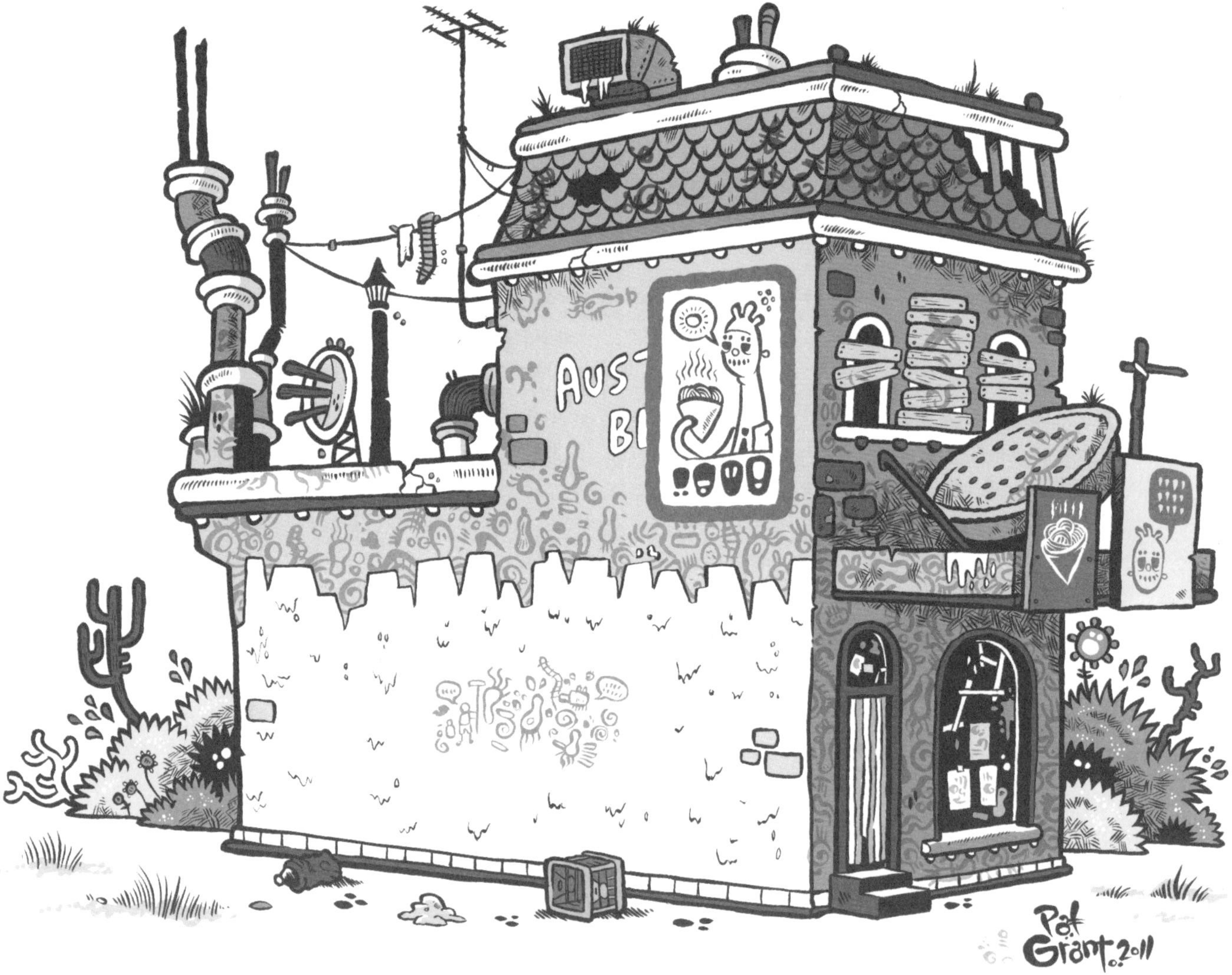
Pat Grant 2011

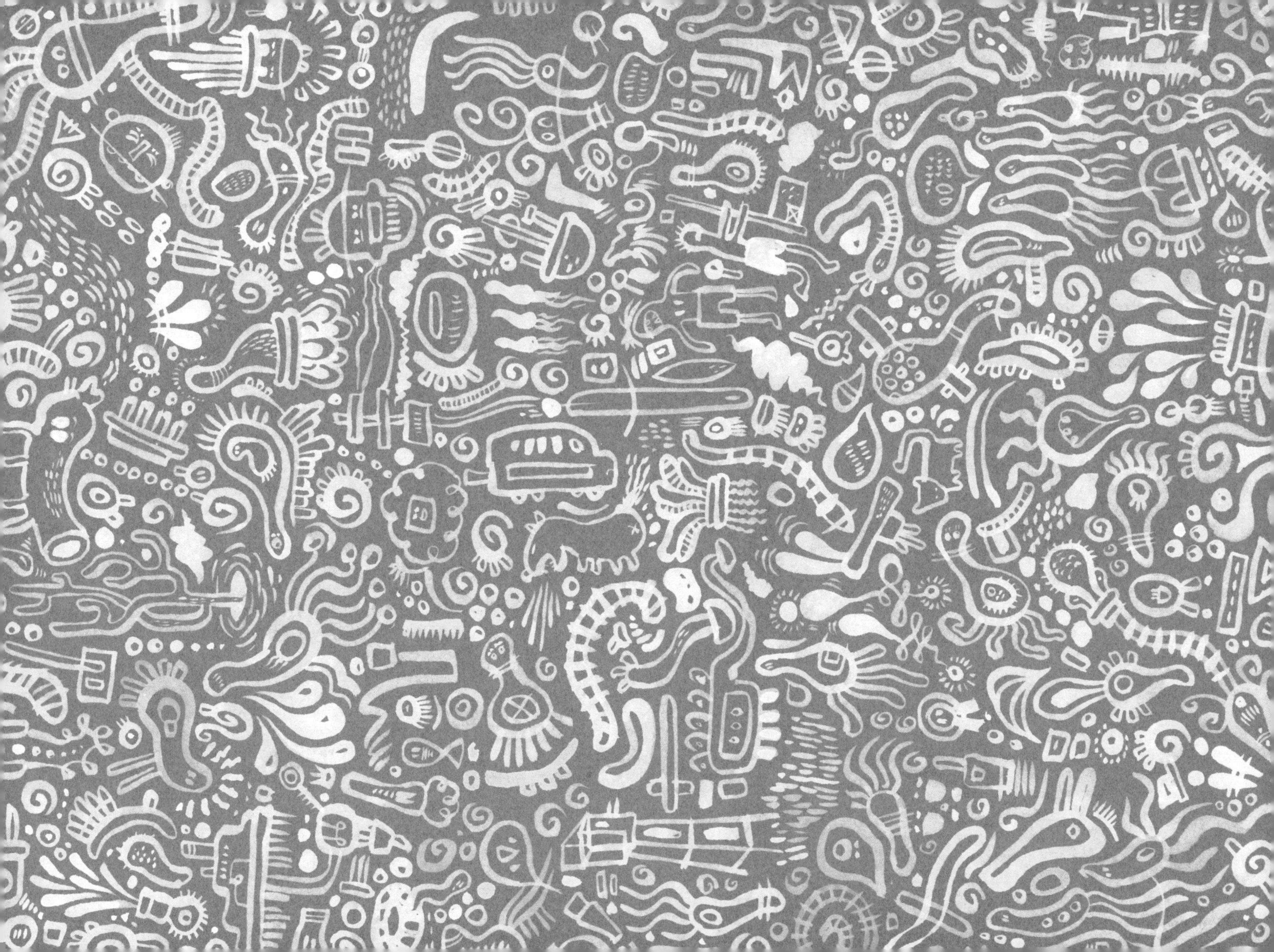

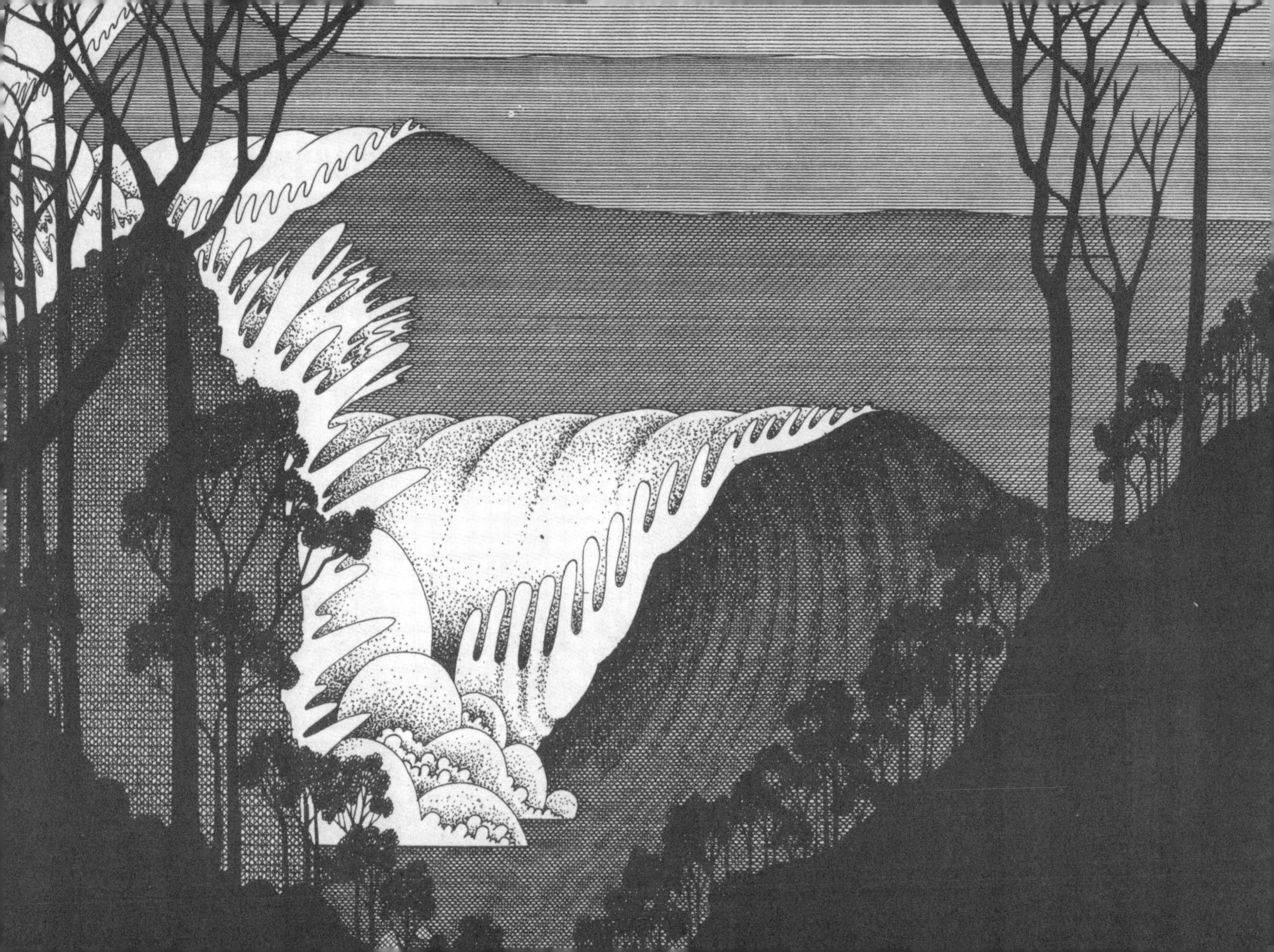

GENEALOGY OF THE BOOFHEAD:

IMAGES, MEMORY AND AUSTRALIAN SURF COMICS

Everything in my comic book *Blue* is bullshit. There is, for instance, no town called Bolton. At least not on the east coast. And not where there were visits from strange, blue-skinned foreigners. And I am not a right-wing crank who works as a painter. But then again, all of it is true. I did steal cigarettes from my dad. I did wag school to go surfing with my friends. And there was a bush track that ran over the creek, under the train line and down to the beach.

The track was a little goat trail that meandered through a patch of scrub behind the Sawtell Golf Course. It ran from the bottom of Newcastle Drive in Toormina to the end of Boronia Street in Sawtell. We'd go to the beach every morning and every afternoon, on skateboards or bikes with surfboards under our arms. We'd cross the handmade plank bridge across the stream that people still call Chinaman's Creek, and follow the track through the spindly thickets of paperbark growing on the clay flats. If it had been a wet year, the track was muddy and often treacherous. If you had a ciggie to smoke, that was where you'd light it up.

I was born in 1982, the same year that Stephen King wrote the excellent novella *The Body*, which most people know as the film *Stand by Me*. You're probably familiar with the story and you've most likely noticed that my narrative has a similar reek. I used the old body-on-the-train-line bit too. But the thing is that one morning, before I saw the film, and long before I read the novella, my friend Benson and I really did follow that bush track to the train line to look at the pieces of a young man's body.

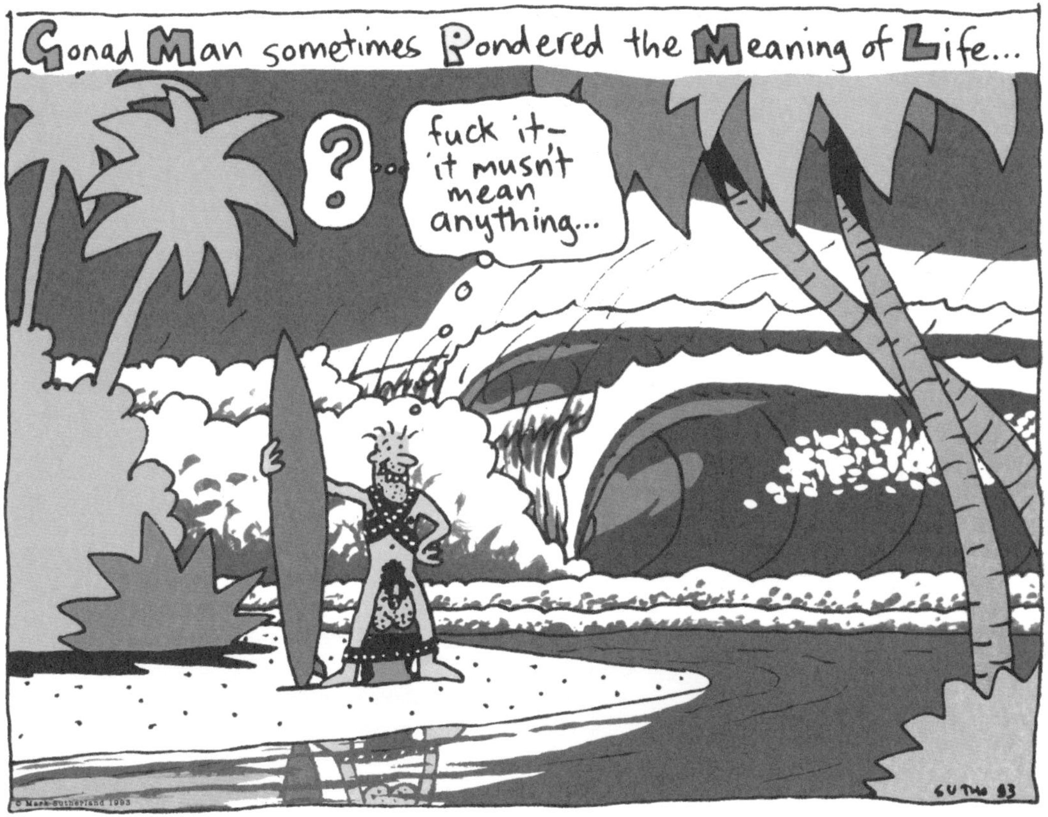
Gonad Man sometimes Pondered the Meaning of Life...
?...
fuck it- it musn't mean anything...
SUTHO 93

The body

We didn't know the kid who died. He was a few years older and had already left school. All we knew was that he was probably walking home drunk, that he had been hit so hard there wasn't much left of him, that the clean-up had been half-arsed, and that the train line was still scattered with pieces of his shredded body. We first heard about it from my best mate Kobus during Mr McRae's English class. He had seen it, he told us, and spent half a period detailing it with visceral precision – a description on par with any of the literary classics Mr McRae was force-feeding us. The word about the dead kid spread and it seemed like half the school was making plans to go and see it.

The next morning I got up while it was still dark. It's always best to arrive at the beach before dawn on that stretch of coast, because the nor'easter picks up early and tends to fuzzy up the waves. That day Benson and I set our alarms even earlier than normal, because we wanted to look at the carnage on the way. We arrived at the place

art seems to be the key that many people need to access a chamber of their psyche that is otherwise locked away from their adult consciousness.

This, I think, is central to the mysterious process of making comics. Good cartooning seems to happen when an artist finds a vocabulary of images that has a certain resonance, not only with the narrative they are writing, but with their own personal story. The slow drama of life that shapes the body of an adult is performed in the nerdy little dance of brush and ink on paper when the artist sits down to draw. This resonance between image, memory and the artist's body is one of the great intangibles in comics, something that can't quite be pinned down. We can see it in Charles Burns, where the pulp horror comics and B-grade sci-fi that he pored over as a kid bleed out of every page he draws as an adult. Similarly, the work of Jim Woodring traces a lifetime devoted to the recreation of forms remembered from disturbing childhood visions and terrifying Fleischer cartoons.

If cartooning is a form of writing interwoven with the act of remembering, then so is comics criticism. At this point in time, when more and more scholars and writers are delving into comics history, it's important for us to be mindful of the pitfalls of writing about a medium so perilously connected to childhood experiences. When I told you about the body at the beginning of this essay, I didn't do it because I felt that *Blue* needs explanation - I did it because to get to the body we had to walk along the bush track. And that muddy trail, the idea of it, is what holds my little comics history together.

Comics history for bogans

Today's 12-year-old will never understand what it was like growing up in an isolated Australian coastal town in the 90s. The nearest comic book store was six hours' drive from my home. The internet was five years late and another five had to pass until it was fast enough to be useful. The media we had access to on the north coast of New South Wales was as bland and lacking in sustenance as the white bread in our lunchboxes.

where the body was before six, when the bush either side of the trail was still and dark. We stopped. The plan was to step off the trail, climb up onto the tracks and examine the gore in the predawn gloom.

My memory of this event brings up feelings of unease similar to those I get when I'm brooding over the themes of *Blue*. I knew I wanted to write about localism, racism and the creepy politics that play out in small town supermarkets and surf club car parks, but the ideas I came up with didn't work until I combined them with the story of some spotty kids who walk up the line to see some human wreckage. It felt right to use the body-on-the-train-line because it was a readymade ripper of a yarn. My only concern was that it had already been put to good use by King.

I showed a draft of *Blue* to Shaun Tan, probably the greatest visual communicator I'm ever likely to meet. He told me that I shouldn't worry about this, about the plot

being clichéd, because it was really a story about memory.

"Comics," he said, "are almost always about memory, about looking back, about making sense of the past."

And I think I agree with him. Many of the important auteur comics of the last half century – the ones I keep rereading, anyway – are about making sense of adolescent or childhood memories, either directly (as in the work of Jeffrey Brown or Gabrielle Bell) or indirectly, in the way the cartoonist has approached the job of making images. It may be that all storytelling is about memory to some extent, but cartooning seems more powerfully linked to juvenile vocabularies of being and knowing than other kinds of writing. Sinking into the story space that comic art affords us – as cartoonists, but also as readers – is to step back into an adolescent or pre-adolescent state, bypassing the analytical and historical filters with which we, as adults, process sensory data. This leaves us exposed to raw, emotive readings of time, space and form. Comic

To add to this, Australia does not have a wealth of comic art history. As a matter of fact, this country has a bad record when it comes to any kind of history. Our way of writing history is to destroy old things pertinent to our landscape and experience, and to import readymade mythologies from overseas. There's not a lot of comic art ephemera floating around Australia, in the way that there is in the US, nor is there a culture of collecting it. If we had a silver or golden age of comics, it's unknown to me. And while there were and are attempts at a publishing industry like that in the States, a truly Australian comics culture has been something of a chimera. That's not to say there weren't or aren't amazing artists or devoted fans, but when it seems like you're on the rock farthest from the bright centre of the comic-book universe, Tatooine syndrome tends to prevail. Success on the sandy planet isn't much success at all, and there's always another womp rat in a Southern Cross singlet looking to tear you down.

When I left home and moved to the city, however, the era of the graphic novel was in full swing. Thick books of thoughtful, sophisticated auteur comics were coming out of North America faster than I could read them. I figured out pretty quickly that I'd be an idiot not to ditch my ambition to write traditional prose and have a go at cartooning.

So with a university degree of questionable value in my back pocket, I began to school myself in comics. I sought out the revered works of the 20th century, taking home what I'd been told were the seminal texts in the Anglophone comics tradition. It's a lineage that has been written and rewritten, an old, well-worn line that runs from Töpffer to Sammy Harkham, passing through the careers of great artists and infamous figures like Outcault, Herriman, McCay, Toth, Kurtzman, Wertham, Kirby, Ditko, Crumb, Eisner, Spiegelman, Miller, Moore, Dan Clowes and Chris Ware. I read *Swamp Thing*, *Cerebus*, Frank Miller's run on *Daredevil*, *Watchmen*, *Sandman*. I read underground comics collections, EC reprints, Ditko's *Spiderman* and reprints of *The Spirit*.

These works were said to have inspired the contemporary comics that I loved, but the feeling I had on reading them was one of disappointment and confusion.

There was a serious disconnect between my own taste and the commonly held opinions of true comic fans. Could no one else see that Frank Miller was a dangerous bigot? That *Cerebus* was so bad it was almost unreadable? That sure, those pages Jack Kirby drew *looked* great, but come on, they're still not that good?

I should say right now that I'm not setting out to discredit the major milestones of 20th century comic art. These were just my first impressions, and I don't necessarily believe them now. But in the first decade of this century, a new book came out every week that knocked my socks off. Meanwhile, all this stuff I was reading to better myself, these classic comics from back in the day, they just seemed fucken stupid. Even Crumb, arguably the most important cartoonist of the 20th century, seemed a little overrated when I compared his work with someone like Dave Cooper (even though Crumb was clearly a powerful inspiration for him). I had come to the world of American comics late. *Jimmy Corrigan* was already on the shelves. I bought it mainly because I liked the book design and it turned out to be the first truly great comic book I ever read. The entire catalogue of the 20th century was something I missed. I tried to catch up, I really did, but I just didn't get it.

Dylan Horrocks, the Kiwi cartoonist who drew a comic so beautiful that it made me choke up and cry in a crowded Melbourne café, said something on the Inkstuds podcast that really changed the way I handle this task of schooling myself in comics:

> During the 70s and the 80s there emerged a whole body of writing about comics. It was the rise of serious comics historiography, but one that really emerged out of fandom. The people who were writing it, I guess they fell in love with comics as 13-year-old boys and retained some of that fannish

1963

50¢

SURFER
CARTOONS

THIS PAGE: RICK GRIFFIN, 1963 // **OPPOSITE:** TONY EDWARDS, FROM CAPTAIN GOODVIBES: THE WHOLE EARTH PIGALOGUE, 1975 // **PREVIOUS RIGHT:** MARK SUTHERLAND, 1993 // **PREVIOUS LEFT:** TONY EDWARDS, 1975 // **NEXT LEFT:** RICK GRIFFIN, 1974 // **NEXT MIDDLE:** VICTOR MOSCOSO, 1994 // **NEXT RIGHT:** RICK GRIFFIN, 1974 //

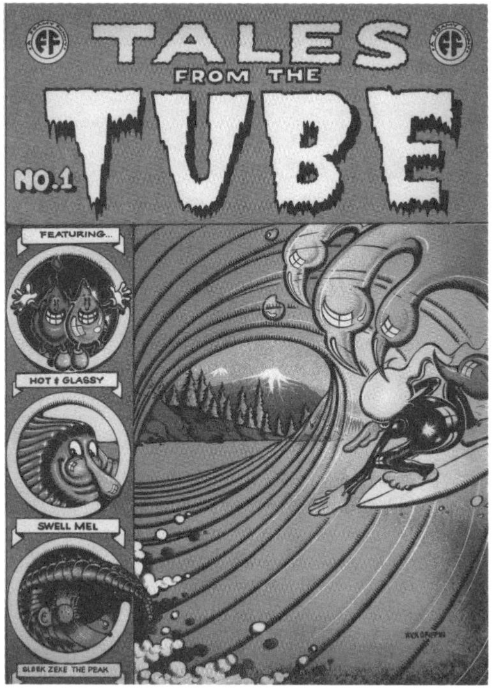
TALES
FROM THE
TUBE
NO.1
FEATURING...
HOT & GLASSY
SWELL MEL
SLEEK ZEKE THE PEAK

> enthusiam. And what 13-year-old boys love is dynamism and energy and kineticism. And so that history came to be written as one where the key figures were people like Joe Kubert, who injected their linework with this incredible dynamism and made the pages really energetic and free. I think there were a lot of forgotten little byways of comics in America which were really just not noticed by the people writing those histories.

What I get from Dylan's interview is that someone like me ought to take the dominant history of comics well salted – not because the line isn't valid, but because I didn't grow up around the corner from a comics store. I never had the chance to be a teenage comic nerd who fell in love with Miller and Kirby. I grew up with other things.

The question then presents itself: When we write about comics, should we screen out our childhood obsessions and work toward something that resembles a stern, adult objectivity? If we want a universal comics history, then yes. But I don't believe such a thing is possible. And for me, the opposite makes more sense. Just as the process of making comics is often interwoven with memory, the writing of comics history is equally personal. The story of comics is a story of love, fandom, fear and uncertainty. So let's resign ourselves to the fact that that when we are writing about comics, we become obsessed 13-year-olds again.

Which is why, in this essay, I'm getting my Howard Zinn on. I'm trying to draw a wobbly new line that represents my childhood obsessions, to map a new genealogy of image-makers. Writing about surf comics is to write about a tradition cluelessly detached from the inner city, from global geek culture. If a comics history is ever going to make sense to me, a boofhead from north coast New South Wales, then I need to write it myself.

Rick Griffin and the first surf comics

During the time that I was trying to better myself as a cartoonist, I would go to the library to read old comics. People really seem to love Jack Kirby, so I picked up *Essential Fantastic Four.* The art in this book is pretty good. One thing that Kirby definitely had going for him was understanding the power of the heroic figure, an iconic form that taps into a storytelling tradition thousands of years old. Kirby connected contemporary graphic design sensibility with all the heady essence of the heroic and biblical texts that underpinned the value systems of boys and young men – and still do. He will never be forgotten, because those who were lucky enough to hold those cheaply printed comic books in the 60s and 70s, and look upon those pictures with the eyes of a nine-year-old, will forever use the art of Jack Kirby as the key to that secret chamber of memory. That's why a copy of *Fantastic Four #48* is worth every penny it goes for on eBay. It's the issue where the Silver Surfer makes his first appearance. But when I made my way through to this comic, looking for whatever it was that everyone else found in it, all I saw was

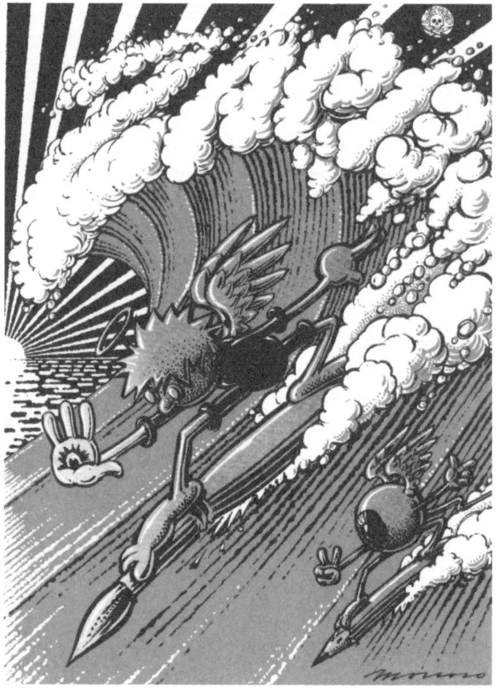

the dickhead on the longboard. My first impression was that old Jack didn't get enough time looking at the fluid dynamics of surfboards and breaking waves, and that the Silver Surfer's stance was just plain stupid. To me, it was self-evident: Kirby don't surf.

After I got bored with Kirby reprints I picked up a few books on underground comics, and things in the monochrome, speckled world of the undergrounds seemed to make a bit more sense. I turned to a spread that had Victor Moscoso's cover for *Zap 13* on one side and a page of surf comics by Rick Griffin on the other. Griffin's page was drawn about the same time Kirby was drawing the Silver Surfer, but unlike Kirby's art, it was something that made an immediate connection with me. The images of breaking waves were so good my bum nearly fell off.

This was the feeling I was looking for, and failing to find, in Kirby. A weird sense of longing and melancholy and what I can only describe as an *understanding*, something deep in my bones that seemed older that I was.

Surf comics start with Rick Griffin. He learned to surf in the late 50s in Palos Verdes, California. He was 14 years old and had a prodigious drawing talent. Most people know Griffin as one of the great poster artists of the Haight Ashbury scene, a central figure in the psychedelic art movement and a key player in the emergence of underground comics. Historian Patrick Rosenkranz calls Griffin the first of the underground cartoonists, not because of his impact on the movement, but because before the countercultural revolution started to build, Griffin was a surf cartoonist. As staff cartoonist for *Surfer* magazine in the early 60s, Griffin's early surf comics have a charming tiki feel, heavily influenced by the commercial design culture of the post-war period. His pages are composed with a minimalism that counterbalances the extreme complexity and fine detail that would characterise his later work, but they still have that unmistakable whiff of the *underground*.

Now, it's really hard to talk about a sport in the abstract without looking like the jock at a poetry night, but I'm going to give it a go. Surfing is as much a sport as it is low-brow performance art, and the surfers that succeed at the form, those that get the best waves, need both physical prowess and a particular way of seeing. The ocean demands a visual literacy if its movements are to be predicted, and the ability to read the ocean translates into a particular visual *sensibility* on dry land. Obsessed surfers spend hours each day looking at waves and movements on the surface of the water. They develop an aesthetic resonance that shudders out into the wider culture. This literacy is something that any surfer worth their salt can immediately sense in the work of Rick Griffin.

Surf art hasn't changed much since Griffin. Even now, 50 years later, the iconic forms of breaking waves, the kooky stances, the longboards and the surf-bum jalopies are the bread and butter of any artist trading in surfer kitsch. But the thing that separates the good surf art from the bad is this understanding of the way water moves

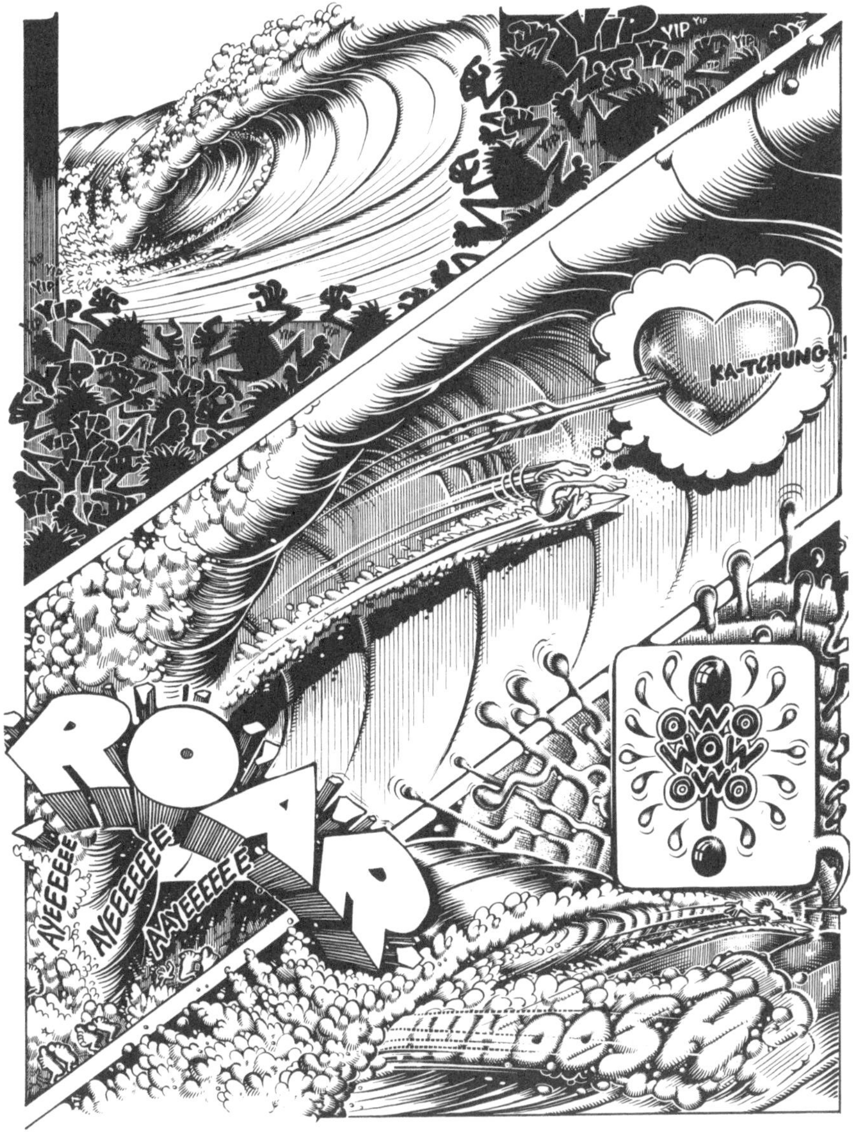
YIP
KA-TCHUNGK!
ROAR

when the ocean meets the land.

Griffin was at *Surfer* when surfing had its first real burst of popularity in California, along with its first crisis of authenticity. American capitalism had swallowed surf culture whole and spat it back out in packaged portions. Surfers were disaffected by the way their culture had been sugared down by beach party films like *Gidget*, *Beach Blanket Bingo* and *Ride the Wild Surf*, and by the increasing use of surfer kitsch to shift any product that needed a youthful image. In the 2004 documentary *Riding Giants*, big wave surfer Greg Noll was asked about the way surfing was depicted in Hollywood. He replied, "It just… Man… It just makes me puke." The importance of by-surfers-for-surfers media had become apparent.

At first glance it seems that most surf comics take their vocabulary from the undergrounds, but the opposite is also true. Noll's surfboard business was booming as the sport increased in popularity, and he subsequently employed Griffin as a designer and illustrator for the company. Shortly after, the two began working on *A Cartoon History of Surfing*, a way for them to take back some of the narrative surrounding the sport. The book has layouts and typography that scream out an underground influence, but it actually preceded the undergrounds by four years or so. Griffin had seen the disconnect between surf culture and its representation in the mass media, and his drawings corrected this, depicting surfers with all the grit and grease and obsession, but without the candy-coated bullshit. Later, when the tiki minimalism wore off, the breaking wave became one of the recurring motifs in Griffin's psychedelic poster design and underground comic art. An example of this later work was what I had stumbled on that day in the library and, as I said, my bum nearly fell off.

Iconic forms and fetishes

The currency that cartoonists trade in is the icon, a simple image drawn in as few lines as possible, signifying a complex but self-contained referent. What cartooning does is translate objects from the outside world into a sequence of icons on the page. Each icon represents not only the sensual experience of the referent, but also its intangible essence. It's about finding the treeness of a tree, or the genuine fuckwittage of a character like Horatio from *CSI: Miami*.

Because of this, the objects that lend themselves most lovingly to cartooning are those that are iconic to begin with. The idealised human body in a dynamic pose, a giant erection, certain makes of automobile, human skulls, a New York City fire hydrant, a particular volcano in Japan. Some things in the world are perfect subjects for cartooning, and a drawing fetish quickly coagulates around them. I can think of very few comic strips that are not built around a particular kind of iconic imagery, and surf comics are no exception. It's a genre defined by the breaking wave.

Just like the 13-year-old Kubert enthusiasts, it's the icons and fetishes from our youth that predispose us to particular traditions. It's something we are almost born into, something over which we have no control. Woodring sat in front of the television watching *Bimbo's Initiation*, for example, while Crumb pored over classic funny animal comics with his older brother. And the surf cartoonists? They looked at the sea.

Crossing the Pacific

As almost all Australians live on the coast, a distinct visual culture has developed alongside Australian surfing, particularly in graphic design, fashion and visual arts. Australian surf art is similar to its Californian and Hawaiian counterparts, but is somehow not quite as clean and wholesome. Australian surfers are dirtier, uglier, frecklier and more blokey, and their art reflects this. But before we had a chance to develop the local style, surf comics and the associated psychedelia were imported from the US.

Australian surfing was preceded by a surf lifesaving tradition as the dominant beach culture. The surf club members – clubbies – were by nature solemn and reasonably conservative. When surfing went through its first waves of popularity in the 50s and early 60s, surf culture emerged as an oppositional force to the sensibility of the clubbies. And in the late 60s the opposition to the

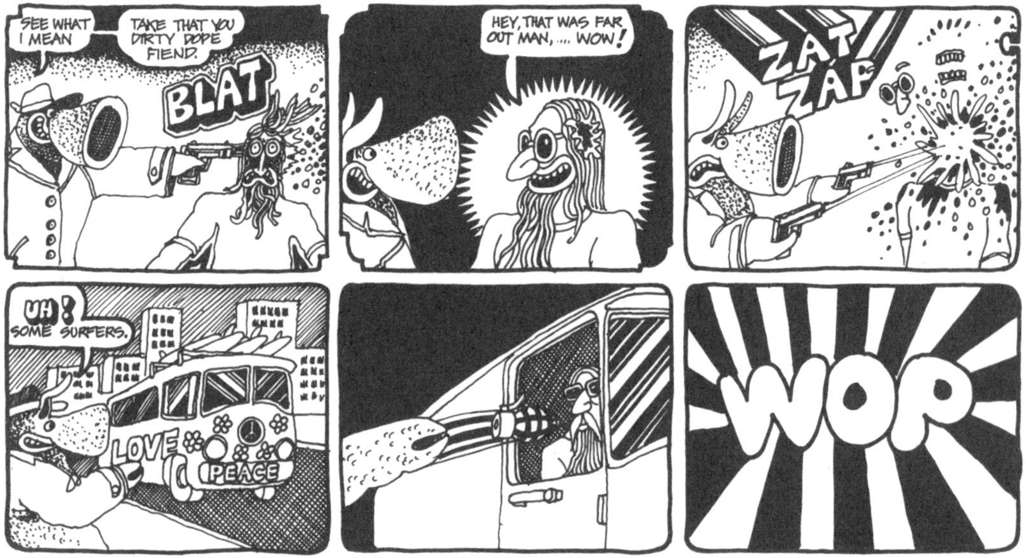
SEE WHAT I MEAN
TAKE THAT YOU DIRTY DOPE FIEND.
BLAT
HEY, THAT WAS FAR OUT MAN,.... WOW!
ZAT
ZAP
UH!
SOME SURFERS.
LOVE
PEACE
WOP

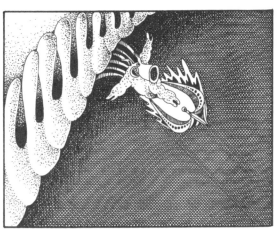

clubbies became an opposition to all forms of authority. Dropping out was the thing to do in 1969, and if you did it Australian style, you ditched your job and drove north chasing the warm weather in a Volkswagen Kombi, the nose of a surfboard poking out the busted back window. Surfing was part of the counterculture in Australia, just as it was in California, and the words *hippie* and *surf-bum* were almost interchangeable.

These days, surf art and kitsch are everywhere and the heavily commodified mainstream surf culture is even more of an embarrassing farce to most surfers. Growing up in the 90s, we guffawed at the absurdity of *Point Break*, just as the grommets of the 60s made fun of *Gidget*. But unlike the situation in the US, in 1960s Australia, no one had figured out that surfing could be a money-spinner. Australian surfers were scruffy, laidback and left-leaning, and were likely to keep a carrot-sized joint in the glovebox. It wasn't surprising then, that when the first underground comics made their way across the Pacific, they made a particular kind of sense to the surfing community here. The Fabulous Furry Freak Brothers were just like the people they knew, and it was no great feat to imagine Fat Freddy's van with surfboards strapped to the roof parked somewhere in the dunes near Byron Bay. The hand-drawn line had already asserted itself as the alternative to the burgeoning design brutalism of the late 20th century. And once Australian surfers had seen the work of Crumb, Gilbert Shelton, S Clay Wilson and, most indelibly, Rick Griffin, the arrival of the Australian surf comic was inevitable.

THIS PAGE: TONY EDWARDS, 1975 // **OPPOSITE:** TONY EDWARDS, 1975 //

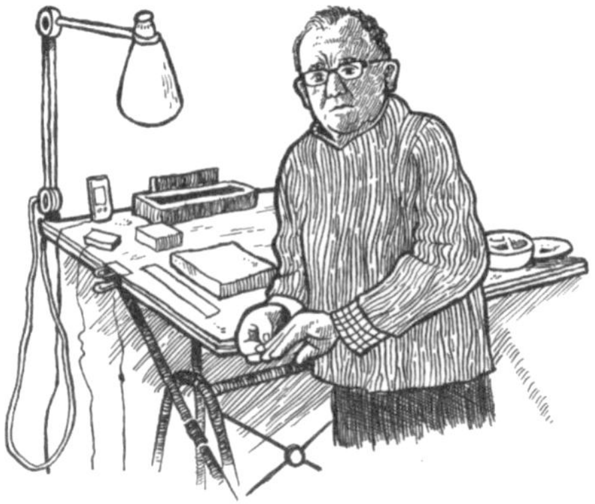

Tony Edwards and Captain Goodvibes

It was 1973 when architectural draughtsman Tony Edwards met John Barnes at a friend's place on Sydney's northern beaches. Barnes was guest editor at a new magazine called *Tracks*, a combination surf mag and underground paper printed on cheap newsprint. Barnes suggested Edwards contribute a black-and-white comic strip similar in tone to the underground comics they'd seen coming out of America. In the third strip he drew for *Tracks* Edwards came up with Captain Goodvibes, a lumpy spotted pig with a prodigious appetite for drugs, booze and boofhead one-liners. The character appeared three more times in the magazine before Edwards lost interest and spiked the strip.

But *Tracks* was still keen, and did what it could to persuade Edwards to keep The Captain going. The next guest editor turned up on his doorstep with fan letters (something Edwards had never seen before), a flagon of white wine and the promise of a full-page spread and $35 a month. "Sal was pregnant and I no longer had a job," Edwards told me, "so I reluctantly and drunkenly agreed."

As always seems to be the case with underground comics, the content is multilayered, either by a deliberate artifice of the author or a beautiful, hapless mistake. In Goodvibes there's a light-hearted surface narrative of counterculture clichés, dole humour, drug binges and encounters with the fuzz that hovers over a latticework of psychedelic imagery, both beautiful and terrifying. Edwards' architectural experience seamlessly inflects the artwork, with surreal Woodring-esque structures blowing the waves out to gargantuan proportions. All the while, a calm, soothing tone to the narration guides our journey on this strange vortex of water, into dreamscapes of wonky acid-creatures and cone-headed sea-gods.

The thing that impresses me most about Edwards is that he was never actually a surfer. He spent his formative years hanging around the beach, like any good surf rat, and he clearly loved to watch the breaking waves, but his reluctance to engage with surf culture as a romantic left him open to more interesting visions of the ocean. The place where the water meets the land – with its strange, soft creatures, its mercurial wave-forms, its hard light and ever present danger – could be psychedelic even without acid.

For my money, Edwards at his best is as good as any of the underground cartoonists to come out of the 60s and 70s. But now, nearly 40 years later, his comic art is almost lost. Like the great American newspaper strips of the 20th century, Goodvibes has existed for decades nowhere other than the garages of leathery old men who collect surf ephemera. Edwards himself, who permanently retired the Pig of Steel in the early 80s to concentrate on painting, doesn't even have a complete collection. He has only a few pieces of original art and a sparse collection of the printed material. The rest has been stolen, sold or donated by Edwards to the State Library of New South Wales. America rediscovered its old newspaper comics through the work of devoted collectors like Bill Blackbeard, and there are several series by artists like George Herriman and Frank King available from publishers like Fantagraphics and Drawn and Quarterly. But this hasn't really happened yet in Australia, and it's astonishing how quickly a decade of comic art can fade from the public consciousness.

I grew up in the 80s and the wonky pink pig has always been familiar to me. The strip had long since finished by the time I was in my surf cap, but the image of Goodvibes was everywhere. Maybe a little faded and creepy in a poster pinned to the club shed, or on the greasy wall of a shaping bay where some grizzled hippie made single-fins, but, nevertheless, everywhere. *Tracks'* circulation was huge during the 70s – 45,000, by unreliable reports – and the strip became so popular that Goodvibes was ripped off for bumper stickers and t-shirts, painted on surfboards and the sides of panel vans. The incredible waves that Edwards drew were burned into my frontal lobe.

But then, by the time I reached adolescence, the newsprint had faded and rotted, and Captain Goodvibes was hardly a glimmer, just something the old blokes used to talk about in the lineup.

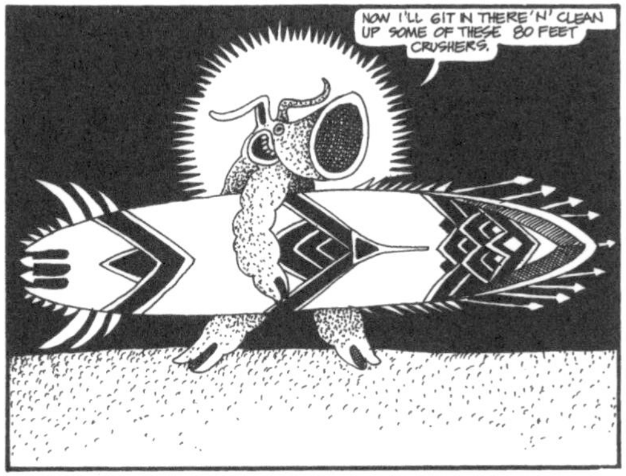

NOW I'LL GIT IN THERE'N' CLEAN UP SOME OF THESE 80 FEET CRUSHERS.

Memory is funny like that: the chambers of the mind go weedy if they don't see any traffic. It worked out the same way with the bush track between Sawtell and Toormina. We did a lot of walking as kids but no adult in Toormina walks anywhere unless there's the threat of a police breathalyser. I stopped using the bush track the day I got my driver's licence. I simply grew up, finished school and moved away like anyone with any sense did, and with a teenager's naivety, I assumed the track would always be there.

The biggest night of the year at the Sawtell pub is Christmas Eve, when all the young people home for the holidays – like me – go to binge drink and shoot the shit. The pub shuts at 12, and with a surly "Merry Christmas", security guards push punters out into the street where they linger, blather, yell, hump each other's legs and square up for drunken brawls.

One Christmas Eve, when I was 21 or 22, I found myself stumbling home on the familiar trail of my morning pilgrimage, past the place where the kid had been killed by the train. As I turned off the road and pushed through the cut-grass into the scrub at the end of Boronia Street, the fluorescent light faded and, to my surprise, the trail faded with it. What was once a clear, clay path was now swamped in weeds and young trees. Granted, I had a belly full of Carlton Draught and my perception was hazy, but the place that was intimately mapped in my memory had changed irrevocably. In the end I had to forget the trail I once knew and blunder through the bush, my hands out in front of my face, in what I thought was the direction home. Lacerated and muddy, I broke out of the trees to find myself looking at the plank bridge across Chinaman's Creek, just as I remembered it, the last kernel of proof that this was one of the highways of my childhood.

As I shambled out of my psychogeographic haze onto the still warm bitumen at the bottom of Newcastle Drive, I sent my old mate Benson a text. I told him the track wasn't there anymore. I needed to know it wasn't just me that had let a chamber of memory go to seed. My phone beeped in response.

"Ha ha," Benson wrote back. "I got caned last time I went through there, ay?"

The art of Rick Griffin and Tony Edwards was not available to me in my teen years, but every drawing of a wave that I pored over between the ages of five and 18 carried the influence of these artists. As did my own drawings when I started to scribble on the inside of my school folder. Only I didn't know it. Because like the track, unless you run back and forth over pop-culture histories, unless you pound the lines and trails with living flesh, they quickly fade into the scrub.

THIS PAGE: MARK SUTHERLAND, 2009 // OPPOSITE: TONY EDWARDS, 1975 // **PORTRAIT:** PAT, 2011 //

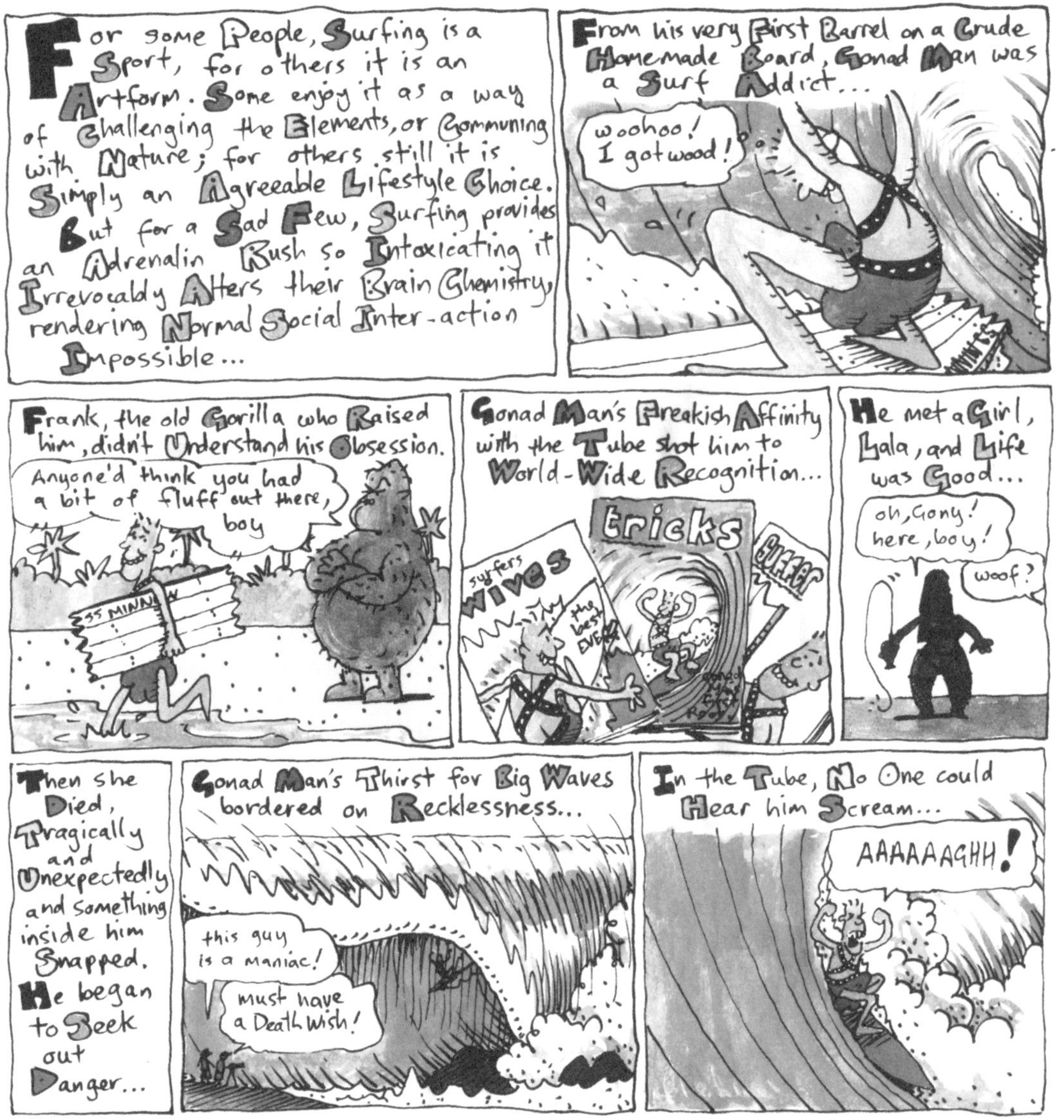
For some People, Surfing is a Sport, for others it is an Artform. Some enjoy it as a way of Challenging the Elements, or Communing with Nature; for others still it is Simply an Agreeable Lifestyle Choice.
But for a Sad Few, Surfing provides an Adrenalin Rush so Intoxicating it Irrevocably Alters their Brain Chemistry, rendering Normal Social Inter-action Impossible...
From his very First Barrel on a Crude Homemade Board, Gonad Man was a Surf Addict...
woohoo! I got wood!
Frank, the old Gorilla who Raised him, didn't Understand his Obsession.
Anyone'd think you had a bit of fluff out there, boy
Gonad Man's Freakish Affinity with the Tube shot him to World-Wide Recognition...
tricks
surfers WIVES
the best EVER
He met a Girl, Lala, and Life was Good...
oh, Gony! here, boy!
woof?
Then she Died, Tragically and Unexpectedly and something inside him Snapped. He began to Seek out Danger...
Gonad Man's Thirst for Big Waves bordered on Recklessness...
this guy is a maniac!
must have a Death Wish!
In the Tube, No One could Hear him Scream...
AAAAAAGHH!

Mark Sutherland and Gonad Man

As I hit adolescence in the mid-90s, and the image of Goodvibes' mottled pink head faded from my consciousness, Mark Sutherland, a trained animator, was holed up in his Bondi studio furiously drawing waves. Sutho had done a painted animated short called *The Dream*, which had impressed Andrew Kidman, then editor of another new surfing magazine called *Waves*. Kidman approached Sutho to start a surf comic for him. It needed to have something of the irreverence of Goodvibes but be appropriate to Kidman's target audience: the squirty little grommets that were swarming the beaches and crowding out the empty breaks in the 80s and 90s. It also had to be called Gonad Man, which was some sort of running joke in the editorial room. Sutho went to work. The product of his labours was an emotionally retarded surfer with a bad temper and an enormous wang.

I was about 12 when I first saw Gonad Man. His beady little eyes gleamed at me and the stray hairs on his bulging bollocks made me jealous. The comic made sense like nothing I had ever seen on paper. I had recently traded in my surf rescue board and clubbie cap for a three-fin thruster, and was just starting to grapple with testosterone in what was, and still is, the sort of social milieu where the emotionally retarded succeed. Gonad Man blundered through life clueless to the pitfalls of drugs, sex and consumer capitalism, leaving broken hearts and disaster in his wake. He was the victim of various cultural predators, but was also a predator himself. In the same way that every nerdy, inner-city kid was captivated by Peter Parker's transformation into a powerful, heroic figure, the grommets of Australia were enthralled by the hapless and boofheaded antics of this poorly drawn man with enormous genitals. Sure, Parker could change into Spiderman, but Gonad Man could stuff his balls up his arse and fart them back out again. We knew what superpower we wanted. We usually bought a copy of *Tracks* or *Australia's Surfing Life* when we had money to burn (and if we didn't have the money, we'd steal it) but Gonad Man was enough to entice us to start pinching *Waves* instead. *Spiderman* wasn't even on our radar.

Later, when I found my way to Crumb in my twenties, I had the same revelation that everyone has. Crumb amplifies the raw artifice of pen drawings, making anyone who ever loved to draw feel not only that it is something they *could* do, but that comics are what they *must* do. But Crumb was not the first to give me this feeling. That credit goes to Mark Sutherland.

The Gonad Man strips weren't slick and angular like the fluorescent surf graphics of the time. They were hand-drawn with a scratchy pen and coloured with simple separations. The drawings of waves were simple but carefully crafted, and the figure of Gonad Man himself had all the ragged power of the swaying cocks scrawled on toilet walls, mixed with the energy of the scribbles we made on desks in class.

Of course, Sutho is nowhere near the draughtsman that Crumb is, but there is a similar frantic quality to the line of both artists. When I went to visit Mark at his home in Nambucca Heads, I saw some of his original art. The Gonad Man originals had been drawn extremely small on thin white paper, with a felt-tip pen balled up in Mark's tense fist. In every line of his comics is the mood of struggle. The draughtsman's struggle to find form, obviously, but this becomes Gonad Man's struggle, and the struggle of every salt-encrusted grommet to find sense in a small country town by the ocean.

The other major theme unleashed in the linework is Sutherland's rage at the state of the surfing culture. Goodvibes had an oppositional relationship with the clubbies and the fuzz, but Gonad Man's enemies were those in the new surfing establishment: the surf brands. By the time I picked up a board, the clueless hippies that ran the show had become, or been replaced by, run-of-the-mill CEOs with the same jelly-chinned affect that the management in any corporation might have. Surf culture is big business, and 70 years shilling boardshorts has changed it into another suburbanite, jock culture.

They were the First Visitors he'd had in Months...
Allah be merciful
hey fuck off!
Gonad Man greeted the Intruders with Suspicion...
Drop in on ME, will ya?
EEYIH! it is the devil himself!

You are more likely to encounter vehement nationalism and territorial violence at the beach than any remnant of a countercultural legacy. Sutherland did, and still does, use Gonad Man to air his grievances with this shift, particularly in his recent online work. That clenched drawing fist keeps moving and Gonad Man rages on.

Gonad Man quickly became as iconic as Captain Goodvibes. His popularity in the 90s was meteoric, and Sutherland was making good money. At one point, a condom manufacturer paid him $25,000 to draw the packaging for an official Gonad Man condom. Goney was the pride of every kid's school folder, and the bane of every deputy principal's decency standards. The logical progression was that Sutherland, with his animation background, would propel his character onto the small screen. Sutho animated a Gonad Man short, which you can still find on YouTube, and that was enough to convince production company Southern Star to dive into full-scale production of a television pilot.

But what seemed like the biggest break in Sutherland's life quickly turned choppy. In production, Gonad Man crossed the line from being a cult surfing celebrity to a product for general consumption. The result was something that Sutherland is, even now, too embarrassed to show anyone. The pilot was never picked up.

"I had a whole production team and everything," he told me. "The problem was that none of them surfed."

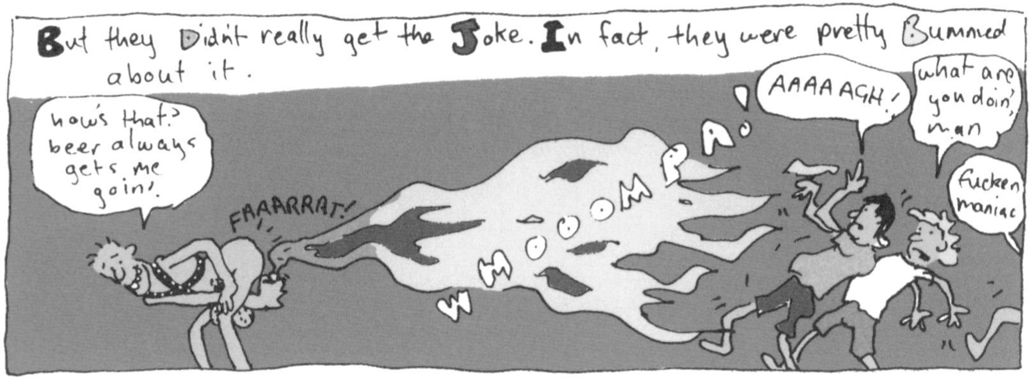
But they Didn't really get the Joke. In fact, they were pretty Bummed about it.
how's that? beer always gets me goin'.
FRAARRRAT!
WHOOOMPA!
AAAAAGH!
what are you doin' man
Fucken maniac

Sandy Bastards

All histories, especially new ones, are the result of naive optimism, the sort that leads a barefoot grommet through a thicket of mud and cut-grass in the hope of discovering a quicker way to the surf, a new lay of the land in the unintelligible tangle. Truth be told, I'm not a very good pop-culture historian. My way of preparing for this essay was to visit Tony Edwards and Mark Sutherland at their studios. At Tony's place we drank coffee and talked about our lives and our art. At Sutho's we went to check the surf at a break called Black Rock near his house while his dog chased seagulls.

But I was bolstered by an essay by Jeet Heer, a real comics scholar, in a book of writing about Chris Ware. Titled "Inventing Cartoon Ancestors: Ware and the comics canon", Heer writes about the way that many of the great contemporary cartoonists, like Chris Ware and Seth, have taken up the task of mapping new historical lines that link lesser known cartoonists of the early 20th century with the work being created in alternative comics right now. In championing and designing reprinted editions of the work of artists like Frank King, Ware has contributed to the preservation of decades of comic art as well as to a rewriting of comics history. His own genealogy traces the careers of artists like George Herriman, Winsor McCay and Gluyas Williams, for whom a cartoon formalism is a greater concern than cinematic realism, and for whom the drama of everyday life is a more worthy subject than that of heroism or adventure. The career of the cartoonist Seth has been informed by a particular tradition of editorial cartooning popular in the hey-day of literary magazines. This is evident in Seth's work in a formal sense, that is, in his cartooning practice, but also in his extra-curricular projects. We can see his efforts to help a reading public rediscover or re-appraise this cartooning tradition in his tiny book *Forty Books of Interest*, a supplement to *Comic Art #8*, and in his design work for Fantagraphics' *The Complete Peanuts*.

Cartooning traditions can completely disappear for a time, skipping generations and re-emerging in unlikely settings. When we compare Ware's *Quimby Mouse* and a *Krazy Kat* reprint, for example, it's clear they're both part of a particular tradition, even though the works are separated by a span of 60 years. One can't lay a Carl Barks story next to Crumb's *Fritz the Cat* and not expect a comics scholar to draw a line between the artists. Only occasionally is the craft passed down through an apprenticeship-like arrangement – in cartooning bullpens, commercial art departments and animation sweatshops – but it's almost always to the detriment of the art. The key to understanding a comic art genealogy is that the texts don't carry the tradition, the *images* do. Great comic pages fade and rot while the forms of fetish recreate themselves over and over, resonating through the decades and drawing bodies.

Thinking back to what Horrocks said, the thing to take from this is that the story of comics is not like that of other art movements. There's no cohesive chain of big names, important events and seminal texts. The narrative is fluid and it depends on the historian's own experience. That's what I was discovering – but couldn't articulate – when I started schooling myself in comics. The history of comics is one that consists of a thousand coming-of-age narratives tangled up together in an unruly lump. I'm adding one more strand.

It's a strand that begins with Griffin, Edwards and Sutherland, and is drawn out to include an array of Australian and American cartoonists. There's Steve Cakebread, who drew a strip called Felch in *Australia's Surfing Life* in the late 90s as a competitor to Gonad Man. And of course there's Ben Brown, the hero of Australian rock 'n' roll graphics, who drew surf comics for *Tracks* in the 90s and is currently working for upstart surf magazine *Stab.* For me, Brown's wave drawings are trumped only by Tony Edwards' in brilliance. A guy by the name of Paul Collins drew a four-page strip in a 1997 issue of *Australia's Surfing Life* named after the magazine's daggy mascot, ASL Man, but that strip never made it to a second issue despite showing promise. I worked for that magazine ten years later and nobody there knew what had happened to Collins.

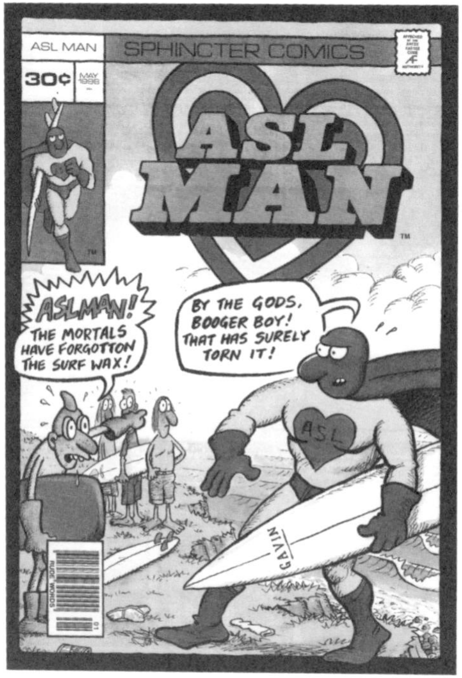
ASL MAN
SPHINCTER COMICS
30¢
MAY
ASL MAN
TM
ASLMAN! THE MORTALS HAVE FORGOTTON THE SURF WAX!
BY THE GODS, BOOGER BOY! THAT HAS SURELY TORN IT!
ASL
GAVIN

It's also a strand that could be extended to include surf comics that weren't part of my childhood. In the 80s, after Captain Goodvibes was retired from *Tracks,* he was replaced by a strip called *Lash Clone* written by DC Green and Adam Ross, and later collected in a 100-page book. Despite its obvious appeal to someone like me, I've never been able to get my hands on a copy.

But I should add a warning: if you follow this thread, if you delve too deeply, you may discover that Australian surf comics are just not very good. You might have the same thing happen to you as happened to me when I picked up the first volume of *Cerebus.* I wouldn't know because I grew up with this stuff. A stern adult judgement of their quality is beyond me.

Last year, as I finished the pencil drawings for *Blue,* I went back home for a high school reunion. Ten years had passed and we all had the beginnings of bald spots and pot bellies. After hours of drinking, I found myself once again on the trek home through sleeping suburbia with some friends. As we hoofed it down the hill on Hulbert's Road, our feet getting soggy with dew, I mentioned the bush track we used to walk on the way to the beach. I remembered out loud for a bit. I told my friends how much time the track used to save us. I told them about the time there were little bits of a human body on the train line.

I started telling the story about that morning, back in Year 10, when Benson and I were on the track, ready to climb up onto the train line and see the body. What I didn't tell them was that despite the plan, despite getting up extra early, despite our anticipation and the hype all through the school, we only paused for a moment. We made an unspoken decision and continued down the track to the beach. We never saw the bits of body and long dark bloodstain. We dogged it.

The friends I was with that night grew up only a short walk from the end of Boronia Street, but not only did they not remember the story of the body, they never even knew about the bush track. The patch of scrub that had been so storied in my mind, that bookmark in my psychogeographic street directory, was blank for them, simply the dead end at the bottom of Newcastle Drive.

The most terrifying thing about this became apparent the next day when, on a whim, I went to walk off my hangover on the old clay trail, and found no trace of any of it in the broad, sober daylight. The plank bridge was gone, the trees had grown and swallowed up the space where the track was. You couldn't imagine anyone passing through the scrub without a machete. The reality of the place now fitted more with my friends' childhood memories than my own. The only proof I had of its existence was the testimony of old locals and a late-night text message.

Part of life when you live at the arse end of the world is that your story never seems to intersect with the grand narratives. Bigger histories from more populous places quickly morph into mythologies, but the smaller stories on the fringes are often nudged out of the collective consciousness and lost forever. If you can imagine, for a second, what would have happened had George Herriman lived in regional Australia and spent a lifetime drawing the rock formations of Arnhem Land into the ever-changing background of his *Krazy Kat* comics. It's likely there would've been no Bill Blackbeard to preserve his genius and no Smithsonian Collection to revive it, and Australian cartoonists like me would still be professing ignorance of a local comics tradition.

Ignorance of history is what destroys it. Hopefully this essay, by mapping a sandy corner of this bastard artform, goes some small way to making sure that a lesser known comic art isn't forgotten. In the end, we write about comics for the same reasons that we draw comics: because the trail is narrow and the weeds are irrepressible.

POST SCRIPT: A few days before this book went to print I got an email from Tony Edwards announcing the release of a Goodvibes omnibus entitled *My Life As A Pork-chop.* It was put together by former *Tracks* editor Sean Doherty. Go get yourself some pig meat it before it disappears again.

THIS PAGE: PAUL COLLINS, 1997 // **OPPOSITE:** TONY EDWARDS, 1979 // **PREVIOUS LEFT:** MARK SUTHERLAND, 2009 // **PREVIOUS RIGHT:** MARK SUTHERLAND, 1997 // **PORTRAIT:** PAT, 2011 //